LET'S HUMOR the OLD MAN

An Old Man's Journey to Salvation

Barry Denzil Haney, MD

Let's Humor the Old Man

Trilogy Christian Publishers
A Wholly Owned Subsidiary of Trinity Broadcasting Network
2442 Michelle Drive, Tustin, CA 92780

Manufactured in the United States of America
10 9 8 7 6 5 4 3 2 1

Library of Congress Cataloging-in-Publication Data is available.

ISBN:978-1-63769-382-7
E-ISBN:978-1-63769-383-4

ENDORSEMENTS

When you read Dr. Barry Haney's writings, I promise you will be impressed with his personal heart, honesty, *and* the depth of his Christian knowledge! That combination will make for a rich, worthwhile reading experience as you share the journey through his spiritual life story.

—Dr. Stan Schilffarth
Staff Chaplain,
University of Cincinnati Medical Center

———————

If you are looking for a book that is inspiring, enter-tain-ing, touching, and enlightening on a number of levels, I may have found your next read. Covering forty topics, the author presents us with his personal journey to salvation. Each chapter contains philosophical insights, scientific knowledge, and colorful personal experiences and then concludes with a thoughtful scriptural perspective and a prayer. The real essence of the book is its message of hope. We all struggle in various ways; yet, we are not forgotten. God is with us through it all.

—Noble J. Burchett
Author of *Song of the Lilies*

———————

This book will inspire those who are looking for salvation or those looking to revitalize their belief in God, Jesus Christ, and the Holy Spirit. It goes beyond the realm of what the Bible teaches us and delves into the darkness of sin and Satan's temptations. The personal experiences of the author are truly enlightening. His forty years of medical practice give a valuable insight into the understanding of selective passages from a physician's perspective. A must-read and hard to put down! You will learn beyond what the Bible teaches you about religion.

—Clay Haney
Stephen Ministries
https://www.stephenministries.org/default.cfm,
https://www.vaamp-productions.com

ACKNOWLEDGEMENTS

This book is dedicated to the following, who were at my side during the writing of this book, providing me the much-needed support and inspiration I needed during my journey to salvation:

- The Holy Spirit, who guided me during the research and writing of this book.

- Pastor Sam Glenn, whose sermons over the past three years have inspired me during my walk with Jesus.

- Pastor Stan Schilffarth, whose friendship and many conversations concerning theology, inspired me during my walk with Jesus.

- My mother and father, Troy and Mary Haney, who guided me and provided me the opportunity to learn about Christianity during my formative years.

- My incredible wife Judy, my angel, sent to me by God over fifty years ago, my partner, whose patience and understanding allowed me to travel along my rocky road to salvation.

- My three beautiful daughters, Tabitha, Andrea, and Kathy, and their godly husbands, Rusty, Jameson, and Ryan, whose lives were significantly affected by my journey and their love and support provided me the inspiration to write this book for them and my precious six grandchildren, Courtney, Briana, Bryson, Landry, Gus, and Molly.

TABLE OF CONTENTS

INTRODUCTION

My Journey to Salvation

In 1920, "Life is a journey and not a destination" was written in a book by Pastor Lynn H. Hough. Many of you have heard this in one form or another over the years. As you know, the meaning of this quote may be different for a Christian and a non-Christian. Les Brown characterized life's journey in this way: "I believe that life is a journey, often difficult and sometimes incredibly cruel, but we are well equipped for it if only we tap into our talents and gifts and allow them to blossom."

In this book, you will travel with me along a portion of my life journey.

Bob Dylan wrote, "A man is a success if he gets up in the morning and gets to bed at night, and in between, he does what he wants to do." According to John D. Rockefeller, "Don't be afraid to give up the good to go for the great." According to these secular, worldly standards, I have lived this version of the "American dream." According to them, I personify the secular world's idea of personal success and achievement.

Joseph Prince writes in *Charisma Magazine,*

> Corporate America measures success based on what you
> have done, what you have accomplished, and what you have
> accumulated. It is based entirely on you focusing all
> your time, energy, and resources in meriting titles and col-
> lecting accomplishments.

Based on these criteria, I am a "poster boy" for what it means to be successful in the secular world. I am successful because of what I have done and accomplished. I have been married for fifty years, have three successful, married daughters and six successful grandchildren. I was a Boy Scout and achieved the rank of Eagle Scout. While I was in college, I was in the Beta Club, on the Dean's List every semester, in the Honors Program, and graduated with high distinction, receiving an undergraduate degree in biology.

I graduated from medical school in 1979. I honorably served in the United States Navy for thirty years, starting as an enlisted sailor in 1969, reaching the rank of Commander. While in the Navy, I received training as a Navy Flight Surgeon, Undersea Medical Officer, Submarine Medical Officer, became a certified Navy Diver, was in charge of a Hyperbaric Treatment Facility, and completed a residency in Diagnostic Radiology with Special Competency in Nuclear Radiology in 1990.

Through all of these years of work and training, I had reached the pinnacle of success, according to the secular worldview. Because of all of these accomplishments and according to the secular worldview, I should have been satisfied and happy when I retired, but I was not! I had a large void in my heart that I could not fill with worldly accomplishments. I began asking, *why?*

Slowly and over a long period of time, I began to discover the answer to this soul-searching question in the Bible. Revelation 3:17 states, "Because thou sayest, I am rich, and increased with goods, and have need of nothing; and knowest not that thou art wretched, and miserable, and poor, and blind, and naked."

I retired from the Navy after thirty years of honorable service in 1999. I retired from my practice of medicine in 2012. After retirement, I again began asking, *what is the meaning of life?*

Over the years, I have tried to find the answer in various places, including science, philosophy, and various religions.

At the age of twelve, I was first baptized at the First Christian Church in Winchester, Kentucky. As a child, I attended Sunday school, Sunday night fellowship, and vacation Bible school.

I was intrigued about God and Jesus as a child, but I was not saved. As a child, I was an introvert. Because of this, my mind was a fertile play-

Barry Denzil Haney, MD

ground for Satan. My first sense I was a sinner occurred when I was twelve years old. This started my journey into the darkness offered by a secular worldview.

Over the years, I have been "saved" at least three times. All three were short walks. I believed I was a Christian. I believed in God and that Jesus was His Son and died on the cross at Calvary. I many times asked God to forgive my sins. But the problem was I did not truly have a repentant heart. I would put demands on God, and when those demands weren't met, I would turn away, blaming God.

You see, I did not give up control of my entire life to Jesus. I did not turn away from my sins, easily giving into temptation when tempted by Satan. I would then get angry at God and blame Him for my inability to control my sinful nature.

According to New York City pastor Tim Keller in his book *Counterfeit Gods*, "More than other idols, personal success and achievement lead to a sense that we ourselves are God, that our security and value rest in our own wisdom, strength, and performance." Satan could count on me! I was in his corner, and he didn't have to spend much time grooming me to be a witness for him. My life was the definition of sin. I was self-absorbed, self-centered, sought self-indulgence, thought about myself to the exclusion of others, and focused my life entirely on myself.

My search for the meaning of life ended in March 2018.

On March 2, 2018, I received devastating news from a close acquaintance. His marriage was threatened because of a secret sin. I was shocked and devastated. He was a good, godly person. His marriage was the "perfect" marriage.

It was at that very moment I realized we are all sinners, and the sinful nature plaguing mankind since the dawn of creation, gives Satan the ability to keep mankind eternally separated from God. I then realized why I had not completely surrendered to God in the past. It was because of my pride and arrogance, my desire to not let anyone control me, my desire to be like God.

For the first time, I finally realized, this was the room I did not let Jesus and the Holy Spirit enter. This was the room where I tried to keep dark secrets hidden from the world and God. This realization and conviction by the Holy Spirit was the chink in Satan's armor; the Holy Spirit used to convict me over the next two days. The Holy Spirit used the Ten Commandments to convict me. I really never understood what sin was until I honestly looked at the Ten Commandments. Through this process, I finally became aware I was truly a sinner who tried for years to control his life, and because I am human, it was impossible for me to change my behavior.

Over the next two days, I realized my lifetime attempt to control my sin had failed miserably. I realized I was guilty of all Ten Commandments in one way or another because nothing is hidden from God—He sees even the thought-life. The Day of Judgement now became a reality for me. On judgment day, I would be found guilty by the holy, just, perfect God, who would judge me according to His perfect standard, and the penalty for my sins would be eternal separation from God, in hell!

Finally, on March 5, 2018, after sixty-seven years of bitterness, anger, unhappiness, loneliness, and separation from God, I received God's grace through faith!

Jo Swinney in *Walking with the Bible* defines "repent" as follows: "Repent—to regret the wrong actions we have done or our failure to do things we should have done, and to turn from such behavior, seeking God's forgiveness."

In Acts 20:21, Luke writes, "Testifying both to the Jews, and also to the Greeks, repentance toward God, and faith toward our Lord Jesus Christ." For the first time in my life, I actually repented of my sins. I not only confessed my sins to God but turned away from them, one hundred and eighty degrees. I turned over my total life to Him, with no room or space in my soul posted with a sign at the door stating, "Do not Enter! Reserved for Barry only!"

I placed my faith and trust in His Son, Jesus Christ, who died on the cross to pay the penalty for my sins, and defeated death by His resurrection on the third day. At that moment, I was reconciled with God through

Barry Denzil Haney, MD

justification by faith. Jesus and the Holy Spirit entered my heart and now lives there. My life has now changed! In 2 Corinthians 5:17, Paul writes, "Therefore if any man be in Christ, he is a new creature: old things are passed away; behold, all things are become new." I now have a new heart and new desires. I am a new creature in Christ. I have been born again with God's Spirit living within me.

Where I once had no interest in the things of God, now I love Him and yearn to please Him. I want to keep His Commandments. I have been converted by the power of the Gospel and hunger for the Word of God through daily study of the Bible with the Holy Spirit's guidance. I want to please Him.

The Bible has now come alive because I now have God's Holy Spirit living in me, leading me into all truth. I believe that Jesus, through the Holy Spirit, gives me cues on what I need to change, nudging me until I make the changes He wants me to make. I try to carry on a conversation with God throughout the day. I listen to Him through daily prayer.

However, my daily walk with Jesus has not been without tribulation!

Since I was saved, the attacks from Satan have intensified. Paul writes in 1 Corinthians 10:13,

> There hath no temptation taken you but such as is common
> to man: but God is faithful, who will not suffer you to be
> tempted above that ye are able; but will with the temptation
> also make a way to escape, that ye may be able to bear it.

But Jesus and the Holy Spirit have given me the power to overcome most of Satan's temptations! However, if I do sin, and I will sin, I am convicted by the Holy Spirit to immediately confess my sin and ask for God's forgiveness. First John 1:8-9 states, "If we say that we have no sin, we deceive ourselves, and the truth is not in us. If we confess our sins, he is faithful and just to forgive us our sins, and to cleanse us from all unrighteousness."

Now, instead of being self-centered, as I was before, I try to follow C. S. Lewis thoughts in *Mere Christianity* by focusing on the needs of others, by focusing away from my own concerns, by considering how I might serve in God's Great Commission to spread the Word of the Gospel throughout the world, by considering how I might encourage others, and by considering how I might help the people I encounter. But don't get me wrong! As I stated earlier, my journey to salvation has been a very long, rocky road!

Satan's attacks have increased. Not only have the number and frequency of attacks increased since I was born again, but the devices Satan has used have become more sinister and deceptive. Being the sly fox he is, Satan has unleashed a myriad of different ways to deceive me, tempt me, and distract me.

But thanks to God's grace, the Holy Spirit strengthens me to resist temptation. James tells us in James 4:7, "Submit yourselves therefore to God. Resist the devil, and he will flee from you." During the weekend of October 18-20, 2019, I experienced a divine appointment with God during my Emmaus Walk. Although on March 5, 2018, I thought I had given "my all" to God, surrendering everything to him, giving him complete control of my life, finally trusting him one hundred percent, I was wrong.

But on October 19, 2019, during the "Dying Moments" ceremony at the Emmaus Walk, I finally laid at the foot of the cross, the one thing that I was still trying to control. The one thing preventing me from having a complete personal relationship with Jesus.

When I gave up control of my life completely to Jesus, at that moment, I finally had one hundred percent trust in Jesus! My chains had been broken; I was set free. His unconditional love now flows through me. I am a conduit through which his unending love, amazing grace, and mercy flow through me to others. Praise God, thank you for your love and mercy. I am now righteous because of Christ's righteousness, holy because of God's holiness!

Although my journey to salvation has been rocky, the journey has been strengthened through the instruction of the Holy Spirit. The Holy Spirit

Barry Denzil Haney, MD

has shown me God created humanity for relationships, relationships with each other; a relationship with nature; a relationship with God.

However, human sin has separated us from God, turning what should have been a loving relationship into one filled with hate and disobedience. But through God's grace, God has built a bridge that allows us to relate to Him. Abraham Kuyper, in his book *Near Unto God,* summarizes this concept for us: "It is good for us to be near God. It is eternity to know Him intimately in our daily lives. That's the mark of believers. They know what joy there is in being near unto God, and they want nothing else."

In Jeremiah 9:23-24, the Bible tells us,

> Thus saith the LORD, Let not the wise man glory in his wisdom, Neither let the mighty man glory in his might, Let not the rich man glory in his riches: But let him that glorieth glory in this, That he understandeth and knoweth me, That I am the LORD which exercise lovingkindness, judgment, and righteousness, in the earth: For in these things I delight, saith the LORD.

I would like to summarize my journey to salvation in this way:

> Since becoming a child of God, each day, I praise God for being my creator and thank Him for His love. I thank Him for loving me and for dying on the cross at Calvary, paying the debt for my sin, enabling me to spend an eternal, loving relationship with Him in heaven. And the good news is, you too, can spend an eternal, loving relationship with God. All you have to do is have faith in Jesus, repent of your sins, and through the grace of God, you will "bask" in the Light of His love for an eternity.

Jennie Riddle, who wrote "The Revelation Song," states in an article she wrote, "I asked the Holy Spirit to help me write a song that painted

Him; a song that the angels and creation were already singing, so that we could join in with *one voice,* as *one bride,* to *one king."* Now that I know I will spend eternity with God, I can truly sing this song of praise, a verse from "The Revelation Song":

Holy, holy, holy is the Lord God Almighty
Who was and is and is to come
With all creation, I sing praise to the King of kings
You are my everything and I will adore You

Billy Graham described the journey of life this way:

The journey God has set before us isn't a freeway: we are
constantly encountering forks and junctions and crossroads.
Which way will we go when we meet them? Life is filled
with decisions, and we can't avoid them.

For me, the meaning of Billy Graham's quote about the journey of life has changed over the years, depending on what season of life I am experiencing at that moment.

On January 1, 2020, I decided to take a journey with God for forty days and entered the "wilderness." During this time, I took a temporary vow of silence for the first few days, adhered to a strict diet of fish, rice, vegetables, fruits, and vitamins. Most importantly, I met with God on His terms, studied and meditated on His Word, and communicated with Him through prayer.

I felt the presence of the Holy Spirit guiding my hand as I wrote the words in this book. I wrote these words to glorify Jesus, my personal Savior. I wrote these words for the unsaved and hope these words provide a chink in Satan's deception, so the Holy Spirit might convict their spirit man, so they too might spend an eternal loving relationship with God. I wrote these words to my brothers and sisters in Christ who might need encouragement during moments of doubt when Satan and his minions are trying to deceive and weaken one's faith—Jesus is all I need—all I need is Jesus.

In this book, I will share with you reflections concerning my journey to salvation. I hope these reflections give you a sense of the changing, chaotic journey to salvation I have experienced. I hope my experiences help you during your life journey!

During my "forty days in the wilderness," the road I took during my journey has been very rocky. But I am grateful to God He was by my side, holding my hand each step of the way. I felt the presence of the Holy Spirit guiding me, instructing me, and teaching me, as I endeavored to give the reader worldly and godly wisdom based on topics I feel are important during your journey to salvation.

God blessed me with a lifetime of diverse experiences! I believe He prepared me to write a book like this by exposing me to varied life experiences during my journey, experiences which forced me to face the topics discussed in this book. For instance, I do not think it is a mistake. I became a physician, became involved with the Church starting in childhood, and, at times, became Satan's right-hand man as I navigated the treacherous waters of the world, sometimes as a "prodigal son."

From these many varied experiences, I hope the reader will sense the worldly wisdom I have gained over the years, tempered by the godly wisdom I have received through study and meditation on God's Word and through daily prayer. I hope you will discover information you might use to help you navigate the treacherous waters you will encounter during your life journey. May God bless you and your family!

—Barry Denzil Haney, MD

ADDENDUM

Since I finished this book in February 2020, I feel like my journey to salvation has been like a roller coaster ride! I have experienced many peaks and valleys the past year.

During the peaks of this ride, I sensed the presence of the Holy Spirit, guiding, instructing, and protecting me during my journey through the treacherous waters of life.

Unfortunately, when I reached the valleys of this ride, I now know Satan was actively involved, attempting to drag me to hell with him through his lies and deceptions.

In the past three weeks, the pastors at my church, Central Church in Georgetown, Kentucky, have been sharing a series of teachings based on the life of William Borden—the heir to the Borden family fortune. Instead of living a life this fortune offered him, he chose a different path, the narrow path, and became a missionary. At the age of twenty-five, his work for God ended when he died of spinal meningitis. Prior to his untimely death, he had inscribed these three phrases in his Bible; *"no reserves, no retreats, no regrets."*

During this roller coaster ride, I have experienced times when I felt defeated, when I had *"no reserves"* during those moments when I am over-whelmed by the secular world engulfing me. At those moments, Satan succeeds in convincing me to alter my course from the narrow path leading to heaven, and to briefly travel along the wide path so many in today's secular world travel along. During this roller coaster ride, when I sensed the presence of the Holy Spirit guiding my journey, I lived by those words William Border inscribed in his Bible, *"no retreats."*

During a recent sermon at my church, Pastor Andrew Glenn offered this about the importance of "*no retreats,*" conviction, and connections during our walk with Jesus:

> We need to step forward with no regrets; we need to remain convicted. When you lose connection, you lose alarm—but we don't want to alarm people. The alarming thing today in today's church is there is no alarm. Instead, we want to be a seeker-friendly church; the odds are one hundred percent of you will stand before your Creator. You will die and stand before Him and be asked what have you done with your time, that ought to alarm us be convicted, so you have "*no regrets*" on that day!

I hope when my journey to salvation ends, I will have "*no regrets.*" However, since I finished this book, which I believe was inspired and co-written with the Holy Spirit, I have already experienced regret. In 2 Corinthians 7:10, Paul tells us this about the importance of sorrow in repentance and forgiveness, "For godly sorrow worketh repentance to salvation not to be repented of: but the sorrow of the world worketh death."

For the past six months after finishing this book, God allowed me to go back into the desert. Although I didn't forsake God, Jesus, or the Holy Spirit, I did turn my back on God. I now know this was a clever plan by Satan to gradually and deceptively limit my daily Bible reading, my daily meditation with God, and my daily instruction by the Holy Spirit.

During this period of time, God allowed Satan to put semi-opaque blinders on my eyes. He allowed me to experience the secular world and taste the pleasures of the world again. He allowed Satan to deceptively and cunningly entice me to follow him, to become his "*right-hand man*" again.

But four weeks prior to signing a contract to have this book published through TBN/Trilogy Christian Publishing, the Holy Spirit used my wife Judy to convict me. God essentially told me to get off the couch, come back out of the desert, publish the book inspired by Him, and begin placing Jesus as the focus of my life.

In His Grand Plan of Salvation, he wanted this book published, so those He had already planned to read this book would be convicted by the Holy Spirit, so they could begin to fulfill their role in His Plan!

All glory to God! Thank You, Jesus!

—Dr. Barry Denzil Haney
April 8, 2021

CHAPTER 1

The Pain of Depression!

But it displeased Jonah exceedingly, and he was very angry.
And he prayed unto the LORD, and said, I pray thee,
O LORD, was not this my saying, when I was yet in my
country? Therefore I fled before unto Tarshish: for I knew
that thou art a gracious God, and merciful, slow to anger,
and of great kindness, and repentest thee of the evil. Therefore now, O LORD, take, I beseech thee, my life from me;
for it is better for me to die than to live… I do well to be
angry, even unto death.

—Jonah 4:1-3, 9

When Jonah becomes angry with God for extending mercy to those he doesn't believe deserving, he descends into a severe depression, wanting to die to escape the pain of depression, overwhelming him at that moment.

What is this thing called depression? What power does it have over the human mind to make death seem to be the only way out?

The Cambridge Dictionary defines depression in this way: "A feeling of sadness or a type of mental illness that causes long periods of unhappiness."

The Dictionary of Bible Themes defines depression in this way: "A deep sense of despondency, discouragement, and sadness, often linked with a sense of personal powerlessness and a loss of meaning in and enthusiasm for life. Many biblical characters show evidence of such behavior which originates in a number of different ways."

How prevalent is depression?

In 2016, the National Institute of Mental Health estimated over sixteen million US adults had at least one major depressive episode.

According to the World Health Organization, more than three hundred million around the world have depression. Research shows women are affected by depression more than men. It is estimated fifteen percent of the adult population will experience depression at some point in their lifetime.

During my thirty-seven-year practice of medicine, depression was commonplace in my patients, in the workplace, and in my social contacts.

Depression has been around for a long time!

In 400 BC, the Greek philosopher and physician Hippocrates believed a condition called "melancholia," caused by an excess of bile, would cause someone to become despondent and fearful, the first term used for depression.

During the Renaissance, the Europeans considered melancholia to be a sign of creative genius. Sigmund Freud's writings in *On Murder, Mourning and Melancholia* helped modernize the concept of melancholia. Because depression is a mood disorder, it causes a persistent feeling of sadness and loss of interest. Although symptoms vary for each individual, the symptoms generally occur most of the day, nearly every day.

For many people, symptoms are usually severe enough to cause problems in daily activities, including but not limited to feelings of sadness, tearfulness, emptiness or hopelessness, angry outbursts, irritability or frustration, loss of interest or pleasure in most activities, sleep disturbances, tiredness, lack of energy, reduced appetite, anxiety, agitation, or restlessness

Although similar to adults, signs and symptoms in children and teens can be different. In younger children, symptoms may include sadness, irritability, clinginess, worry, aches, and pains, refusing to go to school, or being underweight. In teens, symptoms may include sadness, irritability, feeling negative and worthless, anger, poor performance, poor attendance at school, feeling misunderstood, extremely sensitive, using recreations drugs or alcohol, eating or sleeping too much, self-harm, loss of interest in normal activities, and avoidance of social interaction.

In the elderly population, symptoms of depression may be different or less obvious such as memory difficulties or personality changes, physical aches or pain, fatigue, loss of appetite, sleep problems, loss of interest in sex, wanting to stay at home, rather than going out to socialize or doing new things, suicidal thinking or feelings, especially in older men.

How does depression affect the body physiologically?

You might have heard the phrase, one I have used during my medical practice, "depression is caused by a 'chemical imbalance' in the brain." Although the disease of depression and its manifestations can be caused by alterations in brain and body chemicals, research supports a combination of multiple forces are involved, including faulty mood regulation by the brain, genetic vulnerability, stressful life events, medications, and medical problems.

What are the types of depression?

There are many types of depression, from depression caused by events in your life to depression caused by chemical changes in your brain. It is important for health care professionals to make a diagnosis in order to determine the right treatment.

Oftentimes, depression is experienced during the anniversary of a dead relative/spouse or during family get-togethers and holidays, especially Christmas.

In his article "A Letter to the Depressed Christian at Christmas," David Murray speaks of how prevalent depression can be during the Christmas season in the following excerpt taken from that article "Depression is tough at the best of times...the thought of mixing with happy people fills you with dread...the thought of remembering lost loved ones fills you with gloom."

MY PERSONAL EXPERIENCE: SEVERE DEPRESSION!

In the fall of 1992, I found myself in the back of a Navy ambulance, sirens wailing, in the late afternoon one fall day, heading from the Naval Hospital Pensacola to the United States Air Force Keesler Medical Center, located in Biloxi, Mississippi. I was being transferred because the Naval Hospital psychiatrist believed I was a suicide risk, rightly so, because of severe depression.

Two and one-half years earlier, I had arrived at the Naval Hospital Subic Bay, Philippines, depressed, beginning a two-year tour as a staff radiologist, without my wife and three children.

I was not accompanied by my wife and three children because I did not want to expose them to the ordeal of two years living in a strange land, outside the comforts of the United States, and because of the inherent dangers living in that part of the world during the ongoing, sometimes

Barry Denzil Haney, MD

hostile, base treaty negotiations going on between the United States government and the Philippine government, I elected to leave them in Pensacola, Florida. Although at the time, I did not perceive that to be a problem, I came to find out this "arrangement" was devastating to my mental health.

To make matters worse, toward the end of my tour, Mount Pinatubo erupted, leading to a cascade of events that permanently damaged and affected my psyche. Again, not realizing the damage to my mental health, I finished my tour and arrived back in Pensacola, reunited with my family, ready to begin a new life as a staff radiologist at the Naval Hospital in Pensacola!

Sounds like the ending to a beautiful story, a fairy tale ending, right?

No, it was the beginning of what I like to call my "journey into nothingness."

Although I was thrilled to be back home with my family after two years of separation from them, I had this overwhelming sense of emptiness, anxiousness, and sadness.

I couldn't sleep and began to have a loss of interest in things I once thought pleasurable. At work, I had trouble concentrating, remembering details, and making decisions.

I had this overwhelming sense of worthlessness and incompetency, an overwhelming sense of inadequacies. I felt like I was living a lie; they had made a mistake when they gave me a diploma as a physician! In my delusion of self-pity, I started to devise elaborate, bizarre ways of ending this charade of being a doctor. From ways to make me blind so I couldn't read imaging studies to finally ending it all when I held a loaded 357 magnum to my head, in the bathroom at my home, alone, filled with an overwhelming sense of doom, helplessness, nothingness with my wife at work and my two youngest children at school.

In the bathroom, I slowly but deliberately began to squeeze the trigger—but just before the gun went off, the phone rang in the bedroom, startling me, causing me to take my finger from the trigger.

Dazed, I put the gun down onto the bathroom sink, and walked into the bedroom, picked up the phone, and heard the voice of my oldest married daughter, Tabitha.

Now, I don't know what you think, but I feel the Holy Spirit intervened, nudged my daughter to call me because it was not part of God's plan for me to die in this way. I took a shower, put on my uniform, and quickly drove to the Psychiatry Department at the Naval Hospital Pensacola to tell the psychiatrist I needed help!

I was diagnosed with severe depression, secondary to Post Traumatic Stress Disorder (PTSD), caused by the events during my tour in the Philippines.

Over the next two weeks, I underwent group therapy and was started on the drug Elavil, an antidepressant.

Over the next two weeks, I recovered from my "journey to nothingness," with a new appreciation for life and a renewed sense to continue my career as a diagnostic radiologist in the Navy!

But that's not the ending of this story! I spent the next twenty-five years still searching to fill the void in my heart with earthly pleasures. For you see, I still lacked the godly wisdom I needed to finally escape this "journey to nothingness," this struggle with chronic depression I had not fully dealt with.

GODLY WISDOM

What does God tell us in the Bible about how to deal with depression?

In order to replace thoughts of despair with the fruits of the spirit, we need to begin to read the Bible and talk with God daily through effective prayer.

When we accept Jesus as our Savior, have faith in Jesus, the Bible tells us through God's grace, the Holy Spirit will reside in our hearts, along with Jesus.

The Holy Spirit will teach us and instruct us as we read the Bible daily and give us the knowledge we need to replace the thoughts causing our depressed mood with positive thoughts, so the fruits of the Spirit, love, joy, peace, patience, goodness, kindness, gentleness, faithfulness, and self-control now fill our minds instead.

In Ezekiel 36:26, God offers to replace our stony heart with a new heart, "A new heart also will I give you, and a new spirit will I put within you: and I will take away the stony heart out of your flesh, and I will give you a heart of flesh." In the passage 1 Thessalonians 5:16-24, God tells us to accept to rejoice always. Accept to pray continually, accept to thank God for everything, accept to give thanks in all circumstances, accept to change when the Holy Spirit convicts us to change, accept to take God's Word seriously, accept to ask, *"Is this right, in God's sight?"* accept to do right, accept to resist temptation, accept to be who God intended us to be, accept to commit our life to do God's will for our life—not our own, accept to rely on God's power—not our own, to do what we are called to do.

We must be prepared to suffer many adversities, many kinds of trouble during our time on Earth. We must learn to bear them. If we do these things, then we will come to a point where we think of suffering as "sweet and acceptable" for the sake of Christ, as Thomas a Kempis tells us in *The Imitation of Christ*. Remember, when you suffer something for Jesus, He promises great glory is in store for you, and He promises your suffering for Jesus brings great joy to all the saints of God. Thomas a Kempis tells us, "All men praise patience, though there are a few who wish to practice it." Let us strive to be patient! Thomas a Kempis also tells us, "you must leave a dying life; the more man dies to himself, the more he begins to live unto God."

Remember, you must make the right decision, to suffer for Christ rather than enjoying earthly pleasures! Remember, Christ clearly exhorts the disciples and all of us who wish to follow him, "If any man will come after me, let him deny himself, and take up his cross, and follow me" (Matthew 16:24).

We must remember, we are not promised a life without sorrow and pain, but we must also remember we do have hope! If we bear our cross, if we continue to have faith in Jesus, if we continue to try to please God in everything we do, if we do these things, we will be rewarded on Judgment Day, we will receive our gift from God, an eternal relationship with Him in heaven! Remember, we cannot rely upon ourselves because we cannot do any of the things God wants us to do! We must rely on Jesus, who lives in our hearts!

We need to strive to please him in everything we do and place our complete trust in Him. He will give us the strength from heaven to conquer temptation. We must not fear our enemy Satan but armor ourselves with the *"Full Armor of God."* He will help us prevent Satan from succeeding in his ultimate plan, his plan to lead us to eternal separation from God.

Because we were created by God to have a relationship with him, sin has created a separation from God which we experience as a void in our heart. We spend most of our lives trying to fill this void, this emptiness in our heart, with earthly pleasures. Moral relativism teaches, whatever is good for you is good! Moral relativism does not believe in absolute truth.

However, we are born with a sense of right and wrong, the absolute truth of God, placed in us by God at our conception. Because of the separation from our Creator God, we have a longing to have a relationship, to experience the unconditional love God offers us through this relationship.

Because we are separated from God, we search for other things in the secular world to satisfy this craving for love, this craving for joy, this craving for peace. We can never satisfy this longing we have, this longing to have a relationship with God, with anything we do, based on our worldly experience.

But there is hope! This hope resides in Jesus! Jesus, who is God incarnate, who came to this Earth, took on a fleshly form as the man called Jesus came to this Earth to pay the penalty for our sin. Because God is just, our sin demands death based on God's universal law. Because we are all sinners, we are condemned to hell, eternal separation from God. But because God loves us so much, He died on the cross at Calvary, paying the penalty for our sins, so we could be made right in His sight.

Through Christ's death on the cross, the penalty for our sin has been paid. And when Christ rose from the dead three days later, he defeated death and now sits at the right hand of God, where we also sit. *Hallelujah,* praise God!

It doesn't matter who you are or where you are from; depression is a real issue affecting real people all around us. Godly wisdom found in the Bible can help individuals with depression. Here is a synopsis of steps to consider, excerpted from an article by Bruce Hennigan, entitled "Depression: Reject the Guilt, embrace the Cure."

> Be willing to face emotions that may have been ignored or pushed away for years.
>
> Be willing to face these emotions through Christ's strength. As Matthew 5:4 (NKJV) says, "Blessed are those who mourn, for they shall be comforted."

Though not advisable in every situation, medication may provide needed physical help for people struggling with depression. Talk to a doctor about it.

If needed, reach out for Christian counseling for support, to help you address underlying causes of your depression, and to help you develop a plan of action.

ILLUSTRATION

The following illustration concerning temptation is taken from Michael P. Green's book *1500 Illustrations for Biblical Preaching*:

A man and his wife who were on a long trip stopped at a full-service gas station. After the station attendant had washed their car's windshield, the man in the car said to the station attendant, "It's still dirty. Wash it again."

So the station attendant complied. After washing it again, the man in the car angrily said, "It's still dirty. Don't you know how to wash a windshield?"

Just then, the man's wife reached over, removed her husband's glasses from his face, and cleaned them with a tissue. Then he put them back on, and behold—the windshield was clean!

Our mental attitude has a great deal to do with how we look at things. The whole world can appear pretty bleak if we have a depressed mental attitude. Yet, how bright the world can appear if we have a joyful attitude of hope.

———————————

PRAYER

Our heavenly Father,

I don't understand this journey into nothingness I now feel! Although I should be happy, I have lost interest in the things I once thought pleasurable! Please help me to understand! Help me to escape this journey and return to You!

Today, I have an overwhelming sense of worthlessness! I have a profound sense of emptiness, anxiousness, and sadness! Last night I couldn't sleep because I have an overwhelming sense of inadequacies. I feel like I'm living a lie!

But, I also have hope! Because You are a loving God, through the work on the cross, the penalty for my sins have been paid, I have been made right in Your sight, because of the righteousness of Jesus!

Thank You for promising me You will give me rest! Thank You for taking my yoke upon You! Thank You for Your grace! Thank You for Your Son, Jesus!

In the precious name of Jesus Christ our Lord and Savior,

Amen!

CHAPTER 2

The Beginning...Temptation!

That ye put off concerning the former conversation with the old man, which is corrupt according to the deceitful lusts; And be renewed in the spirit of your mind; And that ye put on the new man, which after God is created in righteousness and true holiness.

—Ephesians 4:22-24

———————

WORLDLY WISDOM

In this passage found in Ephesians Chapter 4, the Holy Spirit is teaching me, if we will reject temptation directed at our old flesh by Satan, and let God do, through us and in us, His plan for our life, then we will become more Christ-like during our life journey on earth.

The Cambridge Dictionary defines temptation in this way: "The desire to have or do something, especially something wrong, or something that causes this desire."

In the beginning, every man was originally made in the holy image of God. He was created in righteousness and true holiness. All mankind has fallen by an act of apostasy and rebellion committed first by Adam.

Our God did not create us to be the depraved and sinful beings we are. Because of our earthly affections and supreme love of self, we are sinners and imperfect. The sinfulness of our hearts appears at the very beginning of our life.

Sin entered the world when Adam and Eve believed Satan's lie and disobeyed God!

They obeyed their own will and ate of the tree of the knowledge of good and evil. This act of disobedience led to the corruption of their human nature. All of Adam and Eve's descendants have inherited this original sin.

However, we must remember, temptation does not become sin until conception takes place. This occurs when you consciously agree with whatever you lust after that displeases God. Satan is the one who usually brings about something to entice us to sin and to separate us from God.

In his book *Toxic Spirituality: Four Enduring Temptations of Christian Faith,* Eric Gritsch maintains there are four toxic Christian traditions that ignore and reject:

> The biblical view of Christian life as shaped by the sin of
> idolatry and as an interim between the first and second
> advent of Christ:" anti-Semitism; fundamentalism; trium-

phalism; and moralism. In his view, these four traditions have poisoned the core of Christian tradition by using them "as a means to justify their own ends, the most enduring temptation."

In today's world, we have an incessant quest for pleasure. But that quest has led many in our culture to be "addicted to addictions."

When we temporarily satisfy the pleasure center of our brain when we indulge our addiction, the amount of the neurotransmitter dopamine is increased, which, in turn, drives down the neurotransmitter serotonin, the contentment neurotransmitter, resulting in a vicious cycle. On top of this, chronic stress drives down both neurotransmitters, making matters worse.

Robert Lustig says this:

> Government legislation and subsidies have tolerated ever-available temptation (sugar, tobacco, alcohol, drugs, social media, porn) combined with constant stress (work, money, home, school, cyberbullying, internet), with the end result of an unprecedented epidemic of addiction, anxiety, depression, and chronic disease. Thus, the more pleasure you seek, the more unhappy you get, and the more likely you will slide into addiction or depression.

And if this wasn't enough, Satan has his "tentacles of deception" insinuated into the mix, making it even harder for us to overcome temptation. In her book *Confrontation; Redemption; or the Temptation of Christ in the Wilderness,* Ellen White describes Satan's part in this way:

> Sin is made attractive by the covering of light which Satan throws over it, and he is well pleased when he can hold the Christian world in their daily habits under the tyranny of custom, like the heathen, and allow appetite to govern them.

In the second chapter of biblical counselor Shannon McCoy's mini-book *Help! I'm a Slave to Food!* she shares the following testimony from someone who struggled with overeating:

> My eating was out of control. I ate solely to satisfy whatever
> craving I was having at the time. As a result, my health was
> suffering, and I was not honoring God with my life and
> body he had given me. I was for the first time confronted
> with the fact that the way that I was eating was sinful. I
> knew that my eating was not good, and I never considered
> that my eating was a sin.

I agree with this testimony. Obesity in the United States is a major health issue. People who are obese have an increased risk of certain types of cancer, coronary artery disease, type II diabetes, stroke, as well as significant increases in early mortality.

According to an article dated September 19, 2019, entitled "Obesity in America: A Public Health Crisis," Caitlin Newman writes, according to data published in JAMA in 2018, about ninety-three million people, nearly forty percent of all adults over the age of twenty in the US, are currently obese.

The biblical term for addiction is idolatry. In Proverbs 23:21, it says, "For the drunkard and the glutton shall come to poverty." I believe the sin of overeating is idolatry. I've been on a yo-yo diet most of my life. During my "forty days in the wilderness," I decided to go on a diet of fish, rice, vegetables, nuts, and fruit. I decided to stop worshiping my stomach and appetites by indulging in food and instead worship God.

Before starting my forty-day journey, my wife and I began a monthly seafood membership with the Wild Alaskan Company, a company that delivers a Wild Combo Box of wild seafood caught in forty Marine Protected Areas off the coast of Alaska, where wild salmon and other species of fish are protected from human activity, allowing them to thrive in their natural habitats. I admire this company because of its founder Erin Kahlenberg, whose family has three generations of experience in the Alaskan seafood industry. He believes in providing seafood harvested in "sustainably-managed, wild fisheries."

MY PERSONAL EXPERIENCE: MY ASSOCIATION WITH MY FRIEND, DR. JESS!

During my journey to salvation, from 1990 to 1992, I was stationed in the Philippines at the Naval Hospital in Subic Bay. I had the pleasure of working with Dr. Jess, who was born on February 27, 1927, in the Philippines. Because Jess was a quiet man, I did not know much about his religious views. However, I admired him as a person. He was a man with a big heart, always with a smile on his face, and a humanitarian who cared for the welfare of the Aetas of Zambales.

But I also admired him for his eating habits. As far as I could tell, his diet consisted of fish and rice. He did not appear to have an ounce of body fat!

Like most Filipinos, he was not overweight. He was an inspiration to me then and now as I try to overcome my "addiction" to overeating.

GODLY WISDOM

So, what godly wisdom can be found in the Bible concerning temptation?

In the Gospel of Matthew 4:1-11, we are given an account of the temptation of Christ by Satan:

> Then was Jesus led up of the Spirit into the wilderness to
> be tempted of the devil. And when he had fasted forty days
> and forty nights, he was afterward hungered. And when the
> tempter came to him, he said, If thou be the Son of God,

command that these stones be made bread. But he answered and said, It is written, Man shall not live by bread alone, but by every word that proceedeth out of the mouth of God. Then the devil taketh him up into the holy city, and setteth him on a pinnacle of the temple, And saith unto him, If thou be the Son of God, cast thyself down: for it is written, He shall give his angels charge concerning thee: and in their hands they shall bear thee up, lest at any time thou dash thy foot against a stone. Jesus said unto him, It is written again, Thou shalt not tempt the Lord thy God. Again, the devil taketh him up into an exceeding high mountain, and sheweth him all the kingdoms of the world, and the glory of them; And saith unto him, All these things will I give thee, if thou wilt fall down and worship me. Then saith Jesus unto him, Get thee hence, Satan: for it is written, Thou shalt worship the Lord thy God, and him only shalt thou serve. Then the devil leaveth him, and, behold, angels came and ministered unto him.

In this account, we are told Jesus was withdrawn from beginning the mission God had sent Him to do in order to undergo a three-fold test of temptation in a desolate desert, on behalf of those he had come to redeem.

Christ stood in Adam's place to bear the test he failed to endure in the Garden of Eden. Jesus entered the gloomy wilderness and met with Satan face-to-face! Satan, emboldened by his victory tempting Adam and Eve, boasted to the heavenly angels, he would be triumphant and overcome Christ by his power. In the desert, Satan felt Christ had been humiliated, and because of this humiliation, he would be successful in overcoming Christ. But Satan was wrong. Christ could not be tempted, and Satan failed.

Barry Denzil Haney, MD

What is the meaning and purpose of Jesus' temptations in this passage?

First, Jesus revealed His humanity, expressing feelings humans experience during stressful situations. Second, He displayed His superiority to humans and His knowledge of God's Word to resist Satan's temptations. Finally, Jesus offered us an example of how to deal with Satan when we are tempted. As James tells us in James 1:13-15,

> Let no man say when he is tempted, I am tempted of God:
> for God cannot be tempted with evil, neither tempteth
> he any man: But every man is tempted, when he is drawn
> away of his own lust, and enticed. Then when lust hath
> conceived, it bringeth forth sin: and sin, when it is finished,
> bringeth forth death.

The Bible tells us in 1 Corinthians 10:13,

> There hath no temptation taken you but such as is common
> to man: but God is faithful, who will not suffer you to be
> tempted above that ye are able; but will with the temptation
> also make a way to escape, that ye may be able to bear it.

The Bible tells us to avoid things that might lead to compromising situations and sin. Romans 13:13-14 tells us,

> Let us walk honestly, as in the day; not in rioting and
> drunkenness, not in chambering and wantonness, not in
> strife and envying. But put ye on the Lord Jesus Christ, and
> make not provision for the flesh, to fulfil the lusts thereof.

We become sons of God. Our spirit is then saved, and our spirit will then spend eternity with God in heaven. However, the soul, part of the spirit, still undergoes the process of progressive sanctification, the process of becoming more holy, becoming more Christ-like, as we undergo our journey of salvation while here on Earth. We will fall because Satan is the great deceiver; he will find a way to crack the protection that the Holy Spirit provides the soul.

Why does that happen? Why does God allow the soul part of our Spirit to succumb to Satan's temptation?

Because God loves us so much, He did not want to force us to believe; He did not want to force us to worship him; He did not want to force us to have faith in Jesus; He did not want us to be robots! He gave us free will.

For you see, because God loves us so much, He wants us to willingly have faith in Jesus. He gave us free will and placed the responsibility on us to make the choice, whether we want to spend eternity with Him in the place He has prepared for us in heaven, or to make the only other choice, to be eternally separated from Him, in a place called hell.

The choice is ours!

Because of God's grace and kindness, He has provided a way for us to spend eternity with Him—the plan is simple, a simple formula—but there is only one way, and that is through faith in Jesus.

Thank You for this gift of salvation, our heavenly Father!

ILLUSTRATION

The following illustration concerning temptation is taken from Michael P. Green's book *1500 Illustrations for Biblical Preaching*:

Barry Denzil Haney, MD

A woodpecker is a very interesting bird. The loud rat-a-tat-tat noise he makes as he drills into trees in search of bugs to eat always attracts attention. The secret of his success is simple. When a woodpecker finds a suitable tree, he begins to drill a hole. If the wood is too hard or no bugs are found, he simply moves over a bit and starts again. Over and over, he continues until he meets with success.

Satan uses temptation in much the same way. He will try one temptation on us and then, if not successful, will move over a bit and try another. And so he will continue, over and over again, until he finds a soft spot in us that he can use to his advantage.

PRAYER

Our heavenly Father,

We adore You; we trust You; we love You.

We praise You for being our Creator.

We thank You for Your free gift of salvation You offer us through Your wonderful, merciful grace.

We pray for revival in each of us personally.

We lift up to You in prayer all of those with spoken and unspoken needs. Thank You for Your continued comfort, peace, and healing power in their lives.

We ask that we may know Your love since we ask nothing other than an eternal relationship with You. For You mean everything to us: our life, our light, our salvation, our food, and our drink, our God. Inspire our hearts; we ask You, Jesus, with that breath of your Spirit!

In the precious name of Jesus Christ, our Lord and Savior,

Amen.

CHAPTER 3

Chewy Candy Delight!

Love not the world, neither the things that are in the world.
If any man love the world, the love of the Father is not
in him. For all that is in the world, the lust of the flesh,
and the lust of the eyes, and the pride of life, is not of the
Father, but is of the world. And the world passeth away, and
the lust thereof: but he that doeth the will of God abideth
forever.

—1 John 2:15-17

WORLDLY WISDOM

Although John warns us not to love the world's ways, not to *"lust of the flesh,"* and admonishes us to do the will of God, many people allow themselves to be enslaved by lust.

The Cambridge Dictionary defines lust in this way: "To have a strong desire for something."

The Dictionary of Bible Themes defines lust in this way: "An overpowering and compulsive desire or passion, especially of a sexual nature. Scripture condemns lust of all kinds and urges believers to show self-control."

Where does lust come from, and how long has it been around?

Most would agree; it originates in the mind and has been around since men began living together in communities. In the article called "Seven Deadly Sins," the following excerpted passage describes lust as one of the eight human offenses and human passions to be avoided:

According to *Sacred Origins of Profound Things* by Charles Panati, the theologian Evagrius first drew up a list of eight offenses and wicked human passions. "They were, in order of increasing seriousness: gluttony, lust, avarice, sadness, anger, acedia, vainglory, and pride. Evagrius saw the escalating severity as representing increasing fixation with the self, with pride as the most egregious of the sins."

Is lust a sin?

First of all, I do not believe the thought of initiating lust is a sin until acted upon. At first, Satan may frequently remind you of some memory, tempting you to dwell on it or seduce you to fantasize about a particular person or object. But there is a fine line between the temptation of lust and falling for the temptation and displeasing God.

Lust, the sin, is not temptation, but it becomes sin when you surrender to temptation, when you dwell on the impure thoughts Satan has presented you, or when you act upon the impure thoughts, then lust displeases God and becomes sin.

During my lifetime study of philosophers and great thinkers who lived throughout history, I have discovered, most of the great thinkers agree, "as you think, you shall become."

If you think positive, uplifting, cheerful thoughts, you will become a positive, uplifting, cheerful person. If you think negative, sad, somber thoughts, you will turn out to be a negative, sad, somber person.

MY PERSONAL EXPERIENCE: RED MAN CHEWING TOBACCO!

When I was eleven years old, my parents leased a small country store across the road from Skyview Drive-in, located in Winchester, Kentucky. During tobacco season, farmers, who were cutting tobacco in the early fall, would come to my parent's country store at noon break to buy lunch.

In the store was an old-fashioned meat counter, where my mother would make fresh, huge sandwiches mostly made up of bologna or ham—sliced from a loaf—with mayo or mustard and topped with lettuce and fresh tomatoes right out of the garden!

Everyone who bought one seemed to love them!

I also remember the workers buying small boxes of crackers, Vienna sausage in the can, and other such snacks.

They would gather, just outside the store, sit in the grass, in the cool breeze of a shade tree and talk, while they devoured their lunch!

My brother Clay and I would sit under a tree, as close as we would dare venture, in order to overhear the colorful and sometimes lewd conversations sprinkled with curse words we had never heard before.

I don't remember too much about what was said, but to a young boy of eleven, the stories I heard captivated my imagination.

But the thing I remember the most, the thing that captivated the imagination of a young boy, was the men pulling from their front pocket a beautiful bar, a bar of what appeared to be chewy, delicious candy!

After eating, chowing down the huge sandwiches, dripping with juices mixed with tomato juice from the fresh tomatoes and mayonnaise spread generously on the two slices of bread, barely holding together the mounds of meat stacked high between them, many would pull out of their pockets, a dark bar, usually wrapped in a beautiful, colorful, wrapping of metallic foil, glistening in the noonday sun.

They would quickly tear the wrapping from the bar, then viciously, tear a huge bite from the bar, and then slowly, but deliberately, begin chewing.

The bar they held glistened in the sunlight, with what looked like tendrils of honey dripping from the edges of the bite mark, a delightful, thick, beckoning, I'm sure, sugary, syrupy mixture of chewy delight!

For a time, they seemed to enjoy what they were chewing, but to my amazement, they would, after a few minutes, spit out the juices from their mouth!

I couldn't understand why they would spit out that syrupy, sugary, delightful liquid!

But nevertheless, I remember later sneaking into the store, hiding from my mother's sight, and going to the stand where the beautiful, packaged candy was displayed.

Carefully, I took the one that looked the most inviting to me, hid it in my pocket, then quickly, but stealthily, snuck out of the store, and to my delight, without my mother discovering my presence!

I immediately ran to the back of the barn adjacent to our house.

I quickly unwrapped the beautiful, wrapped foil paper and pulled out this plug, this beautiful, delightful, sweet-looking bar of what I assumed was candy!

I looked around, to make sure no one was watching, and then took a big bite out of this bar and began chewing, but to my horror, I tasted the most horrific thing I had ever tasted, worse than liver, spinach, broccoli, or even all three mixed together, a witches brew—I almost immediately began spitting this vile liquid from my mouth!

I'm sure I turned several shades of green and became sick to my stomach. As you might guess, my chewy candy delight actually was a plug of chewing tobacco, probably the brand Red Man!

Little did I know at that moment, I was being taught a very valuable lesson—not everything in the world is as it appears. Not everything available for me to experience in the world will bring me joy; not every earthly pleasure will fill that void; no earthly pleasure will satisfy that hunger for pleasure, the need for a relationship. Only the unconditional love of God will fill the void through faith in Jesus and by God's grace.

Barry Denzil Haney, MD

GODLY WISDOM

According to godly wisdom, God is not the source of temptation. *If God is not the source, who is?* James resounding answer is the heart of man! "But every man is tempted, when he is drawn away of his own lust, and enticed. Then when lust hath conceived, it bringeth forth sin: and sin, when it is finished, bringeth forth death" (James 1:14-15).

As the Bible goes on further to say in Proverbs 23:7, "As he thinketh in his heart, so is he." In verse 14, James uses the two highly descriptive words *"drawn away"* and *"enticed,"* fishing terms illustrating the seduction of the thought of lust. Like bait seduces a fish to bite a concealed hook, the temptation of lust leads a man down the disastrous road to displeasing God.

Just like in the secular world, I believe the churches today are filled with men and women who live a double life. They, as Keith Drury describes in his book *Spiritual Disciplines for Ordinary People,* are "Jekyll-Hyde Christians." He goes on to say: "These double-minded Christians sneak off to the private closets of their minds. There they dwell on corrupt and sordid thoughts, then cower back full of guilt and despair. This is a wretched way to live."

The temptation of lust is seen on television, in the movies, in our music, in advertisements, during halftime shows, in our books, and in glossy magazine close-ups at the supermarket check-out.

Because it is almost impossible to escape sensuality—lust—in our daily life, how do we get help? How do we use godly wisdom to help us with the overwhelming temptations of lust we are exposed to each day? By daily prayer and daily reading and study of the Word of God, the Holy Spirit will teach and instruct you on how to use the sword of the Spirit to withstand Satan's temptations.

Paul tells us in Galatians 5:16-17,

> This I say then, Walk in the Spirit, and ye shall not fulfil the lust of the flesh. For the flesh lusteth against the Spirit, and

the Spirit against the flesh: and these are contrary the one to the other: so that ye cannot do the things that ye would.

Paul goes on to say in Romans 8:6-11,

> For to be carnally minded is death; but to be spiritually minded is life and peace. Because the carnal mind is enmity against God: for it is not subject to the law of God, neither indeed can be. So then they that are in the flesh cannot please God. But ye are not in the flesh, but in the Spirit, if so be that the Spirit of God dwell in you. Now if any man have not the Spirit of Christ, he is none of his. And if Christ be in you, the body is dead because of sin; but the Spirit is life because of righteousness. But if the Spirit of him that raised up Jesus from the dead dwell in you, he that raised up Christ from the dead shall also quicken your mortal bodies by his Spirit that dwelleth in you.

God loved us so much and didn't want us to be robots forced to worship Him, but instead wanted us to freely worship Him. He gave us the gift of free will. But in doing this, He knew this would usher into His creation the problem of sin and evil and that sin would prevent those He created in His image from spending an eternity with Him. So in His omniscience, before He said, "Let there be light," He imagined His plan of salvation for the world. He gave us the blueprint of this plan of salvation in the form of the Bible.

Barry Denzil Haney, MD

ILLUSTRATION

The following illustration concerning the Devil's Effect on Christians is taken from Michael P. Green's book *1500 Illustrations for Biblical Preaching*:

> An artist carved a woodcut titled "The Knight, the Devil, and Death." The woodcut pictures a gallant knight riding his stallion down a path in the middle of the night. Alongside the path are many creatures and monsters that seem to want to devour the knight. But they can gain no advantage over him because his eyes are on his home; he cannot be bothered.

> Likewise, as long as we keep our eyes on Christ, we will not be devoured by Satan, though he is eagerly awaiting a moment when he might distract us and cause us to sin.

———————

PRAYER

Our heavenly Father,

Thank You for being my Creator; thank You for Your unconditional love, mercy, kindness, and grace; thank You for caring for me so much, You died on the cross at Calvary, so my sins would be forgiven; so I might spend an eternity with You in heaven, even though I don't deserve it.

Thank You, for forgiving my sins; thank You for the hope You give me each day; thank You for the Holy Spirit, who instructs me, teaches me, and protects me from the temptation of lust from Satan; thank You for the opportunity to please You each day; thank You for giving me the opportunity to play a small part in Your grand plan of salvation for the world; thank You for all the blessings You have bestowed on me.

In the precious name of Jesus Christ, our Lord and Savior,

Amen!

CHAPTER 4

A Glimpse of Hell!

But unto every one of us is given grace according to the measure of the gift of Christ. Wherefore he saith, When he ascended up on high, he led captivity captive, and gave gifts unto men. Now that he ascended, what is it but that he also descended first into the lower parts of the earth? He that descended is the same also that ascended up far above all heavens, that he might fill all things.

—Ephesians 4:7-10

WORLDLY WISDOM

In the passage in Ephesians Chapter 4, the Holy Spirit is teaching me the following: each one of us has been given grace, we have been saved; when Christ ascended to sit at the right hand of God, He took captive the sin we were previously enslaved to when He nailed it on the cross at Calvary; and He went from glory to humility, and then from humility back to glory, so we could be filled with the Holy Spirit. Some take the second part of verse 9, "he also descended first into the lower parts of the earth," to mean he descended into hell. But that is controversial, and I leave it to you to pursue further if you are interested.

The Cambridge Dictionary defines hell in this way: "In some religions, the place where some people are believed to go after death to be punished forever for the bad things they have done during their lives."

The Dictionary of Bible Themes defines hell in this way: "The state of final separation from God, and so from all light, love, peace, pleasure, and fulfilment."

MY PERSONAL EXPERIENCE: A TERRIFYING DREAM!

Shortly after my brother Ronnie died in February 2019, I experienced a terrifying dream.

In the dream, I was in a very dark place, without a body, spirit-like, able to think, but unable to experience any other sensation I usually could experience through my ears, nose, mouth, or sense of touch. This was a very dark place, a vast empty space, filled with blackness, containing no other stimulation or sensation, unlike any other place I had ever been. Complete and total darkness seemed to be mysteriously and dangerously enclosing me, embracing me, and enshrouding me!

I could sense no light of any kind, no thoughts other than my own, no emotions other than my own, no love or hate. Curiously, I also noticed no sense of time, something very strange to me, the sense of no time or space, just a sense of nothingness.

I cried out, "Help me, Judy, please help me!" But again, I could only sense nothingness, complete and total darkness, emptiness.

The thought then occurred to me, could this be hell! Have I died and gone to hell! Now convinced I was experiencing hell, I again cried out, with a blood-curdling scream, "Please help me, someone, please help me!"

Barry Denzil Haney, MD

WHAT IS HELL?

When I did a Google search on "What is hell," in 0.57 seconds, I received 777,000,000 results! Wow! Based on the Google results, this is a very popular subject! What is it about the word "hell" that intrigues us? The modern English word hell is derived from old English *hel, helle*. This old English word reaches back into the Anglo-Saxon pagan period. Hell appears in several mythologies and religions, known as the "abode of the dead." Both folklore and religion describe hell as an "afterlife location in which evil souls are subjected to punitive suffering, often torture as eternal punishment after death." Commonly, hell is thought of as a place inhabited by demons and the souls of dead people. Because of this fascination with the concept of hell, it is often depicted in art and literature.

One of the most famous is Dante's *Divine Comedy*. This narrative poem by Dante Alighieri, written between 1308 and 1320, describes Dante's travels through Hell, Purgatory, and Paradise or Heaven. Dante draws heavily on the *Summa Theologica* of Thomas Aquinas; therefore, this poem has been called "the *Summa* in verse."

The first part of the three-part epic poem is called Dante's Inferno, Dante's journey through the nine circles of hell guided by the poet Virgil. Dante describes nine circles of hell in order of entrance and severity as follows: limbo, lust, gluttony, greed, anger, heresy, violence, fraud, and treachery. After making their way through all nine circles of hell, Dante and Virgil reach the center of hell, where they meet Satan.

Satan is described as a three-headed beast, with each mouth busy eating a specific person: the left mouth is eating Brutus; the right mouth is eating Cassius; the center mouth is eating Judas Iscariot. To Dante, these three people represented the greatest sinners because they had consciously committed acts of treachery against their lords, who were appointed by God.

During my Google search, I was alarmed and frightened about how persuasive the word "hell" is in the world's vocabulary today!

In order to convey to you the world's insatiable infatuation with hell, I feel compelled to share with you the following ways the concept of hell has insinuated itself into the very fabric of our entertainment and popular culture, which I discovered through my search about "hell" in Wikipedia.

Some of the most famous depictions of hell can be viewed in many paintings by medieval Dutch painter Hieronymus Bosch, the most famous *The Garden of Delights*. The illustrations for Dante's *Divine Comedy* by Gustav Dore also depict Dante's visit to hell. The sculpture called, *The Gates of Hell* by Auguste Rodin is based on the hell depicted in Dante's *Divine Comedy*.

Our infatuation with "hell" can be seen in cartoons, comics, and televised cartoon series, including the following:

> The character Lobo, in the comic book *DC Universe*, who was banned from hell; in the comic strip *Dilbert*, created by Scott Adams, where a place called "Heck" exists, a lesser version of hell reserved for people who have done misdeeds that are not evil enough to warrant hell; in the comic *Far Side* created by Gary Larson, where hell is featured, among other recurring themes, depicting Satan and his minions as grim looking figures in robes with horns and pitchforks, running the place in a businesslike manner; in the cartoon series *Futurama* the characters go to "Robot Hell," where the robot devil and other evil robots reside; in the comic book series *Ghostwriter*, Johnny Blaze sells his soul to the demon, Mephisto, to cure his adoptive father dying of cancer; in the comic book series *Hellboy*, by award-winning artist Mike Magnolia, hell is depicted as a dark alternate dimension filled with flames and demons, where the infernal capital city of Pandemonium resides; in the comic book series *Spawn* hell and its demons are used as important plot elements; finally hell appears in many episodes of the television series, *South Park*.

Our infatuation with "hell" can be seen in films, including the following:

> The theme of hell appears in many films, including *Haxan, Dante's Inferno, Faust, Cabin in the Sky, Heaven Can Wait, Angel on My Shoulder, Damn Yankees, Santa Claus, Scrooge, Tales from the Crypt, Bill and Ted's Bogus Journey, Friday the 13th, Drag Me to Hell,* and others.

Our infatuation with "hell" can be seen in gaming and video games, including the following:

> Dungeons and Dragons role-playing games, where seven hellish planes, usually called the "Lower Planes," exist in the game; in the game *In Nomine*, the forces of Heaven and Hell fight each other in a modern setting. Many videogames also feature "hell" as a central theme, including *Mortal Kombat, Dante's Inferno, Devil May Cry, Diablo, Dune, Hellgate: London: Minecraft,* and others.

Our infatuation with "hell" can be seen in other literature, including the following:

> Milton's *Paradise Lost*, in which Lucifer and other fallen angels are imprisoned in hell for rebelling against God after the birth of Christ; in Piers Anthony's series, *Incarnations of Immortality*, where Hell, along with Heaven and Purgatory, are actually locations populated by main characters and souls of the dead; in Wayne Barlowe's book *God's Demons*, set in hell, follows the endeavors of a powerful demon, Sargatanas, to achieve redemption; in the novel *City Infernal* by Edward Lee, where hell is depicted as a modern metropolis called the "Mephistopolis," where electricity is provided

by tapping the bio-electricity of tortured souls, chaos and suffering are systematically enforced, organic materials such as blood and bones are used for everything from food and building materials, and everything in between, and vicious horrors, both born and manufactured, run rampant; in Emanuel Swedenborg's book *Heaven and Hell*, where he claims to have visited hell.

Our infatuation with "hell" can be seen in our music, where many songs and albums use the word "hell" to talk about *hell*, including the following:

> In their albums, *Beyond Hell* (2006) and *Hell-O* (1988), the group GWAR uses the word hell and other related concepts; the group Slayers' second studio album entitled *Hell Waits*, where hellish lyrical themes are used; the group Insane Clown Posse's album, entitled *Hell's Pit*, is a concept album, about Hell; the Venom album titled, *Welcome to Hell*, also addresses hell, and was released in 1981.

Our infatuation with "hell" can be seen in television and radio, including the following:

> In *Buffyverse*, several places in the world are depicted that are natural gateways between the underworld and the world of mortals; in *Dr. Who*, the "tenth doctor" comes across a being which identifies itself as "the Beast," who resembles popular interpretations of the devil; in the television series, *Supernatural*, hell is mentioned many times as the place demons originated; in the television series, *Reaper*, the main character Sam is a bounty hunter searching for the devil, who must send escaped souls back to hell; Hell appears in several episodes of *The Twilight Zone*, most notably in,

Barry Denzil Haney, MD

"A Nice Place to Visit," and "The Hunt;" in the television supernatural drama, *Ghost Whisperer*, hell is depicted as a place where ghosts go if they did not crossover into light and instead go to the Dark Side; in the British science fiction sitcom, *Red Dwarf*, several characters make reference to "Silicon Hell," the presumed alternative to the concept of "Silicon Heaven," programmed into most artificially intelligent devices, in order to preserve their loyalty to humanity; finally, the concept of "hell" also appears in *Good Omens*.

What I shared with you is just the tip of the iceberg!

I believe Satan has insinuated his tentacles into every facet of our daily lives and uses lies and deception to keep us from an eternal relationship with God. May this "glimpse of hell" described above be a warning, "to resist the devil, and he will flee from you" (James 4:7).

On a more optimistic note, in the United States, I have witnessed a resurgence in Christian values in entertainment and popular culture. Beautiful works of art can be found with Christian themes. Many books can be found by Christian authors. Many cartoons, comics, and television cartoon series feature Christian-based themes. The popularity of the genre of Christian music attests to the lure of this brand of music. On social media sites, blogs dedicated to Christianity flourish. Even on television and radio, religious networks can be found dedicated to spreading the Good News of the Gospel to the world.

Another area I have not given up hope for is the genre of video gaming. I have been a fan of gaming since I can remember. I owned an Atari and played the game *Pong* religiously during my undergraduate years in college, during the 1970s. As the sophistication of video games increased over the decades, I have played many of the most popular video games, sometimes to excess. Until I completely gave my life to God in 2017, I played *Forge of Empires* for hours a day.

After giving my life completely to God, my time playing video games has significantly decreased. But I will say this, I found, many Christians play video games, usually in secret. I have met several playing the game *Forge of Empires*. In 2019, through inspiration from the Holy Spirit, I founded a guild on Forge of Empires called "IAmAChristian." I formed this guild to witness to other members in the *Forge of Empires* community the good news of the Gospel.

God can use any means for us to witness and make disciples of all men, even video gaming! *Hallelujah!*

ILLUSTRATION

The following illustration concerning hell is taken from Michael P. Green's book *1500 Illustrations for Biblical Preaching*:

> W. C. Fields, following the 1933 earthquake that struck Southern California, said: "We're crazy to live here, but there sure are a lot of us." The same attitude is often displayed by non-Christians, who seem to think that hell will be more tolerable because there will be a crowd down there.

GODLY WISDOM

C.S. Lewis wrote this about hell, "There is no doctrine which I would more willingly remove from Christianity than this, if it lay in my power." For many Christians, hell is a difficult reality. In the New Testament, Jesus speaks about hell more than he did about heaven. Bertrand Russell, a famous skeptic, said in his book *Why I'm Not a Christian*, the following, "Jesus teaching on hell is the one profound defect in Christ's character."

When Jesus was crucified, He appeared to lament the fact He would soon be separated from His Father because of the human sin He would bear and die on the cross for when He cried out, "My God, my God, why have you forsaken me?" (Matthew 27:46 NIV). The Bible describes hell in several verses, including the following sample: "As a place where the wicked will be consigned to a fiery lake of burning sulfur, a second death" (Revelation 21:8); "A very dismal place, where they will receive everlasting destruction, and be shut out from the presence of the Lord in his glory" (2 Thessalonians 1:9); "The wicked shall be thrown into a blazing furnace, there will be weeping and gnashing of teeth" (Matthew 13:50, CSB). From these Bible descriptions, certainly, not a place I want to go to!

Although many people today believe every individual human is going to live forever, some do not believe a loving God would condemn any person to eternal separation from Him in a place called Hell. I disagree with those who believe this, but instead, agree with C.S. Lewis as he puts it:

> Christianity asserts that every individual human being is going to live forever, and this must be either true or false. Now there are a good many things which would not be worth bothering about if I were going to live only seventy years, but which I had better bother about very seriously if I am going to live forever. Perhaps my bad temper or my jealousy are gradually getting worse—so gradually that the increase in seventy years will not be very noticeable. But it might be absolute hell in a million years: in fact, if Christianity is true, hell is the precisely correct technical term for what it would be.

He further elaborates on this subject in other writings in this way:

> Hell begins with a grumbling mood, and yourself still distinct from it: perhaps criticizing it Ye can repent and come out of it again. But there may come a day when you

can do that no longer. Then there will be no you left to crit-icize the mood, nor even to enjoy it, but just the grumble itself going on forever like a machine.

As I see it, unfortunately, we have only two options: live with God in an eternal loving relationship or live eternally separated from God, in a place some call *hell*. I believe, when you say you don't want God's authority but would rather live for yourself, that's hell. C. S. Lewis addresses this issue in *The Great Divorce and The Problem of Pain:*

> In the long run, the answer to all those who object to the doctrine of hell is itself a question: "What are you asking God to do?"…To leave them alone. Alas, I am afraid that is what he does…In the end, there are only two kinds of people—those who say to God "thy will be done" and those to whom God says in the end "thy will be done."

What does it actually mean to spend an eternity in hell?

Descent into hell is a statement of, as Michael Allen likes to call, the God-forsakenness we will experience if we make the wrong choice. Hell is the experience of the absence of God's favor or blessing. Because God is omnipresent, God even exists in hell. God's presence in hell is experienced as his wrath, anger, and vengeance. If a person was literally, completely apart from God in hell, they would cease to exist. Contrary to what some atheists and agnostics believe, when you die, you do not cease to exist; you do not experience annihilation.

Every human being will live forever, either in a glorious eternal relation-ship with God or separated from God. Hell represents the latter! Just like us, when Jesus died on the cross, He not only experienced physical death just as we will eventually do, but He also suffered the "spiritual agony" we all deserve because of our sin. Our hope, because of the work of Jesus on the cross at Calvary, is that if we have faith in Jesus, we will spend an eternal loving relationship with God our Father in heaven.

MY PERSONAL EXPERIENCE: LORD, ARE YOU THERE?

I sometimes wonder, as I lay here talking to You, *Lord Jesus, are You there?* I sometimes wonder, *Am I just talking to myself?* I listen, hoping to hear from You. I know that You are there because of the things that happen in my life, the things that make me aware of Your presence. I do believe You have engineered my walk with You, that everything has been planned for me, and that You do have a plan for my life.

Finally, I understand; all I have to do is just get out of Your way and do Your will. Thank You for that opportunity.

Thank You for the gift of the Holy Spirit to help me understand what it is You would have me do.

PRAYER

Our heavenly Father,

Last night, I experienced a terrifying dream! In the dream, I was in a very dark place, where I could only sense nothingness, complete and total darkness, emptiness, what I believe was a glimpse of hell!

Father, I do not want to experience the absence of Your favor or blessing in the place called hell! I do have hope because of the work of Jesus on the cross at Calvary! Hallelujah!

When I pray, I sometimes wonder are You there! When I pray, I listen, hoping to hear from You! Because of the things happening in my life, I know You are there and have a plan for my life!

Thank You, Jesus!

In the precious name of Jesus Christ our Lord and Savior,

Amen!

Barry Denzil Haney, MD

CHAPTER 5

Loneliness!

"And the LORD God said, It is not good that the man
should be alone; I will make him a help meet for him."

—Genesis 2:18

WORLDLY WISDOM

In the beginning, God realized it was not good for man to be alone. In her
book *Biblical Counseling on Loneliness*, June Hunt tells us the word alone
appears one hundred eighteen times in Scripture, but rarely is it synony-
mous with the word lonely. She also explains the word "lonely" acquired its
present meaning this century, and only in recent years has it been thought
of as a mental condition.

Researchers have found many factors can cause the sense of overwhelming loneliness, including social, mental, emotional, and physical factors,
and loneliness can occur even when people are surrounded by other people.

The Cambridge Dictionary defines loneliness in this way: "The state of
being lonely; furthermore, difficulties with establishing personal contacts,
caused, for instance, by social anxiety."

The Dictionary of Bible Themes describes loneliness in this way: "God
intends human beings to live together in harmony and to value one another,
but Scripture recognizes many reasons for individuals to feel unwanted and
isolated."

Feelings of loneliness and isolation can affect all types and ages of people, especially the adolescent and the elderly.

MY PERSONAL EXPERIENCE: LEFT ALONE!

Before my mother died, she shared with me her regret of leaving me alone when I was an infant while she attended premed classes at the University of Kentucky.

Although she left me with my grandmother, who lived downstairs, my grandmother would sometimes have to leave me for hours while she ran errands or did housework.

Oftentimes, when my mother arrived home, she would hear me crying frantically upstairs in the apartment, alone, in my crib, in the dark.

I try to imagine myself, upstairs alone, separated from the world, in this dark lonely place, crying out for someone to help me, wanting a human touch, needing nourishment, needing cleansing, needing intimacy, needing contact with someone or something…

What causes loneliness?

Loneliness can be caused by a variety of things. In our world, because of computerization, we can isolate ourselves in our homes and not interact with anyone. We can do our shopping on the internet using Amazon Prime; we can do our grocery shopping online and have it delivered to us, we can buy prepared food from a variety of vendors and have it delivered, we can go to "church" using Christian channels, we can have social relationships with other people through various social media platforms such as Facebook or Twitter, we can even plan our funeral via the internet.

We don't have to look at a person anymore; we don't have to talk to a person anymore, because Siri or some other computerized voice will talk to us in our cars, at the airport, even in our homes. Lastly, and to me, the most disturbing, we now can have "virtual sex" online because of the explosive, billion-dollar pornography industry, just a click away on our computers!

The medical world has warned us for years that sitting, smoking, and obesity are linked to chronic disease, but in my practice of medicine, loneliness is another risk factor for chronic health conditions.

I have found personally, loneliness is not necessarily about social isolation but how we perceive our level of connectedness to others. For example, a Franciscan monk may not feel lonely at all, while others may feel lonely, even when surrounded by a crowd. The pain of loneliness can be sensed when listening to the Beatles song, *Eleanor Rigby*, captured by the following stanza:

> *All the lonely people*
> *Where do they all come from?*
> *All the lonely people*
> *Where do they all belong?*

Loneliness tends to increase levels of the stress hormone cortisol in our bodies. Although cortisol can be beneficial, it can also have detrimental physical effects on our bodies, including impairment of cognitive function, compromise of our immune system, increase in the risk for cardiovascular disease, Type II diabetes, arthritis, and other inflammatory diseases.

Loneliness can also impact our mental health adversely, causing problems such as depression and anxiety, and it has been found that lonely people are twice as likely to develop Alzheimer's disease. Loneliness can lead to a chronic stress condition, be harmful to sleep, age the body, and damage overall well-being.

Guy Winch, in his article "Is There a Gene for Loneliness?" states the following:

> While a specific "loneliness gene" has not been isolated (and
> might never be, as loneliness likely relates to a confluence of
> many genes rather than just one), the findings do reinforce

those of other studies that have also found genetic predispositions to loneliness.

In the book *Encyclopedia of Psychology and Counseling*, S. A. Cappas describes loneliness in this way:

> Loneliness is marked by painful feelings of sadness and longing and almost always by the absence of, yet felt desire for, relationship with others. Symptoms can include experiences of isolation and abandonment marked by anger, irritability, crying, agitation, negative ruminative thoughts, and potentially unhealthy behaviors set forth to compensate for these feelings and symptoms.

How do we deal with loneliness?

The secular worldview position is to address both the "emotional and situational dimension" loneliness has, by taking steps to strengthen connections to others, reaching out to people we come into daily contact with, reaching out to those in our social media sites, and, if necessary, seeking a mental health professional to help tailor a strategy to help us cope and meet others.

But, is there another way, a better way to deal with loneliness?

I would say yes to this question—by seeking godly wisdom!

—————

GODLY WISDOM

Godly wisdom tells us Jesus is the ultimate answer to those who feel lonely. When we study the Gospels, we will find Jesus lived a life of loneliness. God understands how we feel; there is not a thought in our mind He doesn't know, as David tells us in Psalm 139:1-4:

Barry Denzil Haney, MD

O LORD, thou hast searched me, and known me. Thou knowest my downsitting and mine uprising, Thou understandest my thought afar off. Thou compassest my path and my lying down, And art acquainted with all my ways. For there is not a word in my tongue, But, lo, O LORD, thou knowest it altogether.

Just as God realized how loneliness adversely affected Adam in Genesis 2:8, loneliness takes on a painful quality in Genesis 3 when Adam and Eve succumb to temptation and experience loneliness when they are alienated from God.

In Christ's crucifixion on the cross at Calvary, even Jesus experiences the epitome of loneliness as told to us in the Gospel of Matthew 27:46, "And about the ninth hour Jesus cried with a loud voice, saying, Eli, Eli, lama sabachthani? that is to say, My God, my God, why hast thou forsaken me?" The Bible is full of other examples of loneliness and solitude, but also with positive examples of the benefits and purpose of the practice of solitude for Christians.

Most counselors would agree, loneliness is a component present in most people seeking counseling. In some cases, loneliness may positively benefit a person's recovery, especially in grief counseling. In her article "Loneliness: God's Remedy," Jayne Clark tells us this:

We want to talk and be heard, known and understood, included and cared about. It isn't what remedies our loneliness, but who remedies it, Jesus Christ, the friend of sinners…God changes our priorities. Rather than being self-absorbed, we become more focused on others…No matter who you are, you will experience loneliness in this fallen world…He has united us to himself and each other in Jesus, and he calls us to enter into the loneliness around us.

MY PERSONAL EXPERIENCE: HELP ME!

I spent my whole life trying to bridge that gap, to have that relationship, seeking someone, seeking something to fill the mind-boggling sense of loneliness; separation from God. I spent my whole life crying out, "*Help me*," searching for the relationship I was created for.

I looked for any means possible, any earthly pleasure, anything, that would fill that void in my heart, to fill that godly container in my heart, in an attempt to overcome this crushing, staggering feeling of loneliness, this sense of existing in a place of complete darkness, a place void of relationship, a place where no stimulation of any kind exists, a place of nothingness; a place called hell.

The problem is, these brief encounters with earthly pleasure, the ecstasy I felt when I filled this void, are quite satisfying but extremely and totally short-lived. I found that whatever earthly pleasure I use requires more and more to achieve the same electrifying, ecstatic, orgasmic response, the same release of dopamine at the cellular level in my brain.

Finally, after seventy years of searching, I realize, what I am really seeking is an eternal loving relationship with my Creator God; He is the answer to my loneliness. I am searching for agape love; I'm searching for His unconditional love, only experienced in God's presence!

Our heavenly Father, you are the beginning and the end, the Alpha and the Omega, You are the divine Creator, You are the great I am, You are my personal Savior, You are my Creator God, You are the one, and only, hallelujah, we bow down before You and praise and worship Your name. Thank You, Lord.

PRAYER

Our heavenly Father,

Thank You for being my Creator; thank You for Your unconditional love, mercy, kindness, and grace; thank You for caring for me so much that You died on the cross at Calvary, so my sins are forgiven. So I might spend an eternity with You in heaven, even though I don't deserve it.

Thank You for forgiving me of my sins. Thank You for the hope that You give me each day. Thank You for the opportunity to please You each day; thank You for giving me the opportunity to play a small part in Your grand plan of salvation for the world; thank You for all the blessings You have bestowed on me.

You are so good, You are so gracious, You are so faithful! Thank You, Lord Jesus. Thank You, Holy Spirit, for teaching me, instructing me, and protecting me.

Thank You, Jesus. Thank You for my family; thank You for my friends!

In the precious name of Jesus Christ, our Lord and Savior,

Amen.

CHAPTER 6

In Darkness...
Let There Be Light!

"Then spake Jesus again unto them, saying, I am the light of the world: he that followeth me shall not walk in darkness, but shall have the light of life."

—John 8:12

WORLDLY WISDOM

The Merriam-Webster Dictionary defines light in these ways:

"Something that makes vision possible; the sensation aroused by stimulation of the visual receptors; spiritual illumination."

The Dictionary of Bible Themes describes light in this way:

"The brightness that enables sight in the darkness; scripture often uses light as a symbol of the saving presence of God in a fallen world, with darkness being used as a symbol of sin or the absence of God."

Most people don't like the darkness. It can be scary. I remember when I was a small child, I was convinced a monster lived under my bed and was waiting in the dark for just the right time to come out and kidnap me and take me away from my mom and dad! There is a good reason humans have learned to be wary of the darkness. Huddled around the warmth and light of a burning campfire, in a cold, damp cave, early man was terrified of the dark because of the danger lurking in the shadows.

In the introduction to *The Shadow* radio program, which aired in August 1930, the actor Frank Readick would read the following introduction to the show, "Who knows what evil lurks in the hearts of men? The Shadow knows!"

What is light?

Light, in the Britannica Dictionary, is defined as electromagnetic radiation that can be detected by the human eye. There is no single answer to the question, "What is light?"

The following list gives an idea of how some might answer this question:

- Light is a primary tool for perceiving the world and communicating within it
- light from the sun warms the Earth, drives global weather patterns, and initiates the life-sustaining process of photosynthesis
- light's interactions with matter have helped shape the structure of the universe
- light provides a window on the universe, from cosmological to atomic scales
- light transmits spatial and temporal information

Physicists have wrestled with the question, "What is light?" for many years.

Since the mid-twentieth century, a comprehensive theory of light, known as quantum electrodynamics, has been regarded by most physicists as complete. This theory combines the ideas of classical electromagnetism, quantum mechanics, and the special theory of relativity.

Although not complete, I will give a very brief history of mankind's study of light leading to the fully developed theory called quantum electrodynamics (many significant and important discoveries by many investigators have not been mentioned for the sake of brevity).

Ancient Greek philosophers are generally credited with the first formal speculations about the nature of light. In 500 BCE, Pythagoras proposed sight is caused by visual rays emanating from the eye and striking objects. In 300 BCE, Epicurus believed that light is emitted by sources other than the eye and that vision is produced when light reflects off objects and enters the eye.

In the thirteenth century, Roger Bacon, a friar and natural philosopher, studied propagation of light through simple lenses and is credited as one of the first to have described the use of lenses to correct vision. In 1608, Hans and Zacharias Jansen first constructed compound microscopes. In 1610, Galileo improved the refracting telescope and used it in his discoveries of the moons of Jupiter and the rings of Saturn.

French philosopher Rene Descartes described light as a pressure wave transmitted at infinite speed through a pervasive elastic medium. In the seventeenth century, Sir Isaac Newton was the most prominent advocate of a particle theory of light.

In 1905, Albert Einstein, in his formulation of special relativity, postulated the speed of light is the same in all reference frames, now accepted as a fundamental constant of nature. The fully developed theory called quantum electrodynamics (QED) followed on the heels of other major discoveries made before its formulation. QED describes the interactions of electromagnetic radiation with charged particles and the interactions of charged particles with one another.

Whew, thought you were back at school again! Don't worry; there is no exam to take at the end of this chapter!

ILLUSTRATION

The following illustration concerning creation is taken from Michael P. Green's book 1500 Illustrations for Biblical Preaching:

> The story is told of a science professor who constructed a planetarium, a precisely scaled model of the universe. A student came into his office and asked him who made it. The professor said, "No one."
>
> The student laughed and asked again, "Come on, who made this fantastic piece of precise work?"
>
> The professor replied, "No one. It just happened." The student became confused and angry, and the professor said, "Well, if you can go out of this class and look at nature around you and believe it just happened, you can also believe this precise piece of work just happened without a creator."

GODLY WISDOM

From the beginning of time, darkness has been symbolic of evil. In the Bible, godly wisdom tells us this in Job 30:26 about darkness and light, "When I looked for good, then evil came unto me: And when I waited for light, there came darkness." And Apostle John, speaking of Jesus as the Light of the world, wrote this in John 3:19-21:

Barry Denzil Haney, MD

And this is the condemnation, that light is come into the world, and men loved darkness rather than light, because their deeds were evil. For everyone that doeth evil hateth the light, neither cometh to the light, lest his deeds should be reproved. But he that doeth truth cometh to the light, that his deeds may be made manifest, that they are wrought in God.

In our world today, we see evil in all of its darkness. One way we see this is through the deeds of ISIS. Recently, I read a story of an ISIS mother who kissed her seven and nine-year-old daughters before she sent them off as homicide bombers! In Genesis 1:3-5, the Holy Spirit teaches us this about light and darkness:

And God said, Let there be light: and there was light. And God saw the light, that it was good: and God divided the light from the darkness. And God called the light Day, and the darkness he called Night. And the evening and the morning were the first day.

Although the light that God called "good" in verse 4 was physical light, it was also more, because God also created, what the authors in their book *Holman Treasury of Key Bible Words:200 Greek and 200 Hebrew Words Defined and Explained 2000*, call "the moral realms of light and darkness." When the Messiah appeared in the New Testament, the people that sat in darkness saw a great light, as foretold in Isaiah 60:2-3:

For, behold, the darkness shall cover the earth, And gross darkness the people: But the LORD shall arise upon thee, And his glory shall be seen upon thee. And the Gentiles shall come to thy light, And kings to the brightness of thy rising.

Then Jesus spoke to them in the passage found in John 8:12, "Then spake Jesus again unto them, saying, I am the light of the world: he that followeth me shall not walk in darkness, but shall have the light of life."

Hesychasm is a type of monastic life in which practitioners seek divine quietness through the contemplation of God in uninterrupted prayer, involving the entire human being, soul, mind, and body, often called pure of intellectual prayer, modeled after Jesus' injunction in the Gospel of Matthew 6:6, "But thou, when thou prayest, enter into thy closet, and when thou hast shut thy door, pray to thy Father which is in secret; and thy Father which seeth in secret shall reward thee openly."

In the book *The Oxford Dictionary of the Christian Church*, the authors make this statement about the importance of "Divine Light" espoused by the Hesychasts:

> The immediate aim of the Hesychasts was to secure what they termed "the union of the mind with the heart," so that their prayer became "prayer of the heart." This prayer of the heart leads eventually, in those who are specially chosen by God, to the vision of the Divine Light, which, it was believed, can be seen—even in this present life—with the material eyes of the body, although it is first necessary for a man's physical faculties to be refined by God's grace and so rendered spiritual.

The Hesychasts held this light to be identical with the light that surrounded the Lord at His transfiguration on Mt. Tabor and to be none other than the uncreated energies of the Godhead. They considered this Light, and not (as in W. theology) God's essence, to be the object of the "Beatific Vision." In the book *Light For Them That Sit in Darkness*, written by John Bunyan in 1674, the editor, George Offor, offers this analysis of why John Bunyan published this book:

Barry Denzil Haney, MD

His object is to prove that all our knowledge of the Saviour must be received directly from the written Word-that to understand these holy oracles, we must seek and obtain Divine light. By this light we shall find that Christ took upon himself our nature, and, by his holy and perfect obedience to the law, and sacrifice of himself as a sin-atoning offering, he redeemed all his saints, paid the FULL price of their redemption, and will present them unblameable, unreproveable, and acceptable to him that is of purer eyes than to behold iniquity.

In the book *Where Is Your God? Responding to the Challenge of Unbelief and Religious Indifference Today*, the authors wrote this about the hope we have about the "light" godly wisdom provides us:

"Faced with the new challenges of unbelief and religious indifference, of the secularization of believers and of the new religiosity of 'me' such are the reasons for hope, based on the Word of God," found in Psalm 119:105: "Thy word is a lamp unto my feet, And a light unto my path."

We don't have to fear the darkness because Jesus, when He came into the world, eliminated darkness, and brought the light of His glory to all! Jesus is the light that shines in the darkness, providing us hope, promise, and joy! Although light is symbolized as goodness, by contrast, darkness is symbolized as evil, sin, and despair.

In the movie *In His Image,* the film, through the testimonies of those who have suffered sexual or gender confusion, talks about the darkness surrounding this subculture in the secular world. The film shows the viewer how God delivered them out of this dark world into the light made possible by Jesus' work on the cross at Calvary! I highly recommend you consider watching this powerful film!

In closing, let me end with this excerpt translated from a sermon given by Dr. A. Tholuck, a German Protestant theologian and church leader, originally delivered at the University at Halle, sometime in the mid-1800s:

We see, moreover, that even among them there must have been hearts with human sympathies and feelings, for did not the centurion exclaim, as the last faint ray of dying light fell from the eye of the Crucified into his heart. "Verily, this was a righteous man!"

PRAYER

Our heavenly Father,

We adore You; we trust You; we love You, we praise You for being our Creator! We thank You for Your free gift of salvation You offer us through Your wonderful, merciful grace.

We pray for revival in each of us personally and in Your church. We lift up to You in prayer all of those with spoken and unspoken needs this morning.

Thank You for Your continued comfort, peace, and healing power in their lives. We ask that we may know what we love, since we ask nothing other than that, You give us Yourself. For You are our all: our life, our light, our salvation, our food, and our drink, our God. Inspire our hearts; we ask You, Jesus, with that breath of Your Spirit.

In the precious name of Jesus Christ, our Lord and Savior,

Amen.

CHAPTER 7

Why Christianity?

"Jesus saith unto him, I am the way, the truth, and the life: no man cometh unto the Father, but by me."

—James 14:6

WORLDLY WISDOM

A long time ago, in a small remote corner of the world, a man called Jesus shook the foundations of the religious world when he proclaimed these words, "I am the way, the truth, and the life: no man cometh unto the Father but by me." What factors account for the rise of Christianity to become the dominant religion in today's world?

In his book *The Rise of Christianity*, Rodney Stark concludes,

> "The primary means of its growth was through the united and motivated efforts of the growing numbers of Christian believers, who invited their friends, relatives, and neighbors to share the 'good news.'"

The Cambridge Dictionary defines Christianity in this way: "The Christian faith, a religion based on the belief in one God and on the teachings of Jesus Christ, as set forth in the Bible."

How is Christianity different from other religions? Why should I believe in the religion called Christianity? Wikipedia states the following statistic concerning religions in the world:

"According to some estimates, there are roughly four thousand, two hundred religions, churches, denominations, religious bodies, faith groups, tribes, cultures, movements, ultimate concerns, etc."

Because of the staggering number of choices, how does one choose what to believe?

In his book *Why is Christianity True?: Christian Evidences,* E.Y. Mullins writes,

Somewhere is to be found a force or principle or bond which unites all things. This is essential to thought, a first principle of all modern research. Neither science nor philosophy will dispute this point, but rather welcome it.

After years of searching, I found a principle that unites all things, Jesus. The following stanza, taken from a poem I wrote, entitled "All I Need is Jesus," sums up my search for truth:

Looked to philosophers, looked to great, religious men,
Looked to men of science, to famous businessmen.
Who talked of worldly truths and worldly pleasures,
And the importance of storing these earthly treasures.

But I knew, in my heart, these were not universal truths,
But instead, represented Satan's lies, Satan's untruths.
The next few years of my life, were very rocky, to say the least,
I tried to fill that void with many sins, offered by the beast.

Looking, for that source, of inexpressible joy,
Only to find out later, it could be found with Jesus, the real McCoy!

During my life journey, I have absorbed many books by philosophers, theologians, atheists, agnostics, and Christians, searching for evidence that Christianity represents the truth or to uncover facts that would devastate Christianity. I have come to the conclusion, through my extensive studies, that Christianity's factual foundation is firm.

What do I base this profound conclusion on?

I based this conclusion on Bible prophecy. Well over two thousand prophecies can be found in the Scripture, and most have already been fulfilled. No predictive prophecies can be found in the writings of Buddha, Confucius, Mohammed, Lao-Tse, or Hinduism. We can have hope for eternal salvation because the Christian God, through Scripture, foretells things that come inevitably to fruition.

Some postmodernists refute Christianity because they do not believe in the inerrancy of the Bible. They believe the meaning of any biblical, or for that matter, any literary text, cannot be separated from the worldview and ideology of the reader, and for that reason, cannot represent absolute truth. Immanuel Kant said reality cannot be truly known. Citing Kant's views concerning the fallibility of truth, minimalists rate the biblical text low for knowledge of the past, therefore inerrant.

According to the editors in the book *CSB and Apologetics Study Bible*, the purpose of the Hebrew writers was didactic: "To teach the reader how God acts in human affairs, what are his purposes, and the consequences of obedience and disobedience to that purpose."

Based on this discussion, I have come to the conclusion that most postmodern thinkers think each individual is trapped in his or her own private reality. Renée Descartes famously said humans seek to become "the masters and possessors of nature."

But I truly believe all Scripture is God-breathed. God spoke the very words that were written. God, the Holy Spirit, is the author of every book and every word of the Bible. Because some seek to become the "masters of nature," as Descartes asserts, the highest intellects throughout history have wrestled with and tried to define morals.

They have all tried to adopt some philosophy whether they be a skeptic, agnostic, atheist, pantheist, or theist. For example, most agnostics would say that humans do not know whether they are responsible for their sins. Some do not want to blame any human for sin. Because of this belief, there must be no free will.

For some, the choice is to believe in mysticism, as Christians do, or believe in rationalism. But I feel it is not a question between mysticism and rationality. In the final analysis, it is a question between mysticism and madness!

Through my studies, I have come to a conclusion, relying merely on logic does not explain the supernatural. Only relying on logic is often what thinkers have relied on in the past, and this has resulted in anarchy, confusion, and passive obedience to worldly desires. This leads to delusions of the mind, fostered by Satan's lies. It appears the roads of logic lead to some form of bedlam or anarchism. This road leads to delusion of mind.

Only through mysticism, the supernatural belief in the Christian God, can a human navigate his life journey with God, the Holy Spirit, and Jesus by his side. It doesn't matter who you might read, philosophers such as Aristotle, Socrates, Plato; atheists such as Ian McEwan, Christopher Hutchens, Richard Dawkins; agnostics/skeptics such as Bart Ehrmann, Aldous Huxley, Mark Twain; early church fathers such as Origen, Augustine, Tertullian; or scientists such as Galileo, Descartes, Sir Isaac Newton. All of them are human and, therefore, sinners, all have a philosophy of life-based on their worldview, and I believe all were created by an intelligent entity.

I believe in the Christian doctrine of God's transcendence, which implies He is wholly independent of the material universe, beyond all

Barry Denzil Haney, MD

known physical laws, rather than God's immanence, which implies He is fully present in the physical world and thus accessible to us in various ways.

Even though I understand this proposition, I still find it difficult to believe I can do nothing to force members of my family, whom I love so much, to accept Jesus as their Savior. It is even more difficult for me now, after my seventy years of struggle, my tumultuous rocky journey of salvation, to admit, I can't make them understand how simple it is, but yet how hard it is to make the right choice.

Each of us is at a crossroads in our life at some point, where we have to make a choice.

But unfortunately, many, when they are at that pivotal crossroad in their life, procrastinate and put off making this crucial, life-changing choice, which may result in eternal consequences. They may use the excuse, "I have too many things to accomplish in the secular world before I can think about spiritual matters."

On a personal note, my fear is that my grandchildren may flippantly respond, *"I'll do it later; I'll take care of that like Poppy did when I'm sixty-eight years old."* But unfortunately, there may not be a later date to make the choice. Tomorrow may not come.

If Tom Horn's prophecy is correct, we have until 2029 to make that choice. But the fact is, the final judgment could take place in a "blink of the eye."

As I used to tell my brother Ronnie, "don't play a con game with God." You can't say, "well, I'll do it later," or feel you can roll the dice and just wait until another time to make that important decision. You may not have that option in the future!

———

ILLUSTRATION

The following illustration concerning Christianity is taken from Michael P. Green's book *1500 Illustrations for Biblical Preaching*:

> A small boy sat in church with his mother and listened to a sermon entitled "What is a Christian?" Every time the minister asked the question, he banged his fist on the pulpit for emphasis.
>
> The tension produced by the sermon built up in the boy, and he finally whispered to his mother, "Mama, do you know? Do *you* know what a Christian is?"
>
> "Yes, dear," she replied. "Now sit still and be quiet."
>
> Finally, as the minister was winding up the sermon, he again thundered, "What is a Christian?" and banged especially hard on the pulpit. This time it was too much for the little boy, so he jumped up and cried out, "Tell him, Mama, tell him!"[1581]

GODLY WISDOM

What godly wisdom about Christianity can be found in the Bible? In Romans 10:9-11, Paul tells us,

> That if thou shalt confess with thy mouth the Lord Jesus, and shalt believe in thine heart that God hath raised him from the dead, thou shalt be saved. For with the heart man believeth unto righteousness; and with the mouth confession is made unto salvation. For the scripture saith, Who-

Barry Denzil Haney, MD

soever believeth on him shall not be ashamed. For there is
no difference between the Jew and the Greek: for the same
Lord over all is rich unto all that call upon him.

It is an honor for me to serve Jesus. I know, when I please Him, I am doing His will and, through the work of the Holy Spirit in me, the fruits of the Spirit will flow through my heart. My heart will be a conduit for God's unconditional love, and others will see in me God's love, God's joy, God's peace, God's patience, God's kindness, God's goodness, God's faithfulness, God's gentleness, and God's self-control.

These attributes of the Holy Spirit will serve as a light, a beacon of light, to those who are unsaved. These fruits of the Spirit will serve as a way for the Holy Spirit to convict the unsaved, so they too might spend an eternity with our Father, God, when they die. Many people are intolerant of Christianity because they believe it is arrogant to say that Jesus is the only way to God. So what does tolerance actually mean in the postmodern world?

Some would say tolerance is the willingness to accept or tolerate somebody or something, especially opinions or behavior that you may not agree with, or people who are not like you. Many in today's world believe whatever is right for you is the truth. They seek commonality between the world's religion, religious tolerance.

For example, the main character in the novel *Chocolat* believes all religions and superstitions are equivalent, a belief held by many in today's society.

John Hick, in his book *Truth and Dialogue*, summarizes the implications of this belief in this way: "To say that whatever is sincerely believed and practiced is, by definition, true would be the end of all critical discrimination, both intellectual and moral."

After seventy years of searching, I have decided to dismiss this madness, this madness of searching for the truth. Instead of falling prey to the antics of boys on the schoolyard, snatching the ball up from the ground, refusing to play the game because others don't agree with my way of thinking, refusing to listen to other opinions, hurrying home, isolating myself from the world, I ended this search into madness, and decided the principle which united all things, provided the universal truth, is Jesus.

I decided, instead of ending up being the scientist who on the day of judgment stands before God and God asks him why he did not believe, why was he an atheist and the scientist answers, "because there was not enough scientific evidence," I would have faith in Jesus.

Some might ask, how can you claim to know the truth if you haven't tried all the alternatives?

My short answer to the question: it would be humanly impossible to look at all of the alternatives. It would be like doing a search for a purple people-eater; after searching the universe and finding one, I would not need to go on searching. The same is true, looking for the universal truth of God. If I conduct a search and I encounter the truth in Christ, I do not need to go on looking elsewhere since I have found what I was looking for.

As I shared in chapter one, "The Pain of Depression," I struggled with suicidal thoughts during my bout with severe depression. During this struggle, I was severely depressed and found myself unable to muster the energy to work or to devote time to my family.

During that season of my life, I did not know Jesus. Instead, I was looking for help in the wrong place. If I had known Jesus, I would have known He was the one person who could help me because He had defeated death, He had overcome the severe depression of being rejected by God, when He took on the sins of the world as His own, He was able to overcome the severe depression and hopelessness He felt when He cried out with agony, "*My God, My God, why hast thou forsaken me!*"

I think if I had looked at Hinduism, Islam, or any one of the other competing religions or other philosophical traditions, I would not have encountered the truth of Christ and would not have been able to complete my journey to salvation, but instead been condemned to eternal separation from God, my Father.

After years of comparing the different worldviews and rival competing claims about universal truth made along historical, philosophical, moral,

Barry Denzil Haney, MD

scientific, or existential grounds, I concluded the Christian worldview provided the most coherent and convincing explanation of reality. Jesus himself encourages us to do the search when he says, "Ask, and it shall be given you; seek, and ye shall find; knock, and it shall be opened unto you" (Matthew 7:7).

I firmly believe that once you become a Christian, this does not mean you close down your mind, but instead it expands your ability, with the help and guidance of the Holy Spirit, to discover God's love and plan for your life, in His grand plan of salvation.

———————

PRAYER

Our heavenly Father,

We rejoice that we may be called Your children. How majestic is Your name in all the universe! Thank You for understanding our tears. When our words get in the way, we know You still hear and feel our hurts deep inside.

Thank You for giving us hope and strength during each trial we face. During our weakest moments, help us to remember You are always present, and during these moments of despair, we ask You to shelter us in Your hands.

Strengthen us in the hope and faith that our lives will surely go the right way, not through our strength but through Your protection. Grant that through Your Spirit we may come to know more and more that You are with us.

Help us to be alert in our daily life and to listen whenever You want to say something to us. Reveal the power and glory of Your kingdom in many people, to the glory of Your name, and hasten the coming on Earth of all that is good and true.

Therefore, with angels and archangels, and with all the company of heaven, we laud and magnify Your glorious name, evermore praising You and saying, Holy, holy, holy, Lord God of hosts, heaven, and Earth are full of Your glory. Glory be to You, O Lord most high!

In the precious name of Jesus Christ, our Lord and Savior,
Amen.

Barry Denzil Haney, MD

CHAPTER 8

The Wonder of It All!

And the Word was made flesh, and dwelt among us, and we beheld his glory, the glory as of the only begotten of the Father, full of grace and truth. John bare witness of him, and cried, saying, This was he of whom I spake, He that cometh after me is preferred before me: for he was before me. And of his fulness have all we received, and grace for grace. For the law was given by Moses, but grace and truth came by Jesus Christ. No man hath seen God at any time; the only begotten Son, which is in the bosom of the Father, he hath declared him.

—John 1:14-18

WORLDLY WISDOM

In this passage, the Holy Spirit is teaching me about the wonder of Jesus through the eyes of John the Baptist. John realized Jesus was the Word, who became flesh to dwell amongst us, and in the man Jesus, he saw the glory of the Father, grace, and truth. John understood this man, called Jesus, who came after him, actually came before him, as the same God who appeared to the Israelites in the tabernacle when they wandered through the desert for forty years.

Although John realized the law given by Moses is demanding, without mercy, he also understood grace and truth came through Jesus, and these two things are sufficient to meet the demands of the Law. He also understood law and grace are not contradictory but supplement one another. Through John's vision, the Holy Spirit is also teaching us no one has ever seen God, but his Son, Jesus, has made Him known to us.

The Cambridge Dictionary defines wonder in this way:

> "A feeling of great surprise and admiration caused by seeing or experiencing something that is strange and new; something beautiful, unexpected, unfamiliar, or inexplicable."

In the article "Americans May Be Getting Less Religious, But Feelings of Spirituality are on the Rise," David Masci and Michael Lipka reported standard measures, such as how important people say religion is to them and their frequency of religious service attendance and prayer, Americans had become less religious in recent years. They went on to say, "But, at the same time, the share of people across a wide variety of religious identities who say they often feel a deep sense of spiritual peace and well-being, as well as a deep sense of wonder about the universe, has risen."

Barry Denzil Haney, MD

This decline of Christianity in the United States continues at a rapid pace, according to an article from the Pew Research Center, October 17, 2019, which reports the following statistics from the Pew Research Center telephone surveys conducted in 2018 and 2019:

> Sixty-five percent of American adults describe themselves as Christians when asked about their religion, down twelve percentage points over the past decade, while the religiously unaffiliated share of the population, consisting of people who describe their religious identity as atheist, agnostic, or "nothing in particular," now stands at twenty-six percent, up from seventeen percent in 2009.

I'm sure these shocking trends have only increased since then! A Christian has a sense of wonder when he views the universe as God's handiwork, and the religiously unaffiliated share a similar sense of wonder when they look at the same universe without the lens of Christian belief. Who is right?

Over the years, I have pondered the same questions philosophers, theologians, apologists, and atheists have pondered: "Where did I come from? What is life's meaning? How do I define right from wrong and what happens to me when I die?" In my life journey, I could never seem to answer these questions to my satisfaction. The answers I found oftentimes seemed meaningless.

In my confusion, I would sometimes beg God to help me, to give me a sign, to give me reassurance that my thoughts were universal truths, not some vain truths imagined by a human mind. You see, these questions I now have, began when God first imagined me in His dreams, continued as my body formed in utero, continued when I took my first breath, continued when I was in the crib, alone, in a dark place, and will continue until the day I take my last breath here on earth.

Then and only then will I no longer be discouraged. All my questions will be answered when I begin an eternal relationship with God in heaven.

Until then, I will search for the answers to these questions, using godly wisdom, not worldly wisdom!

ILLUSTRATION

The following illustration concerning discouragement is taken from Michael P. Green's book *1500 Illustrations for Biblical Preaching*:

The devil decided to have a garage sale. On the day of sale, his tools were placed for public inspection, each being marked with its sale price. There were a treacherous lot of implements: hatred, envy, jealousy, deceit, lust, lying, pride, and so on.

Set apart from the rest was a harmless-looking tool. It was quite worn and yet priced very high.

"What is the name of this tool?" asked one of the customers, pointing to it.

"That is discouragement," Satan replied.

"Why have you priced it so high?"

"Because it is more useful to me than the others. I can pry open and get inside a man's heart with that, even when I cannot get near him with the other tools. It is badly worn because I use it on almost everyone since so few people know it belongs to me."

The devil's price for discouragement was high because it is still his favorite tool, and he is still using it on God's people.

Barry Denzil Haney, MD

GODLY WISDOM

What godly wisdom does the Bible have for us concerning the wonder of the universe we see around us? In Genesis 1:31, we are given a glimpse of God's sense of wonder, as he rejoiced in the completion of the creation of the universe we now live in: "And God saw everything that he had made, and, behold, it was very good. And the evening and the morning were the sixth day."

Although God could have easily made the universe, in the blink of an eye, it would seem He chose to do His handiwork over a period of six days, perhaps, to demonstrate His wisdom, power, and goodness in each part He made, and to show us how "good" things might come into existence from small beginnings. In the Bible, many other beautiful, unexpected, and inexplicable events occur that can give us a sense of wonder, a feeling of surprise, mingled with admiration.

The account of creation described in Genesis gives us a sense of wonder when we consider how God could create the complex, intricate design of the universe we now experience around us. In the book *Redemption; or The Temptation of Christ in the Wilderness,* the authors give this beautiful interpretation of man's decision to sin by displeasing God, resulting in "paradise lost:"

> Adam and Eve should have been perfectly satisfied with
> their knowledge of God derived from his created works
> and received by the instruction of the holy angels. But their
> curiosity was aroused to become acquainted with that of
> which God designed they should have no knowledge. It
> was for their happiness to be ignorant of sin. The high state
> of knowledge to which they thought to attain by eating
> of the forbidden fruit plunged them into the degradation
> of sin and guilt...Adam was driven from Eden, and the
> angels who, before his transgression, had been appointed to
> guard him in his Eden home, were now appointed to guard

the gates of paradise and the way of the tree of life, lest
he should return, gain access to the tree of life, and sin be
immortalized.

Events such as the miracles Jesus performs give many people a sense of
wonder, such as the event described in Matthew 14:22-27, describing how
Jesus walked on the water:

> And straightway Jesus constrained his disciples to get into
> a ship, and to go before him unto the other side, while he
> sent the multitudes away. And when he had sent the multi-
> tudes away, he went up into a mountain apart to pray: and
> when the evening was come, he was there alone. But the
> ship was now in the midst of the sea, tossed with waves: for
> the wind was contrary. And in the fourth watch of the night
> Jesus went unto them, walking on the sea. And when the
> disciples saw him walking on the sea, they were troubled,
> saying, It is a spirit; and they cried out for fear. But straight-
> way Jesus spake unto them, saying, Be of good cheer; it is I;
> be not afraid.

In the book *Redemption; or The Miracles of Christ, the Mighty One*, the
authors give this lengthy, but beautiful interpretation of how we might
react when witnessing such a miracle as this:

> Ardent Peter is nearly beside himself with delight. He
> sees his Master boldly treading the foam-wreathed waves,
> coming to save his followers, and he loves his Lord as never
> before. He yearns to embrace and worship him. He longs
> to meet him and walk by his side upon the stormy water.
> He cries, "Lord, if it be thou, bid me come unto thee on
> the water." Jesus granted his request; but Peter had taken
> only a step upon the surface of the boiling deep, when he

looked back proudly toward his companions to see if they were watching his movements and admiring the ease with which he trod upon the yielding water. In taking his eyes from Jesus, they fell upon the boisterous waves that seemed greedily threatening to swallow him; their roaring filled his ears, his head swam, his heart failed him with fear. As he is sinking, he recovers presence of mind sufficient to remember that there is One near who can rescue him. He stretches out his arms toward Jesus, crying, *"Lord, save me, or I perish!"* The pitying Saviour grasps the trembling hands that are reached toward him and lifts the sinking form beside his own. Never does that kindly face and that arm of strength turn from the supplicating hands that are stretched out for mercy. Peter clings to his Lord with humble trust, while Jesus mildly reproaches him: *"O thou of little faith: wherefore didst thou doubt?"*

The final example of a concept in the Bible giving us a sense of wonder, and undoubtedly, one of the most important concerning our salvation, is the doctrine of atonement, found in Romans, Chapter 5:1-21:

Therefore being justified by faith, we have peace with God through our Lord Jesus Christ: By whom also we have access by faith into this grace wherein we stand and rejoice in hope of the glory of God. And not only so, but we glory in tribulations also: knowing that tribulation worketh patience; And patience, experience; and experience, hope: And hope maketh not ashamed; because the love of God is shed abroad in our hearts by the Holy Ghost which is given unto us. For when we were yet without strength, in due time Christ died for the ungodly. For scarcely for a righteous man will one die: yet peradventure for a good man some would even dare to die. But God commendeth his love toward us, in that, while we were yet sinners, Christ died for us. Much more then, being now justified by his blood, we shall be saved from wrath through him. For if, when we were enemies, we were reconciled to God by the death of his Son, much more, being reconciled, we shall be saved by his life. And not only so, but we also joy in God through our Lord Jesus Christ, by whom we have now received the atonement. Wherefore, as by one man sin entered into the world, and death by sin; and so death passed upon all men, for that all have sinned: (For until the law sin was in the world: but sin is not imputed when there is no law. Nevertheless death reigned from Adam to Moses, even over them that had not sinned after the similitude of Adam's transgression, who is the figure of him that was to come. But not as the offence, so also is the free gift. For if through the offence of one many be dead, much more the grace of God, and the gift by grace, which is by one man, Jesus Christ, hath abounded unto many. And not as it was by one that sinned, so is the gift: for the judgment was by one to condemnation, but the free gift is of many offences unto justification. For if by one man's offence death reigned by one; much more they which receive abundance of grace and of the gift of righteousness shall reign in life by one, Jesus Christ.) Therefore as by the offence of one judgment came upon all men to condemnation; even so by the righteousness of one the free gift came upon all men unto justification of life. For as by one man's disobedience many were made sinners, so by the obedience of one shall many be made righteous. Moreover the law entered, that the offence might abound. But where sin abounded, grace did much more abound: That as sin hath reigned unto death, even so might grace reign through righteousness unto eternal life by Jesus Christ our Lord.

In his book *Atonement and Personality*, R. C. Moberly gives us his account of the relation of Christ to sin, as the Atoner:

> The relation of Christ to sin, as the Atoner, is more myste-
> rious than that of His relation, in obedient life, to holiness.
> But nothing can exceed the directness with which the
> relation to sin is emphasized in Scripture, or the cardinal
> place of this relation in the Christian creed. The relation to
> sin is absolute, unreserved, personal—though the sin is not
> in Himself.

"Him who knew no sin, He made to be sin on our behalf."

Elsewhere the relation to sin is stated in a different way, "God sending His own Son in the likeness of sinful flesh, and as an offering for sin, condemned sin in the flesh." Many other beautiful, unexpected, and inexplicable events can be found in the Bible to give the reader a sense of wonder, a feeling of surprise, mingled with admiration. I invite you to read the Bible and discover why the Bible has been described by some scholars as the "single most important book ever written."

MY PERSONAL EXPERIENCE: THE WONDER OF IT ALL!

During my rocky road to salvation, God has placed key people in my life to help me stay on the narrow path! I would like to share with you one of those people.

I have known Landon for many years. I first met him during my Radiology training at the Naval Hospital Oakland.

Landon is one of those people everyone likes! With his Robert Redford rugged good looks, charming smile, and effervescent personality, you cannot help but like him!

Landon has a passion for the outdoors and hiking. Over the years, he has graciously taken me with him on several memorable hikes, including Glacier National Park, the Canadian Rockies, Zion National Park, and the Sheltowee Trace Trail in the Natural Bridge State Park, located in Kentucky.

During these hikes, I experienced the vastness of God's creation, unhindered by the business of the secular world. I was alone with God!

I marveled at the beauty of his creation as I hiked along the trail. I could sense the presence of God as I viewed the grandeur of his creation, the awesomeness of his power, his omnipotence, his omniscience!

In these moments, I could not understand why such a mighty God would want to bother with us who deserve death because of our trespasses against Him. It was at that moment I understood the significance of God's love for us!

PRAYER

Our heavenly Father,

We come before You today to give You honor and praise. You are the source of all that is good. We thank You for the opportunity to come and gather together with You this day.

We ask for Your hand of blessing on us this day. We open our hearts, minds, and souls to You. We ask that You guide and direct us so that our day is filled with godly wisdom.

Thank You for helping us to accomplish Your work. Help us to love one another as You have commanded us to do. Help us to please You in everything we do this day.

We ask all this in the glorious name of Jesus,

Amen.

CHAPTER 9

Heritage and Legacy

Enter ye in at the strait gate: for wide is the gate, and broad is the way, that leadeth to destruction, and many there be which go in there-at: Because strait is the gate, and narrow is the way, which leadeth unto life, and few there be that find it.

Matthew 7:13

WORLDLY WISDOM

The heritage and legacy of Christianity could probably be summed up by the words Jesus spoke during the sermon on the mount in Matthew 7:13. He seems to be telling us not to look for shortcuts to God; the way to eternal life is vigorous and demands our full attention! In order to understand Christianity, we need to know the difference between heritage and legacy and how they affect our life journey.

The Cambridge Dictionary defines *heritage* in this way:

"Features belonging to the culture of a particular society, such as traditions, languages, or buildings, that were created in the past and still have historical importance."

The Cambridge Dictionary defines *legacy* in this way:

> "Something that is a result of events in the past; something that is a part of your history or that remains from an earlier time; a situation that has developed as a result of past actions and decisions."

From these definitions, a simpler, workable definition would be that heritage refers to material and economic inheritance, while legacy refers to immaterial and cultural inheritance.

Based on the simplified definitions, your heritage might be very important in the secular world. Where you are on the economic ladder would definitely affect your acceptance in the secular world.

But what about your legacy?

This too, could affect how you perceive your position in the world. If you are a Christian, you know you are a child of God and your legacy or inheritance, if you will, in the hope of an eternal relationship with your creator God in heaven. If you are not a Christian, your cultural inheritance would still significantly affect your standing in the world.

I like to think of my heritage and legacy in terms of my family tree. When you look at your family tree, you get a glimpse of your ancestors' life journeys. If I look back at the past three generations of my family tree, many different life journeys are represented. The following list demonstrates some of their life journeys:

> Horse trader; national cutting horse champion; circuit rider for Methodist Church; college football starting fullback; neon glass bending artisan; physician; nurse; engineer; educator; audiologist; physical therapist; music degree; special needs person; teacher assistant; pharmacy tech; photographer; federal prison guard; regional tire salesman

Barry Denzil Haney, MD

and manager; helicopter pilot; IT specialist; sonographer; trucking company supervisor, police officer.

As this list demonstrates, each person's life journey is different.

During a men's Bible study meeting at our new church, we talked about the concepts of heritage and legacy. How these two terms, heritage and legacy, are interrelated and how they apply to the building of our new church. We talked about what these two terms, these two concepts, have to do with our walk with Jesus. The concern was brought up by one of the members about the potential danger facing the new church as we enter into a new period of focus.

The focus for the congregation over the past four years has been to complete the new church building. He wants to make sure during the process of building a church, we don't lose focus on what is the truth, "*Jesus is the subject.*" I think we all agree the danger is always present to lose sight of the purpose, the mission, the focus of what our life and the church's life should be, "*Jesus is the subject.*" Our focus should be all about Jesus!

Each of us travels on a different path in life. One of the byproducts of one's journey is goal attainment. For a Christian, our focus should be Jesus, not the destination. As the Bible tells us, each person, during his life journey, travels along a path, either a broad path that many travel along or a narrow path which only a few travel along.

Which path are you traveling along during your life journey?

GODLY WISDOM

What is the heritage of Christianity?

The tradition of Christianity, its heritage, goes back to Jesus. It goes back to the instructions the resurrected Jesus Christ gave to his disciples to spread his teachings to all the nations of the world, His Great Commission, in Matthew 28:16-20:

> Then the eleven disciples went away into Galilee, into a mountain where Jesus had appointed them. And when they saw him, they worshipped him: but some doubted. And Jesus came and spake unto them, saying, All power is given unto me in heaven and in earth. Go ye therefore, and teach all nations, baptizing them in the name of the Father, and of the Son, and of the Holy Ghost: Teaching them to observe all things whatsoever I have commanded you: and, lo, I am with you always, even unto the end of the world. Amen.

The early Christian community started as a "house" church. The first description of meeting together as a Christian community is recorded in Acts 1:13: "And when they were come in, they went up into an upper room…all continued with one accord in prayer and supplication…"

This tradition of meeting in a house continued as Christianity spread across the Roman Empire. Paul records a group of early Christians meeting in the home of Phebe, "…For she hath been a succourer of many, and of myself also. Greet Priscilla and Aquila my helpers in Christ Jesus…greet the church that is in their house."

This tradition continued the following decades, although because of persecution, Christians were forced underground to meet in the catacombs. After Christianity was legalized in AD 313, church buildings began to multiply. The Reformation in the sixteenth and seventeenth centuries saw an explosion of church building throughout Europe. But Christians continued to meet in homes to supplement their formal church life, which has continued into the twentieth and now the twenty-first century, called by some the "house church movement."

Heritage and tradition have been important in the development of Christianity.

But what about legacy?
What is the legacy of Christ?

The following illustration nicely summarizes what Christ and His work on the cross at Calvary mean:

> *"The legacy of Christ is not tension, but peace.*
> *The legacy of Christ is not war, but peace.*
> *The legacy of Christ is not advice about peace, it is peace!"*

Chuck Stecker, in his book *Men of Honor, Women of Virtue*, offers a wonderful example of the concept of legacy, which he shared at a baseball game with a friend after Mark McGwire hit the first of seventy homers he would hit during the 1998 baseball season:

> A few moments later, as we finally settled back into our seats, the gentleman sitting next to me turned and asked me…, "Chuck, what do you think the legacy of Mark McGwire will be?" I…replied, "I don't think that's really your question. What you are really asking is what I think the final legend of Mark McGwire will be…I'm not sure about Mark McGwire's legacy because that will be determined by the quality of man he is—the fiber and fabric of which he is made. Not knowing McGwire personally, I can't make that assessment. While it's easy to speculate about the legend—the individual records and accomplishments—it's far more difficult to determine the legacy."

As I conclude this chapter on heritage and legacy, I am thinking of my Father, the Son, and the Holy Spirit, the beginning and the end, the Alpha and the Omega, my Creator, the Creator who imagined me in His dreams, who loves me so much that He became the Slain Lamb whose shed blood on the cross at Calvary saves me from sin, the sin which separates me from

God.

But I thank God that if I have faith in His Son, Jesus, I can spend an eternity in a loving relationship with him. I sometimes can't believe God cares so much for me! I am nothing! But, I have to remind myself, I was created by Him in His image. He does love me. He does care for me. He wants me to crawl into his lap, and He wants to envelop me with His loving arms; He wants to have a relationship with me.

Before He said the words, *"Let there be Light,"* He imagined me in His dreams; He imagined me writing this chapter in this book. He worked out all the details of His plan of salvation! Even as He spoke the words, *"Let there be Light,"* the creation event, the blinding flash, the explosion, the finely tuned Big Bang occurring in an instant, He knew I would be a passenger on a small blue planet, traveling through space and time, at this moment in time, in this moment of human history, in this moment of His plan of world salvation, during this moment of my walk with Jesus.

MY PERSONAL EXPERIENCE: MY FRIEND, CAPTAIN NEAL STEWART FLOWERS!

In closing, I would like to tell you about an important part of my legacy, my association with Captain Neal Stewart Flowers.

In 1982, God put Captain Neal Stewart Flowers in my life.

This began a one-year weekly conference, before working hours, where I brought approximately one hundred daily chest radiographs from the Naval Aerospace Medical Institute where I performed prequalification physical examinations on potential Naval aviators to his office at the Naval Hospital Pensacola.

Although our morning get-together was intended to teach me how to read a CXR, it became more like a time of fellowship between a father and son.

Barry Denzil Haney, MD

He taught me much about what it meant to be an honorable Christian man. His testimony of how to live as a man of God is what I remember the most.

He believed in God and Jesus, and his life was a light to me. He was truly a wise man, who God put in my prodigal journey of salvation.

When Neal Flowers died on January 12, 2012, I was unable to attend his funeral.

A few weeks later, his wife Ruby sent me a letter and a gift. In the letter, she told me how fond Neal was of me and that he would want me to have the gift she had sent me. It was his stethoscope he had used for many years as a tool to identify what was wrong with patients who came to him for healing.

It now is clear to me; God used Neal as a tool to help me see what was wrong with me. So I could finally surrender all to Him and finally have one hundred percent trust in Him.

Thank you, Neal, thank You, Jesus!

PRAYER

Our heavenly Father,

Today, help us not deprive ourselves of Your favor by our ingratitude. But instead, allow us to be gently ruled by You and render You our due obedience.

Thank You for Your free gift of salvation, which includes our regeneration, in which You implanted a new life in us, which includes our conversion, or our turning to You as our Lord and Savior through faith and repentance, which includes our justification, or the establishment of our righteous standing before You!

In addition, this includes our adoption or Your gift of grace in which You received us into our church, as one of the Sons of God, which includes our sanctification, the continual process of being made more holy, more Christ-like each day, until glorification takes place at the second coming of the Lord Jesus Christ, when final sanctification takes place and we become entirely like Christ.

We humbly bow down before You this morning in our depraved state and praise You as our Creator and king. We humbly lift up to You in prayer this morning all of these spoken and unspoken needs.

We humbly ask You to continue to provide Your encouragement, comfort, peace, and love to those with needs. We humbly ask You to continue to provide Your Wisdom and guidance to the doctors, nurses, other health care providers, and any other person You have provided to care for those with needs.

We humbly ask that You provide the same encourage-ment, comfort, peace, and love to the family members of those with needs.

We humbly ask that You continue to wrap all of the members of Your church family in Your loving arms and protect them from pain and temptation.

We humbly ask all of these things in the precious name of Jesus Christ our Lord and Savior,

Amen.

Barry Denzil Haney, MD

CHAPTER 10

Worldly or Godly Wisdom?

"And I gave my heart to know wisdom, and to know madness and folly: I perceived that this also is vexation of spirit. For in much wisdom is much grief: and he that increaseth knowledge increaseth sorrow."

—Ecclesiastes 1:17-18

"But the wisdom that is from above is first pure, then peaceable, gentle, and easy to be intreated, full of mercy and good fruits, without partiality, and without hypocrisy."

—James 3:17

WORLDLY WISDOM

In the passage from Ecclesiastes, God is telling me worldly wisdom and experience will not solve every problem in life because worldly experiential knowledge alienates us from God. But God tells us in James, if we live by faith in God's promises He gives us through godly wisdom found in the Bible, we can cease living our lives running in circles, and our life journey here on Earth will have a purpose, as we walk along the narrow path toward the kingdom of God!

The Cambridge Dictionary defines wisdom in this way:

"The ability to make good judgements based on what you have learned from your experience, or the knowledge and understanding that gives you this ability."

The Dictionary of Bible Themes describes wisdom in this way:

"The quality of knowledge, discernment and understanding characteristic of God himself."

True wisdom, seen in the ministry of Jesus Christ, is a gift of the Holy Spirit. Scripture affirms that true human wisdom is a gift from God and points out the folly of trusting in mere human wisdom. During a meeting of the Thursday morning men's connection group at my church, we discussed wisdom. We discussed the differences between worldly wisdom and godly wisdom. We agreed, we receive godly wisdom from God, whereas worldly wisdom comes from our life experiences during our journey of life.

Jen Wilkin, in the article "Why It's Important to Know the Difference Between 'Godly' and 'Worldly' Wisdom," describes worldly wisdom in this way:

Worldly wisdom and godly wisdom are antithetical and adversarial... Worldly wisdom self-promotes... Worldly wisdom seeks the highest place... Worldly wisdom avoids the mirror of the word... Worldly wisdom trusts in earthly possessions... Worldly wisdom boasts... Worldly wisdom says trials will crush you... Worldly wisdom says temptation is no big deal... Worldly wisdom says seeing is believing... Worldly wisdom wields might... Simply put, any thought, word or deed that compromises our ability to love God and neighbor is folly.

Leo Perdue, in his book *The Sword and the Stylus: An Introduction to Wisdom in the Age of Empires*, explains wisdom in this way:

Barry Denzil Haney, MD

"… acquiring of knowledge through empirical experience, rational thought, and comparative analysis, which enable one to reach studied conclusions and to act accordingly… an epistemology… knowledge that is derived from the study of things that may be empirically assayed by the human senses (hearing, seeing, touching, tasting, and smelling)… through rational analysis, may be placed into the configurations of definition and understanding."

In order to understand worldly wisdom, you have to take into account the entire recorded history of worldly knowledge. Worldly knowledge currently available to mankind is overwhelming, representing the accumulated ideology from many contributors throughout the ages. Sources include oral tradition, texts on astrology, cosmology, religion and the gods, nature, science, music, architecture, engineering, mathematics, et cetera.

In an article entitled "How Much Data Is There in the World," the "Global Datasphere" in 2018 reached eighteen zettabytes (18×10^{21})… IDC predicts the world's data will grow to one hundred seventy-five zettabytes in 2025. Another article I read said a 2015 study estimated it would take two percent of the Amazon rainforest to print out the amount of internet data in that year alone.

Wow, that's a lot of knowledge to remember in order to have worldly wisdom!

But wait, is it even possible for the human brain to store this amount of knowledge, much less use it wisely?

Paul Reber, in his article "What Is the Memory Capacity of the Human Brain?" writes:

The human brain consists of about one billion neurons. Each neuron forms about one thousand connections to other neurons, amounting to more than a trillion connections. If each neuron could only help store a single memory, running out of space would be a problem. You might have only a few gigabytes of storage space, similar to the space in an iPod or a USB flash drive. Yet neurons combine so that each one helps with many memories at a time, exponentially increasing the brain's memory storage capacity to something closer to around two and a half petabytes (or a million gigabytes).

For comparison, if your brain worked like a digital video recorder in a television, two and a half petabytes would be enough to hold three million hours of TV shows. You would have to leave the TV running continuously for more than three hundred years to use up all that storage.

Despite the amount of storage the brain apparently has, many believe, no human can know everything there is to know, so does that mean we can never be wise? Karl Pearson, in his book *Grammar of Science,* stated his view that Alexander Humboldt was the last person to know everything:

> At the beginning of this century it was possible for an Alexander von Humboldt to take a survey of the entire domain of the extant science. Such a survey would be impossible for any scientist now, even if gifted with more than Humboldt's powers. Scarcely any specialist of today is really master of all the work which has been done in his own comparatively small field. Facts and their classification have been accumulating at such a rate, that nobody seems to have leisure to recognize the relations of subgroups to the whole. It is as if individual workers in both Europe and America were bringing their stones to one great building and piling them on cementing them together without regard to any general plan or to their individual neighbor's work.

If we can't be assured of being wise through worldly wisdom, what are we to do?

Barry Denzil Haney, MD

The following, taken from Michael Green's book *1500 Illustrations for Biblical Preaching*, illustrates the folly of facing life's struggles without the help of God:

"Man's wisdom is not enough. It is limited, partial wisdom."

T. S. Eliot put it so beautifully when he said in "The Rock:"

All our knowledge brings us nearer to our ignorance,
All our ignorance brings us nearer to death,
But nearness to death no nearer to God.

Then he asks the profound question that hangs over this whole generation:

"Where is the Life we have lost in living?"

ILLUSTRATION

The following illustration concerning wisdom is taken from Michael P. Green's book *1500 Illustrations for Biblical Preaching*:

A man approached a speaker and said, "You Christians are all brainwashed."

The speaker replied, "I think we are all brainwashed to a degree. The important thing is that we Christians choose what we want to wash our brains with."

GODLY WISDOM

Godly wisdom is to be found throughout the Bible: the Old Testament, the book of Proverbs, the book of Ecclesiastes, and the book of Job are generally regarded as wisdom literature. In the New Testament, the words of Jesus are regarded as God's wisdom for us.

Most would agree, as we become older, we become more wise through our life experiences. In Job 12:12, Job reflects, "With the ancient is wisdom; And in length of days understanding."

Paul warns us in 1 Corinthians 3:18-20, the folly of worldly wisdom in the sight of God:

> Let no man deceive himself. If any man among you seemeth to be wise in this world, let him become a fool, that he may be wise. For the wisdom of this world is foolishness with God. For it is written, He taketh the wise in their own craftiness. And again, The Lord knoweth the thoughts of the wise, that they are vain.

In James 3:13-18, James warns us of the dangers of worldly wisdom and why we need to strive for godly wisdom during our life struggles:

> Who is a wise man and endued with knowledge among you? let him shew out of a good conversation his works with meekness of wisdom. But if ye have bitter envying and strife in your hearts, glory not, and lie not against the truth. This wisdom descendeth not from above, but is earthly, sensual, devilish. For where envying and strife is, there is confusion and every evil work. But the wisdom that is from above is first pure, then peaceable, gentle, and easy to be intreated, full of mercy and good fruits, without partiality,

Barry Denzil Haney, MD

and without hypocrisy. And the fruit of righteousness is sown in peace of them that make peace.

How do we obtain godly wisdom?

Godly wisdom comes from daily prayer and the study of the Bible. When we study the inspired Word contained in the Bible, the Holy Spirit guides us and instructs us on what we should do in order to do God's will for our lives. Because of free choice, we can either accept that guidance or not. When we accept God's challenge, then we make him happy.

MY PERSONAL EXPERIENCE: CONVERSATION!

My son-in-law called me one morning and informed me a business venture he had been struggling with for the past few years was about to end. My initial reaction was *hallelujah*, praise God! He has been struggling with this and other matters for many years. I was so glad he now can put this behind him and begin to work on himself.

He told me; he was close to accepting Jesus Christ as his Savior. At the time, I prayed that the Holy Spirit would use me or someone else to convict him, before it is too late! I pray for godly wisdom!

Thankfully, as this book is published, my son-in-law now knows Jesus, serving as a conduit for the Holy Spirit. All glory to God!

I pray God will put someone in everyone's life to help the Holy Spirit convict them to realize their personal salvation is the only thing that really matters in life!

We must turn it all over to God, turn over all control of our life to God, and trust God one hundred percent in this proposition. When we do this, we must also repent of our sins, turn away from our sins. If we are sincere, and God knows our hearts, then we will become a new person, a new creature, a child of God. Jesus will then reside in our heart and do some "housecleaning" in our heart, and the Holy Spirit will also reside in our heart to guide, instruct, and protect us from Satan's temptations that will come our way.

We need to realize that spiritual warfare is occurring around us each moment of our lives! Men spend their whole lives thinking what they experience here on earth is all that there is. But our time here on earth is such a small fragment of eternity!

What we should be doing instead of trying to accumulate wealth and other material things, instead of trying to fill the void in our heart with pleasures the world offers us, instead of fighting with God, instead of trying to control our lives, instead of trying to work everything out for ourselves, which we will fail at, is asking Jesus to come into our lives and take control of our lives.

When we surrender to him completely and honestly, only then will we have the peace that comes from the unconditional love God offers us at that moment. I pray the unsaved reading this book will understand this for their own salvation. They could be such an example to those around them. Because of their jobs and associations, they could be a witness to so many unsaved souls, and maybe from their witness, the Holy Spirit might convict their hearts so they too might spend an eternity with Him.

Because my three sons-in-law know Jesus, they are a witness and a leader in their families. They are able to witness to their wife and children. As Christian men, they try to follow God's Word in the Bible, leading their family, educating them, and bringing their children up according to Your Word.

If you are unsaved, I pray that Jesus brings someone into your life the Holy Spirit can use to convict you, thereby glorifying His kingdom. If you are unsaved and reading this book, you are at a crossroads in your life. I hope you choose the narrow path, leading to eternal salvation!

In conclusion, William P. Brown, in his book *Wisdoms Wonder: Character, Creation, and Crisis in the Bible's Wisdom Literature* sums up godly wisdom very well:

Barry Denzil Haney, MD

Wisdom offers an enduring sense of mystery of all that is, of all that is Other: the reverberating laughter of Wisdom's cosmic delight, the inalienable dignity of creation's denizens, and the unfathomable nature of the God behind it all. Creation remains a central feature of biblical wisdom.

PRAYER

Our heavenly Father,

You tell us, "ask, and it will be given to you, seek, and you will find, knock, and the door will be open."

Father, no matter what difficulty, sickness, or hardship those on our prayer list may be facing this day, we ask that You bless them.

In the Bible, You have soothed us, saying do not fear tomorrow. So, we pray this day that they will know Your peace in their hearts. A peace that surpasses all understanding; a peace that will guard their hearts and minds; a peace they receive from Christ himself.

Father, we pray that You strengthen them during any pain or suffering they might experience, or hardship they may be facing.

Father, during this season of their lives, we would just ask that You come and be present, watching, waiting, moving to help guard every moment during this process.

May they be held in Your loving arms and protect from all harm while they experience Your comforting and sustaining peace. We pray for Your healing power during this time of adversity. We pray You provide their family with the same comfort, strength, and peace.

We ask all of these things in the precious name of Jesus,

Amen.

Barry Denzil Haney, MD

CHAPTER 11

Following the Cross!

Take up your cross and follow Me...

And when he had called the people unto him with his disciples also, he said unto them, Whosoever will come after me, let him deny himself, and take up his cross, and follow me. For whosoever will save his life shall lose it; but whosoever shall lose his life for my sake and the gospel's, the same shall save it. For what shall it profit a man, if he shall gain the whole world, and lose his own soul?

—Mark 8:34-37

———————

WORLDLY WISDOM

In Mark 8:34, in His own words, Jesus tells us what it means to be a disciple. He is outlining the process of discipleship. First, we must "deny ourselves," not give something up but deny our right to run our own lives. Second, He then tells us to "take up his cross;" we are not to be offended or upset by the big or little things of life. Finally, He says, "follow me or obey me."

In a nutshell, Christianity is about following Jesus and doing what he says.

The Cambridge Dictionary defines cross in this way:

"An object in the shape of a cross that people were killed on, used as a symbol of Christianity."

The Dictionary of Bible Themes defines the cross in this way:

An instrument of execution, used especially by the Roman authorities for putting criminals to death. The sufferings of Jesus Christ on the cross, foreshadowed in the OT, are related in the NT gospel accounts. Scripture sees the death of Christ as central to the Christian faith. Through the cross and resurrection of Christ, God achieved the redemption of believers.

Why is the cross important?

For Christians, the cross at Calvary, is where Jesus voluntarily paid the penalty for our sins; although He was innocent and sinless, His torture and death were substitutionary. Because He loved us so much, God developed His plan of salvation, to reconcile us to Himself, to overcome the chasm separating us from Him, allowing us to have an eternal loving relationship with Him.

For non-Christians, the cross may represent a lucky piece of jewelry, a symbol to be idolized, offering power or protection from evil forces. Paul tells us in 1 Corinthians 1:18, in the eyes of "those who are perishing," the "word of the cross" is "folly."

Where did the cross and the concept of crucifixion originate from?

Justin characterized Christ' crucifixion as madness: "They say that our madness consists in the fact that we put a crucified man in second place after the unchangeable and eternal God, the creator of the world" (Apology 1, 13.4).

In his book entitled *Crucifixion: In the Ancient World and the Folly of the Message of the Cross*, Martin Hengel eloquently demonstrates the conclusion of the leaders Pliny, Tacitus, and Caecilius, that the one whom Christians claim as their God is a dead God, through the following oracle of Apollo recorded by Porphyry, preserved by Augustine:

> Let her continue as she pleases, persisting in her vain allusions, and lamenting in song a God who died in delusions, who was condemned by judges whose verdict was just, and executed in the prime of life by the worst of deaths, a death bound with iron.

Hengel goes on to say,

> That although the Hellenistic world was familiar with death of barbarian demigods and heroes of primeval times, the thought that the son of the one and only true God, Redeemer of the world, died the death of a common criminal, could only be regarded as a sign of madness.

Hengel further explains, crucifixion is an offensive affair, a barbaric form of execution of the utmost cruelty and began among the Persians. To the Persians, crucifixion was regarded as a form of execution used by barbarian people, including the Indians, the Assyrians, the Scythians, the Taurinians, then later by the Celts, the Germani, Brittani, and the Carthaginians, probably the people who the Romans learned it from.

Greek and Roman historians stressed barbarian crucifixions. In his course entitled *TH111 Doctrine of Christ and the Church: A Reformed Perspective*, R. Michael Allen laments, "The cross was a brutal thing, a gruesome act of torture and execution, something so heinous that Rome would not inflict it on their own citizens no matter how evil they might have been."

According to Hengel, the following statements characterized crucifixion in the ancient world:

> Crucifixion was a matter of subjecting the victim to the upmost indignity; the form of crucifixion varied; the victim could undergo crucifixion while he was alive or be displayed on the cross as a corpse after he had been executed in a different fashion; living or dead, the victim was either nailed or bound to a stake; in the Roman Empire, the norm for this type of execution was flogging beforehand, followed by the victim caring the cross to the place of execution, followed by nailing to the cross with outstretched arms, followed by raising up the cross and seating it into the ground on a wooden peg; the form of execution could vary considerably, the form of punishment left to the caprice and sadism of the executioners.

Hengel offers us a gruesome, eyewitness account of crucifixion, taken from Josephus, of the fate of Jewish fugitives who attempted to escape from the siege of Jerusalem in 70 AD:

> When they were going to be taken (by the Romans), they were forced to defend themselves, and after they had fought,

Barry Denzil Haney, MD

they thought it too late to make any supplications for mercy: so they were first whipped and then tormented with all sorts of tortures, before they died and were then crucified before the wall of the city. Titus felt pity for them, but as their number—given as up to five hundred a day—was too great for him to risk either letting them go or putting them under guard, he allowed his soldiers to have their way, especially as he hoped that the gruesome sight of the countless crosses might move the besieged to surrender: "So the soldiers, out of the rage and hatred they bore the prisoners, nailed those they caught, in different postures, to the crosses, by way of jest and their number was so great that there was not enough room for the crosses and not enough crosses for the bodies."

In conclusion, Hengel writes:

"Crucifixion as a penalty was remarkably widespread in antiquity."

Crucifixion appears in various forms among numerous peoples of the ancient world, even among the Greeks. There was evidently neither the desire nor the power to abolish it, even where people were fully aware of its extreme cruelty.

It thus formed a harsh contradiction to the idealistic picture of antiquity which was inaugurated by Winckelmann in terms of "noble simplicity and quiet greatness" (*edle Einfalt und stille Grösse*). Our own age, which is proud of its humanity and its progress, but which sees the use of the death penalty, torture, and terror increasing in the world rather than decreasing, can hardly pride itself on having overcome this ancient contradiction.

ILLUSTRATION

The following illustration concerning crucifixion is taken from Michael P. Green's book *1500 Illustrations for Biblical Preaching*:

> The unnatural position used in crucifixion made every movement painful; the lacerated veins and crushed tendons throbbed with incessant anguish; the wounds, inflamed by exposure, gradually gangrened; the arteries—especially at the head and stomach—became swollen and oppressed with surcharged blood; and while each variety of misery went on gradually increasing, there was added to them the intolerable pang of a burning and raging thirst; and all these physical complications caused an internal excitement and anxiety, which made the prospect of death itself—of death, the unknown enemy, at whose approach man usually shudders most—bear the aspect of a delicious and exquisite release.

GODLY WISDOM

The Bible tells us to deny ourselves and to take up the cross and follow Jesus!

Sometimes it's hard and difficult to deny yourself while here on earth, to deny the pleasures one receives from doing what makes you feel good.

However, it will be much harder to hear this final word on judgment day, spoken by Jesus in Matthew 25:41: "Depart from me, ye cursed, into everlasting fire." If we learn to hear the word of the cross and follow it willingly now, we will not have to fear we will hear eternal damnation on the day of judgment. *It seems crazy we would actually fear to take up the cross, when doing so, will win us an eternal relationship with God in heaven.*

Barry Denzil Haney, MD

Thomas a Kempis believed,

> The cross offers us salvation, the cross is life, in the cross is
> protection from our enemies, in the cross is the sweetness
> and peace of heaven, in the cross is inexpressible joy, in the
> cross is strength of mind, in the cross is perfect holiness.

As Thomas a Kempis tells us in *The Imitation of Christ*,

> There is no salvation of soul nor hope of everlasting life but
> in the cross... You can spend your entire life searching for
> an elusive pleasure to fill the void in your heart, but you will
> never find a safer way than the way of the cross to fill that
> void. We will face trials and tribulations during our journey
> to salvation, but we must learn to "bear these for as long
> as God wills this to occur in our lives because he wishes
> us to learn to bear any trial without consolation to submit
> ourselves wholly to him that we may become more humble
> through suffering.

Pride and arrogance are the greatest sins. It is through humility that
God brings us to our knees. Only then will we finally realize we cannot
control ourselves; we must turn it all over to God and let the Holy Spirit
work through us. Only God can control the sinful nature in us. We must
learn to carry our cross and do so willingly. If we throw away the trial we
currently face, another one, possibly even a heavier one, may come. Even
Jesus Christ, our Lord took on a cross every hour He was on the earth. He
experienced the pain of his passion! We must remember, as we become
more holy, as we make more spiritual progress in our journey to salvation,
our cross will become heavier because as the unconditional love of God
increases, the pain of the separation from Him also increases.

But we do have hope because we know there is a great reward coming
to us when we bear our cross. We must remember, although it is sometimes

difficult to face our trials, and we sometimes desire to escape from them, we will be strengthened by the grace of God within us. We must remember that we are not promised a life without sorrow and pain, but we must also remember that we do have hope, if we bear our cross, if we continue to have faith in Jesus, if we continue to try to please God in everything we do, if we do these things, we will be rewarded on Judgment Day, we will receive our gift from God, an eternal relationship with Him in heaven.

Remember, we cannot rely upon ourselves because we cannot do any of the things God wants us to do. We must rely on Jesus, who lives in our hearts. We need to strive to please him in everything we do and place our complete trust in Him. He will give us the strength from heaven to conquer temptation. We must not fear our enemy Satan but armor ourselves with the full armor of God. He will help us prevent Satan from succeeding in his ultimate plan, his plan to lead us to eternal separation from God. We must be prepared to suffer many adversities, many kinds of trouble during our time on earth. We must learn to bear them.

If we just do these things, then we will come to a point where we think of suffering as "sweet and acceptable" for the sake of Christ, as Thomas a Kempis tells us in, *The Imitation of Christ*. For then, you have actually found paradise, heaven on earth!

But if we let suffering upset us, and we continually try to escape from the suffering, this will only make it easier for Satan to follow us everywhere. Remember, when you suffer something for Jesus, he promises great glory is in store for you, and he promises your suffering brings great joy to all the saints of God.

Thomas a Kempis tells us that "All men praise patience, though there are a few who wish to practice it." *Let us strive to be patient!* Thomas a Kempis also tells us that "You must leave a dying life; the more man dies to himself, the more he begins to live unto God." So, Jesus should be the subject! Thank You, Jesus, for loving us so much!

In his book *Jesus B,* Jim Lyon declares this:

Barry Denzil Haney, MD

You became flesh. You, as God incarnate, became the man known as Jesus, and walked among us, here on earth. You showed us, it is possible to live without sin, because Jesus did. You gave us a small glimpse of Heaven on earth, what it will be like when we get to heaven, a glimpse of what it is to live without sin, to have an eternal relationship, with the Father in Heaven.

———————

PRAYER

Our heavenly Father,

Thank You for being our Creator, for imagining us in Your dreams, then creating us in Your image. Thank You for allowing us to live in Your dreams and help us to live our lives according to Your will.

Thank You for Your unchanging love. Thank You for Your mercy.

Thank You for providing for us all our daily physical and spiritual needs. Thank You for Your total provision in the building of Your Church.

Thank You for protecting us. Thank You for sending Your Son to walk among us, to show us how to live in holiness.

Thank You for Your free gift of salvation, granted to those who have faith in Your Son Jesus, who shed his blood on the cross at Calvary, to pay the penalty for our sins.

Thank You for Your immutable promise to us, that whoever believes in Your Son will not perish, but have everlasting, eternal life in a loving relationship with You.

Thank You for giving us Your wisdom, through Your inspired Word contained in the Bible, to teach us how to please You and to become more holy while we reside here on Earth.

Thank You for the Holy Spirit, to guide us, to instruct us, and for giving us strength to withstand temptation as we travel along the road of salvation while we are here on Earth.

Thank You for Your immutable promise that the destination during our travel along this road of salvation is heaven. Thank You for erecting large warning signs along this road of salvation, written in scripture, to help us as we travel along this road of salvation.

Thank You for being with us, holding our hand, as we travel along this road of salvation and for taking over the lead, when needed, during desperate times.

Thank You for the assurance that You will deliver us from our enemies. We honor as holy and sacred, Your name.

We ask that Your perfect will take place on Earth.

We ask, You forgive the wrong things we have done, as we forgive those who have injured us.

We pray for protection from all the things that trip us up and undo us. We thank You for, and ask for, Your continual comfort, peace, and divine healing power, for those with both spoken and unspoken physical and spiritual needs.

In the precious name of Jesus Christ, our Savior, we ask these things.

Amen!

CHAPTER 12

Accountability

Brethren, if a man be overtaken in a fault, ye which are spiritual, restore such a one in the spirit of meekness; considering thyself, lest thou also be tempted. Bear ye one another's burdens, and so fulfil the law of Christ. For if a man think himself to be something, when he is nothing, he deceiveth himself. But let every man prove his own work, and then shall he have rejoicing in himself alone, and not in another. For every man shall bear his own burden.

—Galatians 6:1-5

WORLDLY WISDOM

The Cambridge Dictionary defines accountability in the following way:

"The fact of being responsible for what you do and able to give a satisfactory reason for it, or the degree to which this happens."

MY PERSONAL EXPERIENCE: STRANGE DREAM!

I awoke one morning from a disturbing and strange dream, a dream about the nonsensical search for God many experience throughout their lives, characterized by disappointments and tragedies.

In the dream, I was struck by the ridiculousness of searching in the wrong places, searching for earthly pleasures to fill the void, the chasm separating us from God. Satan uses this knowledge about us to attack us through lies and deception, trying to prevent us from filling the void in our hearts with God's love.

In order to get off this roller coaster ride, this nonsensical search for God, the Scripture tells us we need to have faith in Jesus. *But, how do we combat the temptation we will face once we have faith in Jesus?* Well, one tool we can use is the concept of accountability.

The following taken from *Adventist Men's Ministries Curriculum,* describes successful accountability in this way: "Successful accountability requires a commitment to honest, systematic sharing, and the willingness to act on the recommendations received."

We all need to learn how to listen, keep things to ourselves, and withhold judgment statements. We need to make sure others know we are not condemning them or making value judgments on their integrity. The time of sharing should be voluntary, and the ultimate purpose should be to glorify God's kingdom by helping us along the road of progressive sanctification as we become better here on Earth.

What are some of the desired qualities of an accountability partner or group? Many believe accountability works best in one-on-one encounters or in small groups. Stan Toler, in his book *Rethink Your Life: A Unique Diet to Renew Your Mind,* lists the following qualities of an accountability partner or group:

Choose an accountability partner of the same sex; choose a peer; choose someone who is spiritually maturing; choose a person who is nonjudgmental; choose someone who understands his own brokenness; choose a person who is trustworthy; choose someone who can speak the truth in love to you.

MY PERSONAL EXPERIENCE: UNEXPECTED TEXT!

Later that day, I received a text message from a friend I met at my Emmaus Walk in October. I was so excited to get this text message because he was the person I connected with and shared the most with during that time.

I know God placed him in my life. He is a clinical psychologist by trade and a Christian therapist, a very wise man.

During one of our conversations, he related to me the importance of accountability partners for Christians as a tool to combat temptation.

Because of this conversation, I now, wholeheartedly, believe in this principle and have implemented this strategy in my walk with Jesus.

Because the qualifications for an accountability partner are quite high, it may take a while to find the right person. Trust in God; He will lead you to the right person in His timing. You should pray to God to direct you to the person.

As the Bible tells us in Mark 11:24, "Therefore I say unto you, What things soever ye desire, when ye pray, believe that ye receive them, and ye shall have them." You can always talk to your pastor or another leader at your church. They can often assist you in finding the right person to hold you accountable. But don't base your decision on who the right accountability partner for you is on their recommendations alone. Because God gives us free choice, you're the one who ultimately needs to make that decision; after all, you have the most to gain and lose.

The following, taken from the *Adventist Men's Ministries Curriculum*, captures nicely the idea of accountability with another person:

> The idea of being accountable is not that one man is lording it over the life decisions of another. Neither is it a guilt trip, a burden that the man soon wants to be rid of. The best situation arises in small-group and one-on-one friendships, where the participants frequently share the developments in key aspects of their lives, without fear of condemnation or betrayal. They learn from each other and are challenged to improve, so growing into the pure and contented souls God originally created us to be.

GODLY WISDOM

What does the Bible tell us about the importance of accountability in our walk with Jesus?

In recent years, the term "accountability partner" has surfaced. Although not found in Scripture, James implies a prayer partner in James 5:16: "Confess your faults one to another, and pray one for another, that ye may be healed. The effectual fervent prayer of a righteous man availeth much." But we need to remember what the Bible tells us in 1 John 1:9 about confessing our sins to God: "If we confess our sins, he is faithful and just to forgive us our sins, and to cleanse us from all unrighteousness."

However, even taking into account this admonition from God, we should be able to share our temptations with another Christian, with the caveat, choosing such a person should be done carefully. For the Christian, there are two types of accountability: accountability to God; and account-

Barry Denzil Haney, MD

ability to another Christian. David illustrates the idea of accountability to God in the following beautiful and exemplary prayer: "Search me, O God, and know my heart: Try me, and know my thoughts: And see if there be any wicked way in me And lead me in the way everlasting" (Psalm 139:23-24).

The godly wisdom of seeking accountability with other like-minded is Christians can be seen in the following passage in James 5:13-16:

> Is any among you afflicted? let him pray. Is any merry? let him sing psalms. Is any sick among you? let him call for the elders of the church; and let them pray over him, anointing him with oil in the name of the Lord: And the prayer of faith shall save the sick, and the Lord shall raise him up; and if he have committed sins, they shall be forgiven him. Confess your faults one to another, and pray one for another, that ye may be healed. The effectual fervent prayer of a righteous man availeth much.

All of us are sinners; therefore we need to realize, whatever we are struggling with, we are not alone.

The Bible tells us in 1 Corinthians 10:13,

> There hath no temptation taken you but such as is common to man: but God is faithful, who will not suffer you to be tempted above that ye are able; but will with the temptation also make a way to escape, that ye may be able to bear it.

The Bible tells us, God keeps a record of our life journey in the book of life:

> Then I saw a great white throne and him who was seated on it. From his presence earth and sky fled away, and no place was found for them. And I saw the dead, great and small,

standing before the throne, and books were opened. Then another book was opened, which is the book of life. And the dead were judged by what was written in the books, according to what they had done. And the sea gave up the dead who were in it, Death and Hades gave up the dead who were in them, and they were judged, each one of them, according to what they had done. Then Death and Hades were thrown into the lake of fire. This is the second death, the lake of fire. And if anyone's name was not found written in the book of life, he was thrown into the lake of fire.

I believe the Bible is authoritative and life-changing, sufficient to solve any problem. From the passage above, we should take warning and heed the advice God gives us! Remember, in the book of life is recorded the choice each of us makes each time we are tempted by Satan, through his lifetime onslaught of lies and deceptions.

PRAYER

Our heavenly Father,

I don't understand the nonsensical search for God I see so many experience throughout their lives! They appear to be searching in the wrong places, searching for earthly pleasures to fill the void, the chasm separating them from God!

I pray for the conviction of the Holy Spirit to prevent Satan from using this knowledge to attack, through lies and deceptions! His goal is to prevent us from filling the void in our hearts with God's love!

We ask that the Holy Spirit guide us to an "accountability partner" to help us learn from one another during our journey to salvation! A person who can help us resist the devil! Help us find an accountability partner who loves Jesus and whose purpose each day is to please Jesus in everything they do!

In the precious name of Jesus Christ our Lord and Savior,

Amen!

CHAPTER 13

The Outhouse!

And he said, A certain man had two sons: And the younger of them said to his father, Father, give me the portion of goods that falleth to me. And he divided unto them his living. And not many days after the younger son gathered all together, and took his journey into a far country, and there wasted his substance with riotous living. And when he had spent all, there arose a mighty famine in that land; and he began to be in want. And he went and joined himself to a citizen of that country; and he sent him into his fields to feed swine. And he would fain have filled his belly with the husks that the swine did eat and no man gave unto him. And when he came to himself, he said, How many hired servants of my fathers have bread enough and to spare, and I perish with hunger! I will arise and go to my father, and will say unto him, Father, I have sinned against heaven, and before thee, And am no more worthy to be called thy son: make me as one of thy hired servants. And he arose and came to his father. But when he was yet a great way off, his father saw him, and had compassion, and ran, and fell on his neck, and kissed him. And the son said unto him, Father, I have sinned against heaven, and in thy sight, and am no more worthy to be called thy son. But the father said to his servants, Bring forth the best robe, and put it on him; and put a ring on his hand, and shoes on his feet: And bring hither the fatted calf, and kill it; and let us eat, and be merry: For this my son was dead, and is alive again; he was lost, and is found. And they began to be merry. Now his elder son was in the field: and as he came and drew nigh to the house, he heard music and dancing. And he called one of the servants and asked what these things meant. And he said unto him, Thy brother is come; and thy father hath killed the fatted calf, because he hath received him safe and sound. And he was angry and would not go in: therefore came his father out, and intreated him. And he answering said to his father, Lo, these many years do I serve thee, neither transgressed I at any time thy commandment: and yet thou never gavest me a kid, that I might make merry with my friends: But as soon as this thy son was come, which hath devoured thy living with harlots, thou hast killed for him the fatted calf. And he said unto him, Son, thou art ever with me, and all that I have is thine. It was meet that we should make merry and be glad: for this thy brother was dead, and is alive again; and was lost, and is found.

—Luke 15:11-32

Barry Denzil Haney, MD

WORLDY WISDOM

In the parable of the prodigal son, I believe Jesus uses this story to teach us of God the Father's love for each of us and how willing He is to accept us back, no matter what sin we might have committed.

The Cambridge Dictionary defines prodigal son in this way: "A man or boy who has left his family in order to do something that the family disapprove of and has now returned home feeling sorry for what he has done."

The story of the prodigal son illustrates a spiritual point: no matter why we search for earthly pleasures, try to fill the void, the separation from God that we experience in our heart, He will always accept us back, if we believe in Him, repent, and allow Him to control our lives.

MY PERSONAL EXPERIENCE: THE OUTHOUSE!

This reminds me of a story about "the outhouse." When I was a child, I always enjoyed going to my grandmother's house. One such visit stands out vividly in my memory today. I'm not sure what the occasion was, but I remember my father, mother, siblings Clay, Carole, and Ronnie, and I went to my grandmother's house for a family get-together in Mount Sterling, Kentucky, during the late summer.

My grandmother lived in a farmhouse adjacent to a large cornfield. I remember the farmhouse as being quaint, neat, comfortable, and cozy, but without indoor plumbing or bathroom facilities. Water was brought into the house from a well. The bathroom was an outhouse, located separate from the house.

On that particular day, when I walked into her house, I was greeted with the familiar, chaotic but comfortable atmosphere I had remembered from previous visits: the delectable, heavenly smells floating through the house coming from the kitchen; the incessant hum of conversation from the kitchen and living room; the bustling scene of the women in the kitchen, the counters and tables stuffed with pots, pans, utensils, food dishes, piles of dinner rolls, plates of biscuits, chocolate meringue pies, cakes, cookies and candy; my anticipation of how wonderful it was going to be when I would be able to eat the sugary delights on display; the women bustling about, busy preparing the feast we would soon enjoy; the delicious smell of fried chicken and gravy, the odor of pungent onions, the scrumptious smell of cinnamon and apple from the apple pie baking in the oven, all of the smells and aromas from the foods being prepared, blending into the heavenly smell enjoyed by all, both inside and outside the farmhouse; being chased out of the kitchen when discovered trying to reach for a cookie; the sound of boisterous, conversation from the men in the living room, who were deep in conversation about world and local events, offering solutions to the problems we faced, spontaneous bouts of laughter, after the telling of a hilarious joke or story; and hearing other such good conversation about things grown-ups seemed to enjoy chattering about during these family get-togethers.

After the usual attention paid to the children who arrived, my siblings and I were soon forgotten. We were then allowed to begin our exploration of the mysterious world awaiting us outside grandmother's front door.

Although inside my grandmother's farmhouse, I felt comfort, peace, and love, the outdoors was wild and exciting, offering a different kind of pleasure. The farmyard was bustling with activity: chickens frantically scratching, pecking, and sharpening their beaks; cows in the field slowly grazing and chewing; horses in the distance running and neighing; buzzards flying, circling overhead; songbirds constantly chirping and singing; the continuous, resounding pulsation of sound from the katydids. Of course, the first thing my brother Clay and I did, was run into the large, vast, mysterious cornfield adjacent to my grandmother's house.

It was a beautiful day, with white clouds billowing overhead, framed against the backdrop of a deep blue sky, framing the entrance to the corn-

Barry Denzil Haney, MD

field. As soon as we pushed our way through the cornstalks, we entered another planet.

Before us was a strange, vast landscape, one unlike any other we had ever known. The ground was uneven, rocky, flat, deeply rutted, and relatively empty, except for endless standing rows of tall, perpendicular, dry cornstalks, arising from the dry, rocky ground, appearing to stretch for miles in every direction.

As the wind blew, I could hear the leaves of the corn stalks scrape their adjacent brethren, a beautiful song being orchestrated for my hearing pleasure.

But otherwise, my overwhelming sense was how eerily quiet the cornfield was. I was also struck by the relative absence of other living things, except for the occasional spider, grasshopper, or ant that would pass by. I could hear a train apparently slipping through the jungles of corn on the horizon.

My brother and I would chase each other down furrows of ripened corn. As we stumbled our way through the cornfield, the cornstalks scratched our arms and legs as we pushed them aside with one hand and tried to maintain our balance with the other as we ran in a frantic, crosscutting pattern. When my brother and I found ourselves in the middle of the cornfield, I could sense our separateness and loneliness, our vulnerability within this mysterious world.

At that moment, I could imagine a civil war battle taking place or Indians hiding in the rows of corn, ready to ambush any clueless settler who might be wandering through the rows of corn.

But, I will admit, I was terrified by the cornfield, as well. I imagined being cold, wet, and scared, huddled amongst the tall cornstalks, hoping someone would soon find me. Furthermore, I could imagine monsters of all descriptions living within the tall cornfield.

But the thing I remember most about this visit was the outhouse!

Now, just what is it about an outhouse that intrigues a young boy?

There's nothing special about the appearance of an outhouse. It is constructed from roughhewn old planks of grey, weathered hardwood. No apparent architectural marvel was used in its construction. It is rectangle in shape, with a stiff, hard-to-open door, and sits over a deep pit in the ground.

However, to an adventurous young boy, it was a palace, the "Taj Mahal," a getaway, something that Tom Sawyer would live in, a palace to live in on a tropical island, or in a forest, a place where you could hideout from pirates, those out to get you.

When I forcibly pulled open the outhouse door, I entered into a different world.

I'm not sure what fascinated me about the outhouse.

It didn't particularly have a good smell; there was nothing attractive, glittering, or beautiful about the inside. Nevertheless, it was very intriguing; the old, tattered Sears catalog with missing pages; a roll of yellow, water stained, wrinkled toilet paper hanging on a nail on the wall; old newspapers plastered against the walls, I guess to keep out the cold air in winter, and then, of course, the smell. It wasn't a bad smell, to a young boy, it was a very interesting smell.

Although the odor from an outhouse has been described as the vilest smell imaginable, the loose boards on the sides of the outhouse provided air blasts from outside when the wind howled, which mixed the smells of the outside cornfield, wildflowers, and plants with the vile smell emanating from the outhouse pit, providing for a most interesting smell, a smell I'm sure my dog would take delight in!

Of course, the thing that intrigued me most was the seat you sat on.

In this particular outhouse were two seats, made by carving out two adjacent holes into a long, rough board. The actual hole you sat on had been meticulously carved and sanded down to form two elliptical holes, with a smooth surface and a perfect contour to accommodate your "behind" comfortably, a perfect throne, if you will, on which you could "relieve yourself."

Of course, being the mischievous boy I was, I wanted to peer down into the dark hole beneath me, to investigate the very deep, dark space below me, to discover what might lie beyond the world I perceived in this strange, mysterious place beneath my naked butt!

Barry Denzil Haney, MD

What I saw when I peered into that dark hole at first startled me, but then amazed me—what I saw was mounds of mysterious stuff! Although I thought I knew what that "stuff" was, it was still mysterious and evocative, drawing me into a new world, reminding me of my desire to see and do new things, because after all, I was my own man, I was no longer a child, I was my own master…

Suddenly, I heard the clanging of the dinner bell, "Dinner's ready! Come and get it!" clamored my grandmother from the backdoor. I stood up and ran from the outhouse, back to the safety of her home, to ravage the meal that awaited me!

Like the prodigal son's journey from the safety and security of his father's house, the lure of the outhouse represented my desire to experience what the outside world offered, to escape the known, to experience the unknown.

Using the following analogy, albeit I admit, a bit of a stretch, I was like the prodigal son, an abuser of the unmerited grace I received from my grandmother, provided me through the comforts of her home, and traded that hospitality for the worldly pleasures I thought I found in the outhouse.

As Isaiah 53:6 (NIV) tells us,

"We all, like sheep, have gone astray, each of us has turned to our own way."

When I heard the dinner bell ring, I realized the outhouse was a worthless treasure, and what I truly needed was the comfort within my grandmother's house, the reassuring, comforting arms my grandmother's house offered me, much more exciting than the cold, drafty, smelly outhouse!

But, in all fairness, I was a young lad who was really hungry. So, seeing the light in the darkness, I scurried back into the loving arms of my grandmother's house, where I received not only grace, through the comfort my grandmother's house provided, but also would be able to satisfy my primal urge of hunger, would be able to satisfy the earthly pleasure of devouring the wonderful meal I would soon enjoy in my grandmother's house!

The prodigal son parable has appealed to people throughout the centuries.

In her essay *The Prodigal Son: An Essay in Literary Criticism from a Psychoanalytic Perspective*, Mary Ann Tolbert describes this appeal in this way:

> "The wish to restore a unity, a harmony among the conflicting elements of one's life is an almost universal desire." She goes on to say, the Prodigal Son "expresses a basic human desire for unity and wholeness in life."

Charles Dickens reportedly called the Prodigal Son "the greatest short story ever told."

Most would agree it is a story of real life.

It's almost impossible to read this parable without seeing someone you know or yourself in it.

What is your "prodigal moment," and do you respond to it with worldly wisdom, or do you seek godly wisdom to help you?

———————

GODLY WISDOM

What is the meaning of the prodigal son parable found in the New Testament of the Bible in Luke 15:11-32? Jesus appears to be talking to the religious leaders and teachers of the law, pleading with them to flee from their own righteousness and works-based religion, asking them to experience salvation by God's grace through their faith.

As Jesus tells us in Matthew 5:3, "Blessed are the poor in spirit for theirs is the kingdom of heaven." We need to realize, we are unworthy and, therefore, can only be saved when we reach out for help and when we have

Barry Denzil Haney, MD

faith in Jesus, who paid the ultimate penalty for our sin, giving us hope for an eternal loving relationship with God in heaven.

Many of us will face a prodigal moment in our life, and God tells us if we place our trust in Him, we will overcome the trial and tribulations we will experience during that season of our life. For those parents reading this book, who are facing a prodigal situation, Kyle Idleman, in his book *Praying for Your Prodigal*, offers the following hope: "Find hope in the fact that we serve a God who loves your prodigal even more deeply than you do…He is the Father who waits just as eagerly for your prodigal's return."

These brief encounters with earthly pleasure we all experience, the ecstasy we temporarily experience when we fill this void, are fleeting. We find whatever earthly pleasure we use to fill the void in our heart requires more and more to achieve the same electrifying, ecstatic, orgasmic response, the same release of dopamine at the cellular level in our brain.

Ultimately, we need to realize; we are really seeking an eternal loving relationship with our Creator God; we are searching for agape love; we are searching for the unconditional love only experienced in God's presence. My spirit man has been saved and made righteous because of Christ's righteousness; my spirit man is holy because of Christ's holiness. The void, the chasm, the separation from God has been removed. Because of His shed blood on the cross at Calvary, my sins have been forgiven. I've been made right in the eyes of God. I've been justified in the sight of God. Sin no longer separates me from Him.

I know I was created in His image to spend eternity with Him in a loving relationship. I know this search throughout my life to fill this void, this empty godly container in my heart, with earthly pleasures, was an unsuccessful attempt to fill that void, to bridge that chasm, to remove that separation, to satisfy that unquenchable hunger, for a relationship with God!

PRAYER

Our heavenly Father,

We look forward to the day when You come back and we are gathered up into the clouds with You, to be united with You, to sit at the right hand of God in heaven.

We also realize that day will be a sad day for You because as You have told us in Your Word, many will choose not to follow You, but will instead choose to be eternally separated from You.

Oh, I pray that each person will have a renewal of their mind and see the light. I pray You will become the light, in their world of darkness, so they will not spend an eternity in the dark, cold, place of nothingness, called hell.

I pray they will not be the baby crying out in the dark for help in a cold, dark, empty, black place of nothingness, where no relationship is possible, no intimacy exists, no stimulation exists, only nothingness prevails for an eternity in a place called hell.

Thank You, for the hope you have given me. I know my spirit will be with You in heaven for an eternity. Thank You, Lord Jesus; I bow down before You in praise and worship.

You are the beginning and the end; You are the Alpha and the Omega; You are my Creator God.

Thank You for imagining me in Your dreams. Thank You for giving me the opportunity to worship You for an eternity; thank You, Father, thank You, Jesus; thank You, Holy Spirit.

In the precious name of Jesus, our Lord and Savior,

Amen!

Barry Denzil Haney, MD

CHAPTER 14

Unconditional Love or Love with Conditions?

In this was manifested the love of God toward us, because that God sent his only begotten Son into the world, that we might live through him. Herein is love, not that we loved God, but that he loved us, and sent his Son to be the propitiation for our sins. Beloved, if God so loved us, we ought also to love one another.

—1 John 4:9-11

WORLDLY WISDOM

In 1 John 4:9-11, the Holy Spirit is instructing me, Jesus came to satisfy justice, to meet the demands of a broken law, to pay the full debt, to satisfy the penalty. He is instructing me not to ignore this fact; God's love is also just; therefore, the only love worth talking about is a love that satisfies justice. Because of this, all of us "*owe it*" to love one another because if God so loved us, we also should love one another with a non-judgmental love, not basing it on the qualities we see in the other person.

The Cambridge Dictionary defines love in this way: "To have a strong affection for someone, which can be combined with a strong romantic attraction; to like something very much."

The Dictionary of Biblical Themes defines love in this way: "In his words and actions, and supremely in the death of Jesus Christ on the cross, God demonstrates the nature of love and defines the direction in which human love in all its forms should develop."

My first recollection of God's love is when I was taught the song as a young child, "Jesus loves me, this I know…" Although I was taught this concept, what that actually meant was hard to understand. Like many others, I have had a difficult time understanding, believing, or accepting God's love.

MY PERSONAL EXPERIENCE: CONVERSATION WITH STAN!

On November 25, 2019, at approximately 2 p.m., Stan called me while on his way to work as a hospital chaplain at the University of Cincinnati Hospital. I respect Stan very much; he is a pastor and has a doctorate in Ministry from Emory University. I asked him to review a podcast by Brad Freeman entitled "LGBT." I was told by a friend that he had a problem with that particular podcast because he thought Brad's views on the subject were not completely scriptural and wanted me to beware of recommending his site to others.

I told him I would review this particular podcast and get back to him. After reviewing this podcast, I could see where my friend was having a problem with some of the things said in this podcast, but I felt that there was nothing unscriptural in my mind that would prevent me from recommending this podcast to others. Because I respect my friend as well as Stan, I asked Stan to review this for me and give me an honest opinion of what Brad Freeman was saying in this podcast.

Stan got back to me and gave me his usual scholarly interpretation after listening to this podcast. First, he said that as Jim Lyon said in a regional conference in 2015 concerning sexuality and sins of sexuality, we need to look at both a person's posture concerning these topics as well as his position. According to Stan, he feels Brad Freeman's posture is great, that it is Jesus-like. However, his position is difficult for him to figure out, muddy or unclear in position.

According to Stan, when talking about these particular issues in the LGBT community, he tries to divide them up into two categories:

- Those of same-sex attraction but those who don't actually act out, and

- those who are acting out homosexually

These two categories in his mind are very different. Stan related that in Ephesians 2:10, the doctrine of being saved by faith and not works is espoused.

In Acts 2:40, Peter seems to tell us works may be involved, "And with many other words did he testify and exhort, saying, 'Save yourself from this untoward generation.'"

Stan likened this to a receiver in football. After a quarterback throws a beautiful spiral pass deep into the end zone and the receiver runs and positions himself in just the right spot to catch this pass, then catches it. He really didn't have anything to do with the perfect pass but only positioned himself to catch it.

This is like avoiding sin; we work to get ourselves in a position to receive God's grace. Although Stan understands Brad Freeman to believe in the concept of God's unconditional love, he wonders if there might be a hint of universalism in what he is saying in the podcast. Stan believes in the concept of God's unconditional love as well as the concept; love needs to be conditionally received. We should repent and believe the good news.

Wesley, in his discussion of sanctification, talks about two things. He says some things are "sins properly called" and "sins not so properly called." Wesley speaks of sin as "infirmities." He likens sin to a long division problem worked out in the traditional method; sin is like when you make a mathematical mistake while working out the problem and get the wrong answer. Sin is a voluntary transgression of a known law. Wesley also asks, "what if we involuntarily or unintentionally break a known law, is that sin?"

Stan also talks about the paradox between "don't beat yourself up" after you are saved, and on the other end of that paradox, "we want God to perfect us, we want to be sensitive to him." Charles Wesley sums the second part of this paradox in his hymn entitled "I Want a Principal Within:"

> I want a principle within
> Of watchful, godly fear,
> A sensibility of sin,
> A pain to feel it near.
> I want the first approach to feel
> Of pride or wrong desire,
> To catch the wandering of my will,
> And quench the kindling fire.
>
> From Thee that I no more may part,
> No more Thy goodness grieve,
> The filial awe, the fleshly heart,
> The tender conscience, give.
> Quick as the apple of an eye,
> O God, my conscience make;
> Awake my soul when sin is nigh,
> And keep it still awake.
>
> Almighty God of truth and love,
> To me Thy power impart;
> The mountain from my soul remove,
> The hardness from my heart.
> Oh, may the least omission pain
> My reawakened soul,
> And drive me to that blood again,

Barry Denzil Haney, MD

Which makes the wounded whole.

Both parts of this paradox are true, and you need both! As Howard A. Snyder tells us in his article "Is God's Love Unconditional?" "If God loved unconditionally in the Rogerian sense of offering unconditional positive regard, He would forgive and accept every person no matter what, requiring no cross." Therefore, for us to experience God's love, two conditions are necessary; Jesus' death on the cross and our genuine faith.

Thank you, Stan. I really respect and admire Stan's wisdom. Also, I believe my friend is a wiser man than I thought. I do believe God directs us to seek out other Christian's views concerning matters of truth and to correct them when they wander from the truth. In James 5:19-20 (NLT), James tells us:

> My dear brothers and sisters, if someone among you
> wanders away from the truth and is brought back, you can
> be sure that whoever brings the sinner back from wander-
> ing will save that person from death and bring about the
> forgiveness of many sins.

But also, we need to study the Word found in the Bible for ourselves, allowing the Holy Spirit to teach us God's Word and help us understand what is scriptural. We should never be judgmental or quick to judge others. We all are undergoing progressive sanctification, we all are sinners, and we all can learn from one another. Brad Freeman does ask each person who listens to his podcasts to contact him about anything causing the listener concern because he is more than happy to listen to others' concerns and criticisms. Thank You, Jesus.

———

GODLY WISDOM

Which is it, unconditional love or love with conditions? The term unconditional love cannot be found in Scripture. I have come to the conclusion, after a review of the literature, that the concept of unconditional love is a myth.

Some secular humanists believe people need to be loved and accepted unconditionally. Although many have bought into this notion and believe they can love unconditionally, if they are truly honest, because of self-bias and a deceitful heart, they actually place all kinds of conditions on this proposition.

James Dobson, a chief proponent of unconditional love, maintains this: "I'm convinced the human spirit craves this kind of unconditional love and experiences something akin to 'soul hunger' when it cannot be achieved." He goes on to say, "God's acceptance is unconditional."

However, I believe many who agree with Dobson have a misunderstanding of what Paul calls in Ephesians 3:19, "love of Christ which passeth knowledge."

According to Tom Scottsay, et al., in *Unconditional Love and Acceptance?*

> "The thrust of this word in humanistic psychology has been both to give and to expect unconditional love from one another with no strings attached."

He goes on to further say,

> The best kind of love is unconditional love…the highest love secular humanists know…a love that makes no demands for performance, good behavior…associated with a kind of permissiveness…even though the promoters of the unconditional love jargon would say that unconditional love does not have to dispense with discipline.

Barry Denzil Haney, MD

Although God's love is unconditional and unlimited, it is a love with conditions.

Christians believe in salvation by grace received through faith, not on universalism which believes all people are saved. Theodore Jungkuntz describes grace and its relationship with unconditional love in this way:

> God's unconditional love pictures the deity as a permissive parent who has no other motivating power than the unconditional acceptance of every human being regardless of that person's response. God's free gift always implies an unqualified demand.

Jesus told the disciples in John 14:21, "He that hath my commandments, and keepeth them, he it is that loveth me: and he that loveth me shall be loved of my Father, and I will love him, and will manifest myself to him."

God's love requires two conditions to be met. The first condition was met by the death of Jesus on the cross at Calvary when he paid the price for our sins. The second condition is met by the believer, by God's grace through faith. Tom Scottsay, et al., says this in another way: "God's love extended to a person is conditioned by His plan to give eternal life to those whom He has enabled to believe in His Son. The conditions of God's love are resident within Himself."

Rather than use the expression *"unconditional love,"* when describing God's love, perhaps we should use the words found in 1 John 4:8-10,16:

> He that loveth not knoweth not God; for God is love. In this was manifested the love of God toward us, because that God sent his only begotten Son into the world, that we might live through him...Herein is love, not that we loved God, but that he loved us, and sent his Son to be the propitiation for our sins...And we have known and believed the

love that God hath to us. God is love; and he that dwelleth
in love dwelleth in God, and God in him.

Those who believe God would relate to us in unconditional love need
to seek God through the study of His Word and through prayer. Since the
time of Christ's crucifixion, man has searched for God. Augustine captured
this frantic search, in this prayer, near the end of his book *Confessions:*

Late have I loved you, beauty so old and so new: late have
I loved you. And see, you were within and I was in the
external world and sought you there, and in my unlovely
state I plunged into those love created things which you
made. You were with me, and I was not with you. The
lovely things kept me far from you, though if they did not
have their existence in you, they had no existence at all. You
called and cried out loud and shattered my deafness. You
were radiant and resplendent, you put to flight my blind-
ness. You were fragrant, and I drew in my breath and now
pant after you. I tasted you, and I feel but hunger and thirst
for you. You touched me, and I am set on fire to attain the
peace which is yours.

ILLUSTRATION

The following, taken from Michael P. Green's book *1500 Illustrations for
Biblical Preaching*, nicely illustrates many people's understanding of God's
love:

One Sunday, a little boy looked up at his dad and asked,
"Daddy, how does God love us?"

His father answered, "Son, God loves us with an unconditional love."

The lad thought for a moment and then asked, "Daddy, what kind of love is unconditional love?"

After a few minutes of silence, his father answered, "Do you remember the two boys who used to live next door to us and the cute little puppy they got last Christmas?"

"Yes—"

"Do you remember how they used to tease it, throw sticks and even rocks at it?"

"Yes—"

"Do you also remember how the puppy would always greet them with a wagging tail and would try to lick their faces?"

"Yes—"

"Well, that puppy had unconditional love for those two boys. They certainly didn't deserve his love for them because they were mean to him. But he loved them anyway." The father then made his point: "God's love for us is also unconditional. Men threw rocks at His Son, Jesus, and hit Him with sticks. They even killed Him. But Jesus loved them anyway."

I would like to close this chapter about the concept of God's love, with the following, taken from the book *At the Heart of the White Rose: Letters and Diaries of Hans and Sophie Scholl*, written by Hans Scholl et al., taken from a letter written by Sophie Scholl, who died as a martyr at the age of twenty-two, when she was executed by the Nazis, because of her resistance against the atrocities she perceived of that regime:

The only remedy for a barren heart is prayer, however poor and inadequate…if I can't write anything else just now, it's only because there's a terrible absurdity about a drowning man who, instead of calling for help, launches into a scientific, philosophical, or theological dissertation while the sinister tentacles of the creatures on the seabed are encircling his arms and legs, and the waves are breaking over him. It's only because I'm filled with fear, that and nothing else, and feel an undivided yearning for him who can relieve me of it.…But prayer is the only remedy for that, and however many little devils scurry around inside me, I shall cling to the rope God has thrown me in Jesus Christ, even if my numb hands can no longer feel it.

PRAYER

Our heavenly Father,

Thank You for another wonderful day to know You and to bring You glory. We humbly thank You for Your presence this day. We praise You for the brilliant design of Your creation.

Lord, we lift up a prayer for our country. Sometimes it feels like our country is drifting away from a biblical worldview to a secular worldview, a worldview based on individual and cultural relativism rather than Your absolute truth. We ask that You bless our country with Your wisdom, Your love, and Your compassion.

We ask for blessings on our leaders. May they take their responsibility seriously and do their very best each day. We

Barry Denzil Haney, MD

ask that they realize their need for you and for Your Word in order to direct them. When they make decisions, we pray that they hear Your voice and that they follow Your guidance.

Lord we lift up a prayer for our troops. We ask that You bless them. We ask that You place them in Your loving arms and protect them from all harm, both here and around the world. We are grateful for their service and their dedication to keeping our nation safe.

Lord, we lift up the men and women in the work of ministry and missions. We ask that they understand and appreciate the benefits of implementing godly principles and the God-given scriptural roles of men and women in their homes, so Your name is glorified in their lives and homes.

Lord, we lift up prayer for the youth. In today's world, our youth is strongly influenced by the popular culture, a secular worldview that does not believe in Your absolute truth but instead on personal choice and tolerance. We pray that You would keep them from being influenced by the tempting things of the world and desires of the sin nature and protect them from the deceptions of the enemy who would seek to disrupt their walk with You and fellowship with the Father. We ask that You give them grace and wisdom as they face the challenges of life.

Lord, we lift up prayer to the those who are unsaved in the Church. We pray that with true contrition of heart, they confess and repent of their sins to You, ask forgiveness of their sins, realize they are powerless to control their sinful nature, commit to placing their lives into Your loving arms, and ask You into their hearts as their Lord and Savior.

We ask all these things in the precious name of Jesus Christ our Lord and Savior,

Amen!

CHAPTER 15

Misplaced Anger

For we know that the law is spiritual: but I am carnal, sold under sin. For that which I do I allow not: for what I would, that do I not; but what I hate, that do I. If then I do that which I would not, I consent unto the law that it is good. Now then it is no more I that do it, but sin that dwelleth in me. For I know that in me (that is, in my flesh,) dwelleth no good thing: for to will is present with me; but how to perform that which is good I find not. For the good that I would I do not: but the evil which I would not, that I do. Now if I do that I would not, it is no more I that do it, but sin that dwelleth in me. I find then a law, that, when I would do good, evil is present with me. For I delight in the law of God after the inward man: But I see another law in my members, warring against the law of my mind, and bringing me into captivity to the law of sin which is in my members. O wretched man that I am! who shall deliver me from the body of this death? I thank God through Jesus Christ our Lord. So then with the mind I myself serve the law of God; but with the flesh the law of sin.

—Romans 7:14-25

WORLDLY WISDOM

This passage in Romans is one of the most famous and controversial texts in the book of Romans. I believe the Holy Spirit inspired Paul to write this passage in order to teach us that the Christian experience will have instances when we do what we don't want to do, causing us anger, but if we put our trust in Jesus, then get out of His way, and do His plan for our life, not our own, we will find our anger has been misplaced.

The Cambridge Dictionary defines anger as,

> "The feeling people get when something unfair, painful, or bad happens."

In his book *Surviving in an Angry World*, Josh Hunt tells us the following:

> "Anger is a response to some event or situation in life that causes us irritation, frustration, pain, or other displeasure."

Like other emotions, anger is experienced in our bodies as well as in our minds. In fact, there is a complex series of physiological (body) events that occur as we become angry.

Emotions more or less begin inside two almond-shaped structures in our brains which are called the amygdala. The amygdala is the part of the brain responsible for identifying threats to our well-being and for sending out an alarm when threats are identified that results in us taking steps to protect ourselves.

When this alarm is sounded, the brain releases neurotransmitter chemicals known as catecholamines, causing our body to experience a burst of energy, lasting up to several minutes. These neurotransmitters cause your heart rate to increase, your blood pressure to rise, and your rate of breathing to increase. Your face may flush as your body prepares for physical action. Your attention then narrows, fixating on the target of your anger.

Your body is now ready for *"fight or flight."* At this point, it is possible for your emotions to rage out of control. However, the prefrontal cortex, located just behind the forehead, handles judgment and can keep in check the amygdala's output of emotion. If the amygdala handles emotion, the prefrontal cortex handles judgment. The left prefrontal cortex can switch off your emotions. It serves an executive role to keep things under control.

There are ways to help your prefrontal cortex get the upper hand over the amygdala: through relaxation techniques that decrease amygdala activity, thereby reducing your arousal, practicing judgment by the use of cognitive control techniques to help you practice overriding your emotional reactions. From a biblical perspective, this is accomplished through prayer, meditation, and through the protection, instruction, and teaching we receive from the Holy Spirit during our daily study and reading of God's inspired Word.

Physiologically, our bodies require a wind-down phase, as well, which can last for a long time, hours to days, depending on the stress. Anger lowers our anger threshold, making it easier to become angry again. Because our anger threshold has been lowered, minor irritations that usually would not bother us can make us angry. Because anger can interfere with our ability to concentrate, it is sometimes difficult to remember details of our angry outbursts.

Whether we have a biblical or secular worldview, our worldview often can be inadequate to restrain a sudden, uncontrolled flash of anger directed toward someone who frustrates us. Many have grown up with a disproportionate sense of self-righteous wrath. These two events oftentimes lead to inappropriate anger. In her article "Dereliction of Duty: Be Angry," Laura England says this about inappropriate anger:

> I am too often inappropriately angry. I repent and retrace the path of the tornado, retrieving my words that have deeply wended their targets, but I can never retrieve the relationships lost to the whirlwind of hurtful words.

Thanks to the work of Jesus on the cross at Calvary, it is possible for us to be courageous, joyful, humble, confident, and angry simultaneously. Laura England goes on to say:

> "We must be angry at nothing but sin. It's bad enough we sin in our anger, what's worse, we neglect to be angry at all when a defense against a holy God demands righteous anger."

So, in a nutshell, what can we do to stop anger the moment it creeps into our mind?

Barney Fife on the *Andy Griffith Show* used this idiomatic expression, "Nip it, nip it in the bud!"

That's what Paul is telling us to do in Ephesians 4:26: "Be ye angry, and sin not: let not the sun go down upon your wrath." When many people become angry, they will pout and gripe until the perceived harm they experienced has been solved, or in the worse circumstances, explode in front

Barry Denzil Haney, MD

of their loved ones, placing blame on others for their anger, sometimes verbally assaulting the other person or persons involved.

Oftentimes, the best course of action to take, in this case, is to ignore the matter until both parties have had time to *"cool off."* Another important concept to grasp is dealing with irritation quickly in our lives. If we do this, the small irritations we encounter during our life journey rarely will become a problem. But if we ignore them, these small irritations may blossom and tend to get worse and worse until an emotional explosion takes place.

In his book *The Wisdom of the Desert*, James Hannay says the following:

> Men are of three kinds, according to the place which anger finds in them. He who is hurt and injured, and yet spares his persecutor, is a man after the pattern of Christ. He who is neither hurt himself, nor desires to hurt another, is a man after the pattern of Adam. He who hurts or slanders another is a man after the pattern of the Devil.

I think most people reading this book would want to follow the pattern of Christ.

How do we do this?

GODLY WISDOM

PERSONAL EXPERIENCE: I'M ANGRY!

I share this entry from my journal, from November 2019:

"I got angry twice today, and I'm so sorry. First, I got angry because I couldn't find the keys to the car when I took an elderly man from my church family to a doctor's appointment. My wife hung them on the key rack; I'm sure out of love. But they were in a place I had never seen her put her keys before. Also, I got angry at her tonight when she placed the antacids I take when I have breakthrough regurgitation in a different place than I had placed them. I'm sure she was trying to help and placed them where I could find them, but because of my memory problems, I couldn't find them. Then in anger, I lashed out at her. Oh, Jesus, I'm so confused! I'm still struggling with misplaced anger and a loose tongue. Help me, Holy Spirit."

The Bible tells us this concerning anger in Ephesians 4:26-32:

Be ye angry, and sin not: let not the sun go down upon your wrath: Neither give place to the devil. Let him that stole steal no more: but rather let him labour, working with his hands the thing, which is good, that he may have to give to him that needeth. Let no corrupt communication proceed out of your mouth, but that which is good to the use of edifying, that it may minister grace unto the hearers. And grieve not the holy Spirit of God, whereby ye are sealed unto the day of redemption. Let all bitterness, and wrath, and anger, and clamour, and evil speaking, be put away from you, with all malice: And be ye kind one to another, tenderhearted, forgiving one another, even as God for Christ's sake hath forgiven you.

Barry Denzil Haney, MD

In her book *Biblical Counseling Keys on Anger: Facing the Fire Within,* June Hunt gives us her interpretation of God's analysis of anger:

> Anger is appropriate at certain times; anger must be resolved, or it becomes sinful; anger can be curtailed; anger, if prolonged, gives ground to Satan; anger can lead to corrupt, unwholesome, degrading talk; anger can grieve the Holy Spirit; anger can be totally cancelled, anger becomes sin when it results in bitterness; anger must be eradicated before it turns into rage; anger must be forfeited before it leads to fighting; anger must be stopped before it becomes slander; anger must be mastered before it becomes malicious; anger must be defeated through forgiveness.

Through daily Bible reading and prayer, the Holy Spirit will teach us and instruct us on how to deal with anger. The first thing we need to do is understand anger from a biblical perspective. In his article "Anger Part 1: Understanding Anger," David Powlison discusses God's anger:

> The Bible is about anger; the angriest person in the Bible is God. He is also the most loving person in the Bible. God expresses his love for his people by each of three ways he expresses anger at wrong: (1) In love, the anger your sin deserves fell on Jesus; (2) in love, God's anger works to disarm the power of your sin; (3) in love, God's anger will deliver you from the pain of others' sins. Anger is something you do with all you are as a person; it occurs not only in the mind but breaks out into behavior. Anger is bodily, emotional, mental, behavioral. Anger is natural because we were created in God's image; because we fell into sin. Anger is taught and modeled to us; it is practiced, and can become second nature, a habitual manner of life. Anger is an intrinsically moral matter. Learning the difference between righ-

teous and sinful anger is important. Anger is interpersonal, always having to do with God and often other people.

Based on the above, it seems God is angry because of our sin, and rightly so. Anger can be seen in our body language, through our emotions, affect our mental makeup, and cause us to act out. Worst of all, anger can become habitual, a second-hand reaction when we feel harmed by others, damaging our relationships with them. In her article "Dereliction of Duty: Be Angry," Laura England says this about God's anger:

> God's anger is perfect. This is something that is very difficult for many Christians to accept. A.W. Pink notes sadly that some even feel compelled to apologize for this aspect of God's nature. The truth is, there are more references to God's anger and wrath in Scripture than there are to His love and mercy. Psalm 7:11 settles the matter most succinctly: *"God is a just judge, and God is angry with the wicked every day."*

Further, she goes on to say this:

> "The wrath of God is as much a Divine perfection as is His faithfulness, power or mercy," notes Pink. Being perfect, His is never a vindictive anger, but a wrath steeped in justice, righteousness, and holiness. God's anger is an extension of His judgment, devoid of fury and frenzy. God *acts* out of justice; He never *reacts* out of frustration. I believe this is what the Old Testament writers had in mind when they said that God is "slow to anger."

God has shown, by example, how we should handle anger in our daily lives, and God goes on in his inspired Word to give these guiding principles: "A gift in secret pacifieth anger: And a reward in the bosom strong wrath" (Psalm 21:14). "The north wind driveth away rain: So doth an angry countenance a backbiting tongue" (Proverbs 25:23).

"Wrath is cruel, and anger is outrageous; But who is able to stand before envy?" (Proverbs 27:4). "A fool uttereth all his mind: But a wise man keepeth it in till afterwards" (Proverbs 29:11). "When the righteous are in authority, the people rejoice: But when the wicked beareth rule, the people mourn" (Proverbs 29:22). "Surely the churning of milk bringeth forth butter, And the wringing of the nose bringeth forth blood: So the forcing of wrath bringeth forth strife" (Proverbs 30:33).

In her book *God, Anger and Ideology: The Anger of God in Joshua and Judges in Relation to Deuteronomy and the Priestly Writings*, Kari Latvus gives the world hope for anger:

> One of the central paradigms in Deuteronomistic theology
> was that life, land, people around, food, and so on, are a gift
> from God, totally given by grace without being earned—
> this theological statement is still worth exploring as a sign of
> hope in the modern world.

These words of godly wisdom concerning anger can be found in Proverbs 15:1:

> "A soft answer turneth away wrath: But grievous words stir
> up anger." In conclusion, even though I know I am saved,
> I still sin. My spirit has been saved and made righteous
> because of Christ's righteousness; my spirit is holy because
> of Christ's holiness.

The void, the chasm, this separation from God have been removed. Because of His shed blood on the cross of Calvary my sins have been forgiven. I've been made right in the sight of God. I've been justified in the sight of God. Sin no longer separates me from Him.

I know I was created in his image to spend an eternity with him in a loving relationship. I know my search throughout life to fill this void in my heart, with earthly pleasures, has been an unsuccessful attempt to fill a void, to bridge a chasm, to remove a separation.

Despite knowing this truth, I still succumb to Satan's temptation; like Paul, I struggle. I am a wretched man, but like Paul, I have hope because of Jesus. Thank You, Jesus!

ILLUSTRATION

The following illustration concerning witness is taken from Michael P. Green's book *1500 Illustrations for Biblical Preaching*:

A boy once asked, "Dad, how do wars begin?"

"Well, take the First World War," said his father. "That got started when Germany invaded Belgium."

Immediately his wife interrupted him: "Tell the boy the truth. It began because somebody was murdered."

The husband drew himself up with an air of superiority and snapped back, "Are *you* answering the question, or am I?"

Turning her back upon him in a huff, the wife walked out of the room and slammed the door as hard as she could.

When the dishes stopped rattling in the cupboard, an uneasy silence followed, broken at length by the son when he said, "Daddy, you don't have to tell me anymore; I know now!"

Barry Denzil Haney, MD

PRAYER

Our heavenly Father

Help us face our denial; help us admit we are powerless to control our sinful nature; help us realize faith in Jesus Christ, even as small as a mustard seed is the way to receive Your free gift of salvation.

In Your Word, You have shown us Jesus Christ can restore us to our sanity. Jesus Christ can provide us with the strength, acceptance, new life, integrity, and trust needed to make sane decisions based on His truth.

Help us to be open to hope we can only find in Him. Please help us to start living our lives one day at a time. Through Your precious gift, the freedom to choose, we have the opportunity to choose freedom over our self-will, which always fails us.

Help us use this wonderful gift of choice in a way pleasing to You. Please continue to help us overcome our hurts, hang-ups, and habits and may victory over them help others as they see Your power at work in changing our life.

Help us understand how we can use the knowledge we gained today to glorify Your kingdom during the coming week. If we are ready, help us take action and take the next step to commit our lives into Your hands and to ask You into our hearts as our Lord and Savior.

In the precious name of Jesus, we pray,

Amen.

CHAPTER 16

Recurring Childhood Nightmare!

"Thou shalt not be afraid for the terror by night; Nor for the arrow that flieth by day; Nor for the pestilence that walketh in darkness; Nor for the destruction that wasteth at noonday."

—Psalm 91:5-6

WORLDLY WISDOM

In today's secular world, we live in a world gripped by fear, understandably so with endless stories of mass shootings, global threats, violence, and rumors of war we are exposed to through the 24/7 news coverage! But the Holy Spirit is teaching Christians; we need not be afraid because God will protect us from the terrors in this world. He has promised us a better, brighter, eternal future because of our faith in Jesus!

The Cambridge Dictionary defines nightmare as, "A very upsetting or frightening dream, or an extremely unpleasant event or experience."

MY PERSONAL EXPERIENCE:
THE RECURRING NIGHTMARE!

When I was a young child, I remember a recurring, terrifying nightmare. In the dream, I would be in a very dark place; then, all of a sudden, a very bright laser beam of intense, blue-white light would appear.

I was present, somehow, existing within this beam of light, but not in bodily form. I seemed to be traveling within this light, although no landmarks were present to give me the sense of motion, only background nothingness.

Associated with this sense of motion along this intense beam of light was a very high-pitched sound, a shrill, deafening, high-pitched sound! A dreadful, irritating, frightening, foreboding kind of sound, causing a feeling of impending doom, impending death within the fabric of my soul.

The nightmare seemed real! I sensed weightless motion within empty space, within total darkness, within this laser-like beam of intense blue-white light, accompanied by this very high-pitched sound! Although I sensed I was going somewhere, I knew not where I could not sense any ending to this unpleasant, terrifying nightmare!

Just as quickly, this terrifying nightmare would end. I would then be in total darkness, with no interaction, no external stimuli. I could sense only blackness. Then, a veiled face would suddenly appear in the dark void. Distant at first, the face would move slowly toward me, surrounded by a glowing blue light.

As it came closer, the facial features would become more clear. The face appeared elderly, perhaps a woman's face, wrinkled, haggard, witch-like in appearance, with a wide, sinister, toothless grin.

Just as quickly, the face would disappear, and I would then be in this beautiful place, earth-like, with trees, grass, waterfalls, Eden-like—I also sensed I was weightless, able to jump easily over trees and able to fly, soar through the air like an eagle! Then this serene, beautiful place would disappear, the face would return, followed by the terrifying nightmare!

Barry Denzil Haney, MD

Again I would be traveling along the intense beam of light! This would go on and on. I remember becoming more and more terrified, alone, wanting to escape this terrible dream I was experiencing; I wanted someone to help me. I remember crying out for help, but there was no one there—I felt paralyzed. Finally, I remember awakening terrified and trembling, remembering the nightmare in vivid color. It seemed so real!

I remember my mother sometimes would be there when I awoke, trying to arouse me from my slumber, asking what happened, why was I crying out, but I don't remember sharing with her what I had experienced, at least I don't remember talking to her about it.

It seems like this dream happened every night for many of my early childhood years.

Over the years, I've always wondered what this dream meant. Could this dream be God speaking to me as He did to Job? Was God revealing to me something that would occur in the future?

One night in November 2019, I began listening to a video entitled "The Wormwood Prophecy." In the video, Tom Horn (long-time television and radio personality, author of dozens of best-selling books and publisher of many others, serves as the Chief Executive Officer of SkyWatchTV), talked about his new book being released that November. He shared his theory about an asteroid called Apophis, apparently on a collision course with the Earth. He thinks this could be the Wormwood star spoke of in Revelation.

Could this be the interpretation of my recurring childhood nightmare? I was given a glimpse of the end times, as I hurtled through space, along-side the Apophis asteroid, with the final destination, a collision with Earth?

Could the high-pitched sound I hear be the sound generated by the magnetic field of the asteroid as it streaks through the fabric of space at over 28,000 miles per hour, the sound of the third angel's trumpet spoke of in Revelation? Is the vision of the Eden-like place in my nightmare a vision of Earth just prior to the collision? Is the face I see Satan?

Am I actually witnessing this doomsday event described in Revelation 8:1-11?

Could "junk DNA" found in the human genome actually be God's sealed instructions, given to us during dreams and nightmares, to be unsealed according to God's timing? Has the "junk DNA" in my mind now been unsealed, allowing me to interpret the recurring nightmare I experienced as a child?

GODLY WISDOM

What godly wisdom is in the Bible concerning dreams?

In his book *A Letter That Has Not Been Read: Dreams in the Hebrew Bible*, Shaul Bar classifies dream reports into three categories: prophetic dreams, subdivided into dreams of encouragement and dreams of admonition; symbolic dreams; and visions.

A prophetic dream is described in the following passage in 1 Kings 3:5-15:

> In Gibeon the LORD appeared to Solomon in a dream
> by night: and God said, Ask what I shall give thee. And
> Solomon said, Thou hast shewed unto thy servant David
> my father great mercy, according as he walked before thee
> in truth, and in righteousness, and in uprightness of heart
> with thee; and thou hast kept for him this great kindness,
> that thou hast given him a son to sit on his throne, as it
> is this day. And now, O LORD my God, thou hast made
> thy servant king instead of David my father: and I am
> but a little child: I know not how to go out or come in.
> And thy servant is in the midst of thy people which thou
> hast chosen, a great people, that cannot be numbered

nor counted for multitude. Give therefore thy servant an understanding heart to judge thy people, that I may discern between good and bad: for who is able to judge this thy so great a people? And the speech pleased the Lord, that Solomon had asked this thing. And God said unto him, Because thou hast asked this thing, and hast not asked for thyself long life; neither hast asked riches for thyself, nor hast asked the life of thine enemies; but hast asked for thyself understanding to discern judgment; Behold, I have done according to thy words: lo, I have given thee a wise and an understanding heart; so that there was none like thee before thee, neither after thee shall any arise like unto thee. And I have also given thee that which thou hast not asked, both riches, and honour: so that there shall not be any among the kings like unto thee all thy days. And if thou wilt walk in my ways, to keep my statutes and my commandments, as thy father David did walk, then I will lengthen thy days. And Solomon awoke; and, behold, it was a dream. And he came to Jerusalem and stood before the ark of the covenant of the LORD, and offered up burnt offerings, and offered peace offerings, and made a feast to all his servants.

A symbolic dream is described in the following passage in Genesis 37:5-11 (NLT):

One night, Joseph had a dream, and when he told his brothers about it, they hated him more than ever. "Listen to this dream," he said. "We were out in the field, tying up bundles of grain. Suddenly my bundle stood up, and your bundles all gathered around and bowed low before mine!" His brothers responded, "So you think you will be our king, do you? Do you actually think you will reign over us?" And they hated him all the more because of his dreams and the way he talked about them. Soon Joseph had another dream, and again he told his brothers about it. "Listen, I have had another dream," he said. "The sun, moon, and eleven stars bowed low before me!" This time he told the dream to his father as well as to his brothers, but his father scolded him. "What kind of dream is that?" he asked. "Will your mother and I and your brothers actually come and bow to the ground before you?" But while his brothers were jealous of Joseph, his father wondered what the dreams meant.

A vision is described in the following passage in 1 Samuel 3:2-14 (NLT):

One night, Eli, who was almost blind by now, had gone to bed. The lamp of God had not yet gone out, and Samuel was sleeping in the Tabernacle near the Ark of God. Suddenly the LORD called out, "Samuel!" "Yes?" Samuel replied. "What is it?" He got up and ran to Eli. "Here I am. Did you call me?" "didn't call you," Eli replied. "Go back to bed." So he did. Then the LORD called out again, "Samuel!" Again Samuel got up and went to Eli. "Here I am. Did you call me?" "I didn't call you, my son," Eli said. "Go back to bed" Samuel did not yet know the LORD because he had never had a message from the LORD before. So the LORD called a third time, and once more Samuel got up and went to Eli. "Here I am. Did you call me?" Then Eli realized it was the LORD who was calling the boy. So he said to Samuel, "Go and lie down again, and if someone calls again, say, 'Speak, LORD, your servant is listening.'" So Samuel went back to bed. And the LORD came and called as before, "Samuel! Samuel!" And Samuel replied, "Speak, your servant is listening." Then the LORD said to

Barry Denzil Haney, MD

Samuel, "I am about to do a shocking thing in Israel. I am going to carry out all my threats against Eli and his family, from beginning to end. I have warned him that judgment is coming upon his family forever, because his sons are blaspheming God and he hasn't disciplined them. So I have vowed that the sins of Eli and his sons will never be forgiven by sacrifices or offerings.

Although my dream, my nightmare, on the one hand, terrifies me, on the other hand, I am joyful! Joyful because this would mean that God's plan of salvation for the world is coming to a close. If true, I am even more determined to be a beacon of light for the unsaved, to spread the good news of the Gospel to the broken-hearted, allowing the Holy Spirit to convict, so they too, might have the opportunity to spend an eternity with God.

In Job 33:14-16 (NKJV), the Bible tells us this:

For God may speak in one way, or in another, Yet man does not perceive it. In a dream, in a vision of the night, When deep sleep falls upon men, While slumbering on their beds, Then He opens the ears of men And seals their instruction.

_____

PRAYER

Our heavenly Father,

We bless You; we praise You; we adore You. We give You the love of our whole heart. It is our one business, to worship You and love You without thought of anything else.

In the coming year, be our guide, our companion, our counselor, our provider, and our help in time of need. We pray for the anointing of the Holy Spirit to work upon the lives of those with prayer needs.

Bring healing where healing is needed. Bring the comfort and peace of the Holy Spirit. Help us to see that You are there and that You are God Almighty, heavenly Father.

May we fall at Your feet in awe of who You are. May we know Your love. May we know Your care. May we feel it and embrace it.

In the name of Jesus Christ, our Lord and Savior,

Amen.

CHAPTER 17

Unfounded Fear!

"Wherefore I put thee in remembrance that thou stir up the gift of God, which is in thee by the putting on of my hands. For God hath not given us the spirit of fear; but of power, and of love, and of a sound mind."

—2 Timothy 1:6-7

WORLDLY WISDOM

In this passage, the Holy Spirit is telling me, "even if your mind is tempted by Satan to succumb to fear, God will rescue you." He promises all of us a sound mind, allowing us to declare by faith that our mind is sound, safe, and secure when Satan tempts us, allowing us to *resist the devil, and he will flee from you,"* as James tells us in James 4:7.

The Cambridge Dictionary defines fear in this way: "A strong emotion caused by great worry about something dangerous, painful, or unknown that is happening or might happen."

The Dictionary of Bible Themes defines fear in this way: "An attitude of anxiety or distress, caused by concern over a threat to one's future."

Scripture provides numerous examples of situations in which fear is experienced; it declares, however, that God alone is to be feared, and moments of human fear can be opportunities for deepening faith in him.

We all face fears in our daily lives. In his book *Fear Fighters*, Jentezen Franklin says, "There can be no progress in life without taking risks." He goes on to offer this amusing story as an illustration of what the consequences are of not taking risks:

> *There was a very cautious man*
> *Who never laughed or played;*
> *He never risked, he never tried,*
> *He never sang or prayed.*
> *And when he one day passed away*
> *His insurance was denied;*
> *For since he never really lived,*
> *They claimed he never died!*

What is fear?

Psychologists would say fear is an emotional response induced by a perceived threat that causes physiological changes in brain and organ function, as well as behavioral changes such as fleeing, hiding, or freezing from perceived traumatic events. Fear occurs as a response to a certain stimulus occurring in the present or in anticipation of a future threat perceived as a risk to oneself. This leads to the "fight or flight" physiological response, which in severe cases can lead to a freeze or paralysis response.

For humans, fear is regulated by the process of cognition and learning. Our brain judges fear as either rational or irrational. An irrational fear is called a phobia. Psychologists have suggested fear is included in a small set of human emotions. This set includes acute stress reaction, anger, angst, anxiety, fright, horror, joy, panic, and sadness.

Neurobehavioral researchers have discovered a possible neural pathway in the brain, as cited in the excerpt taken from the article "Emotion Regulation and the Anxiety Disorders":

Barry Denzil Haney, MD

Zinbarg (1998) speculated that future neurobehavioral research would further clarify the boundaries of the unitary higher-order fear construct. Consistent with this prediction, a wealth of data demonstrates that the amygdala, a neural structure in the medial temporal lobes of the brain, is a critical structure mediating behavioral, cognitive, and physiological indicators of fear (Kim & Jung, 2006; LeDoux, 2000; Myers & Davis, 2007; Quinn & Fanselow, 2006).

Throughout our lives, many of us experience fear.

MY PERSONAL EXPERIENCE: CHILDHOOD FEARS!

I experienced fear as a child in the form of a monster I knew lived under my bed! While in grade school, I experienced fear when I stood in a line and wondered if I would be picked to play in the backyard basketball game. In high school, I experienced fear when calling a girl on the phone for a date. Later in life, anxiety reared its ugly head, each time I was transferred to a new duty station while I served in the United States Navy.

Phobia is an extreme, irrational fear of a specific object or situation. A phobia is considered a type of anxiety disorder. They are thought to be learned emotional responses.

Hundreds of words have been coined to specify the nature of the fear by prefixing phobia with the Greek word for the object feared. Although I will not try to describe all the recognized irrational fears mankind suffers, I will discuss the phobia of fear of death.

Death anxiety is multifaceted and includes fears related to one's own death, the death of others, fear of the unknown after death, fear of obliteration, fear of the dying process, and fear of a slow or painful death. When death anxiety is severe, keeping a person from living their life, it is called Thanatophobia.

In the article "Study Into Who is Least Afraid of Death," researcher at the University of Oxford makes the following statement: "The very religious and atheists are the groups who do not fear death as much as much as those in-between in a paper published in the journal *Religion, Brain and Behavior*."

In this same article, Dr. Jonathan Jong, Research Associate of the Institute of Cognitive and Evolutionary Anthropology, makes the following claim: "Religious people are less afraid of death than nonreligious people. It may well be that atheism also provides comfort from death…"

In Godly Wisdom, I will discuss why religious people, especially Christians are less afraid of death, but why would atheism provide comfort from death? In the *Daily Dish*, from the magazine *The Atlantic*, dated May 16, 2010, one atheist shared this reason why atheism provides comfort from death:

> I think that when I die I'll cease to exist, and in some
> ways I'm happy about that. Life is hard work. Life is good,
> worthy work that I'm proud of and that makes me feel
> good, for the most part, but even though I'll probably be
> sad to die (and I'd hate to think I was about to die any time
> soon), I'm still glad, in principle, that someday life will
> cease, and my burdens will dissolve with my joys. I don't
> want to live forever.

From my perspective as a Christian, this statement makes me sad because this person does not have the hope I have because of my faith in Jesus.

———————

Barry Denzil Haney, MD

GODLY WISDOM

I believe fear is a natural response when we feel threatened emotionally or physically, a gift from God. As discussed in worldly wisdom, severe fear can sometimes lead to a freeze or paralysis response. I believe fear is a paralyzing spirit that can keep us from God's grace.

In the Bible, what does godly wisdom tell us about fear?

In Isaiah 33:5-6, the Holy Spirit is telling us the first step to overcoming our fear, is the fear of the Lord:

> The LORD is exalted; for he dwelleth on high: He hath filled
> Zion with judgment and righteousness. And wisdom and knowl-
> edge shall be The stability of thy times, and strength of salvation:
> The fear of the LORD is his treasure.

When we have the fear of the Lord, we can unlock the gifts of grace and salvation, wisdom, and knowledge, found in God's Word. In his book *A Treatise of the Fear of God*, John Bunyan says this about the grace of fear:

> This grace of fear is that which, as I may so say, first affects
> the hearts of saints with judgments, after we have sinned,
> and so is as a beginning grace to bring again that to rights
> that by sin is put out of frame. O it is a precious grace of
> God! I know what I say in this matter, and also where I had
> been long ago, through the power of my lusts, and the wiles
> of the devil, had it not been for the fear of God.

As a child, I often would awake in a cold sweat, in the grip of terror and dread of the panic attack caused by the recurring nightmare I described in

Chapter sixteen, "The Recurring Nightmare!" I would lie trembling in my bed, too terrified to get up and switch on the light.

But we can take heed in 2 Timothy 1:7, where Timothy says, "God hath not given us the spirit of fear: but of power, and of love, and of a sound mind."

Proverbs 3:24-26 provides us comfort when we are afraid:

> When thou liest down, thou shalt not be afraid: Yea, thou shalt lie down, and thy sleep shall be sweet. Be not afraid of sudden fear, Neither of the desolation of the wicked, when it cometh. For the LORD shall be thy confidence and shall keep thy foot from being taken.

In the Bible, what does godly wisdom instruct us to do when fear overcomes us?

In Deuteronomy 20:3-4, the Holy Spirit tells us not to panic or be overcome with fear, but to put our faith in God:

> And shall say unto them, Hear, O Israel, ye approach this day unto battle against your enemies: let not your hearts faint, fear not, and do not tremble, neither be ye terrified because of them; For the LORD your God is he that goeth with you, to fight for you against your enemies, to save you.

In closing, we need to read and reread Psalm 23, when we are troubled by fear, because it contains truths to give us comfort, restoration, and peace, even in times of suffering:

> The LORD is my shepherd; I shall not want. He maketh me to lie down in green pastures: He leadeth me beside the still waters. He restoreth my soul: He leadeth me in

the paths of righteousness for his name's sake. Yea, though I walk through the valley of the shadow of death, I will fear no evil: for thou art with me; Thy rod and thy staff they comfort me. Thou preparest a table before me in the presence of mine enemies: Thou anointest my head with oil; my cup runneth over. Surely goodness and mercy shall follow me all the days of my life: And I will dwell in the house of the LORD forever.

PRAYER

Our heavenly Father,

Thank You for giving us strength during our times of fear, thank You for being by our side, holding our hand! Because of Your strength, power, and love, we can always find hope to dispel our doubts!

I have allowed fear to sometimes control my life, and this lack of faith in You is sin. Thank You, for your forgiveness! Please reveal all-controlling fears in my life. Lord, You've been so good to me. Without You in control of my life, what a messy bunch of sinners we would be, with no hope and no peace and no grace!

But because of Your grace and love, You died for us, paying the penalty for our sins. Now we are forgiven and will spend eternity with you, because of Your grace, that's all from You!

Satan is a roaring lion, and he would love to devour me as his prey. He wants to make my life a mess, he wants to steal, kill, and destroy, but You won't let him! You are our refuge, our fortress, and our strength and You protect us from a life that could have been many times more broken, so thank You, God.

And now, I pray that throughout the rest of this week and so much further beyond, we would pray to You as people who need it. Keep us desperate, God!

Help us to hunger and to thirst for You. Help us to believe that our families, our finances, and especially our faith would be nothing without You…but only with You!

God, thank You for your goodness; thank You for our stories! We pray that in the years to come, we would bless You, and find many more reasons to praise and worship Your holy name!

We lift up to You in prayer all of our spoken and unspoken prayer requests. Thank You for Your comfort, peace and healing power. You are the true hero, the perfect judge, the righteous redeemer!

In the precious name of Jesus Christ our Lord and Savior,

Amen!

CHAPTER 18

Who Is God?
Who Is Jesus?

And I give unto them eternal life; and they shall never
perish, neither shall any man pluck them out of my hand.
My Father, which gave them me, is greater than all; and no
man is able to pluck them out of my Father's hand. I and
my Father are one.

—John 10:28-30

WORLDLY WISDOM

In this passage, the Holy Spirit is teaching me four things: There are two
eternal destinies, eternal life and eternal punishment. We are assured the
forces of evil, actively at work, will not succeed in their attempt to snatch
the believer out of Jesus' hand; salvation, once attained, is eternally secure,
and cannot be lost; Jesus and God are the same, a reference to the triune.

The Cambridge Dictionary defines God as,

"(esp. in Christian, Jewish, and Muslim belief), the being
that created and rules the universe, the earth, and its
people." The Cambridge Dictionary defines Jesus as, "The

Jewish religious teacher believed by those who follow him
to be the son of God, whose teachings and life Christianity
developed from."

When Charles Lindbergh flew his plane, the Spirit of St. Louis, he saw
before him all the stars of God's universe he could see in the night sky, that
part of our Milky Way, how beautiful that must have been for him to view
God's handiwork in the night sky as he made the long journey to Europe!

But we now know that what Charles Lindbergh must have marveled at
during his night times of flying across the Atlantic Ocean is just a tiny part
of the universe. We now know the universe contains billions of galaxies,
billions and billions and billions of stars and planets and other celestial
bodies. For the Christian, the nighttime sky is the handiwork of the omni-
scient, omnipotent, omnipresent God of the Bible. But what does the word
"god" mean to non-religious people, humanists?

First, what does the word humanist mean?

In the article "Humanism," a humanist is defined in this way:

> Non-religious people who have believed that this life is the
> only life we have, that the universe is a natural phenome-
> non with no supernatural side, and that we can live ethical
> and fulfilling lives on the basis of reason and humanity.
> They have trusted to the scientific method, evidence, and
> reason to discover truths about the universe and have placed
> human welfare and happiness at the canter of their ethical
> decision-making.

In my discussion, I would place into this general category "humanist"
the following list of secular worldviews:

- Atheist

- Agnostic

- Skeptics

- Freethinker

- Rationalist

- Secularist

- Moral relativism

- Perennialism

- Ecumenism

- Religious pluralism

The traditions of humanist thinking can be traced back at least two thousand, five hundred years. Many people through the centuries have thought and expressed humanist ideas, and some have believed in a god or gods. The first recorded humanist thinking can be found in writings from China, India, Greece, and Rome, from figures such as Aesop, Democritus, Epictetus, Epicurus, and Protagoras. A brief sample of other notable humanists include (but not intended to be a complete list):

> In the Renaissance, Aphra Behn, and Shakespeare; in the
> Enlightenment, Immanuel Kant, David Hum, Thomas
> Paine, Voltaire; in the nineteenth century, freethinkers,
> Charles Darwin, George Eliot, T H Huxley, Robert G
> Ingersoll, John Stuart Mill; in the twentieth and twenty-first
> centuries, Joseph Conrad, E M Forster, Sigmund Freud,
> Thomas Hardy, Julian Huxley, Margaret Knight, Gene
> Roddenberry, Bertrand Russell, John Maynard Smith, Peter
> Singer, Richard Dawkins, Stephen Hawking, Christopher
> Hitchens, Michael Martin.

These Non-Christians, if they believe in a god, believe the universe has created god, a finite god. They want to bring a child face to face with the universe, not with a god. Therefore, non-Christian education is God-less education. This Godless education denies man was created with a responsibility to live a life pleasing to God.

This belief implies sin is not a transgression of God's law. This belief naturally becomes humanistic, man-centered. Man can live for himself, do what feels right, what is right for him, live a self-centered life rather than a God-centered life.

This quotation by Bertrand Russell, taken from his lecture, *Why I am Not a Christian,* summarizes, I believe, the sentiments of most who consider themselves "humanists:" "A good world needs knowledge, kindness, and courage; it does not need a regretful hankering after the past, or a fettering of the free intelligence by the words uttered long ago by ignorant men…"

It is my contention, the "utterings" of those men and women, who call themselves "humanists," are but a vain, futile attempt by the "createe," like Adam and Satan, to become god, rather than submit to the Creator God, have faith in Jesus, thereby securing an eternal relationship with Him, in heaven!

ILLUSTRATION

The following illustration concerning God's love is taken from Michael P. Green's book *1500 Illustrations for Biblical Preaching*:

> One day a single friend asked a father of four, "Why do you love your kids?"
>
> The father thought for a minute, but the only answer he could come up with was, "Because they're mine."

The children had no need to do anything to prove themselves to this father. He took them just as they were. So it is with God's love for us. He loves us as we are, and it is His love that motivates us to trust and obey Him in return.

GODLY WISDOM

According to godly wisdom found in the Bible, who is this Christian God? The Bible tells us in Genesis 1:1: "In the beginning, God created the heaven and the earth."

God, existing equally in three persons, the triune, existed alone. There was no heaven, no earth, no universe, no angels, nothing, from everlasting. He *"was alone, self-contained, self-sufficient, in need of nothing."*

The Bible goes on to tell us He is the source of all life in Colossians 1:16-18:

> For by him were all things created, that are in heaven,
> and that are in earth, visible and invisible, whether they
> be thrones, or dominions, or principalities, or powers: all
> things were created by him, and for him: And he is before
> all things, and by him all things consist.. And he is the head
> of the body, the church: who is the beginning, the firstborn
> from the dead; that in all things he might have the preemi-
> nence.

The Bible tells us God is Sovereign in Isaiah 40:13-14:

> Who hath directed the Spirit of the LORD, or being his
> counselor hath taught him? With whom took he counsel,
> and who instructed him, and taught him in the path of

judgment, and taught him knowledge, and shewed to him the way of understanding?

The Bible tells us in Romans 11:33; God is infinite in his knowledge: "O the depth of the riches both of the wisdom and knowledge of God! how unsearchable are his judgments, and his ways past finding out!"

The Bible tells us in Psalm 115:3; God is independent: "But our God is in the heavens: He hath done whatsoever he hath pleased." The Bible tells us in Isaiah 46:10-11; God is immutable:

> Declaring the end from the beginning, And from ancient times the things that are not yet done, Saying, My counsel shall stand, And I will do all my pleasure: Calling a ravenous bird from the east, The man that executeth my counsel from a far country: Yea, I have spoken it, I will also bring it to pass; I have purposed it, I will also do it.

Now that we know what the Bible tells us about God, what godly wisdom can we find in the Bible about who Jesus is? The Bible tells us in Luke 1:32-33 Jesus' identity:

> He shall be great and shall be called the Son of the Highest: and the Lord God shall give unto him the throne of his father David: And he shall reign over the house of Jacob forever; and of his kingdom there shall be no end.

In the first major speech of Peter at Pentecost in Acts 2:22-36, the ramifications of the angelic prophecy are explained to us:

> Ye men of Israel, hear these words; Jesus of Nazareth, a man approved of God among you by miracles and wonders and signs, which God did by him in the midst of you, as ye

Barry Denzil Haney, MD

yourselves also know: Him, being delivered by the determinate counsel and foreknowledge of God, ye have taken, and by wicked hands have crucified and slain: Whom God hath raised up, having loosed the pains of death: because it was not possible that he should be holden of it. For David speaketh concerning him, I foresaw the Lord always before my face, for he is on my right hand, that I should not be moved: Therefore did my heart rejoice, and my tongue was glad; moreover also my flesh shall rest in hope: Because thou wilt not leave my soul in hell, neither wilt thou suffer thine Holy One to see corruption. Thou hast made known to me the ways of life; thou shalt make me full of joy with thy countenance. Men and brethren, let me freely speak unto you of the patriarch David, that he is both dead and buried, and his sepulchre is with us unto this day. Therefore being a prophet and knowing that God had sworn with an oath to him, that of the fruit of his loins, according to the flesh, he would raise up Christ to sit on his throne; He seeing this before spake of the resurrection of Christ, that his soul was not left in hell, neither his flesh did see corruption. This Jesus hath God raised up, whereof we all are witnesses. Therefore being by the right hand of God exalted and having received of the Father the promise of the Holy Ghost, he hath shed forth this, which ye now see and hear. For David is not ascended into the heavens: but he saith himself, The LORD said unto my Lord, Sit thou on my right hand, Until I make thy foes thy footstool. Therefore let all the house of Israel know assuredly, that God hath made that same Jesus, whom ye have crucified, both Lord and Christ.

The Bible tells us in 1 John 1:1-3, who Jesus is:

> That which was from the beginning, which we have heard, which we have seen with our eyes, which we have looked upon, and our hands have handled, of the Word of life; (For the life was manifested, and we have seen it, and bear witness, and shew unto you that eternal life, which was with the Father, and was manifested unto us;) That which we have seen and heard declare we unto you, that ye also may have fellowship with us: and truly our fellowship is with the Father, and with his Son Jesus Christ.

Finally, Jesus tells us He is the only way to the Father, the only way we are able to spend an eternity with our Creator God in heaven: "Jesus saith unto him, I am the way, the truth, and the life: no man cometh unto the Father, but by me" (John 14:6).

In this chapter, I have briefly introduced to you what worldly wisdom tells us about the concept of God, then recorded scriptural references for you to consider about who the Christian God and Jesus are. The first verse in the Bible introduces the Christian God, *"In the beginning, God…"* Where did God come from? How could He just suddenly appear? The Bible tells us He came from nothing, but how can that be?

The answer to that question is an age-old mystery, controversial, still debated today, yet by faith, we believe that God had no beginning and has no end. You can't put God in a test tube, you can't make a mathematical formula to describe him as Einstein did with relativity, but you can except by faith He is the Creator of the entire universe, and by doing so, spend an eternity with Him in heaven.

I truly believe, once we have asked Jesus into our lives, once we have faith in Jesus, once we have turned complete control of our lives over to Him, then, and only then, we will begin to do His will for our lives. I feel at that moment; we begin to fulfill God's plan for our life. Thank You, Lord Jesus, for leading me. I thank God for helping me to wake up each morning, trying to please Him. I know by pleasing Him, I will be fulfilling His plan for my life, in His grand plan of salvation, for the world.

PRAYER

Our heavenly Father,

We pray for revival. So many of Your people have believed Satan's lies and succumbed to his temptations. Our world so desperately needs Your grace.

We pray for an outpouring of the Holy Spirit and Your grace on all mankind because Your children need Your love and care at this present time.

We pray that You let Your light shine on us. We ask You to convict us with a longing for the Holy Spirit, a thirst, a sacred thirst and longing that will carry us on toward perfection.

We know revival must first begin with us. We ask that the Holy Spirit continue to work within us to make us more holy, more Christ-like each day as we pray and as we study Your word. Through this process, may others see in us the fruits of the spirit, providing Your light to the unsaved, allowing the Holy Spirit to convict them so they too may spend an eternity in fellowship with you. As You remind us in Nehemiah, it is never too late for a new beginning, and we are all in need of rebuilding within.

In the coming year, be our guide, our companion, our counselor, our provider, and our help in time of need. We pray for the anointing of the Holy Spirit of work upon the lives of those with prayer needs. Bring healing, where healing is needed. Bring the comfort and peace of the Holy Spirit to all of those with prayer needs and to their families.

Help us to realize that You are always there and that You are God Almighty. Help us to realize we have been redeemed and have been set free. Help us to realize we can stop fighting because the battle has already been won when Christ spilled His blood at Mount Calvary.

In the precious name of Jesus Christ, our Lord and Savior,

Amen

Barry Denzil Haney, MD

CHAPTER 19

The Mysterious Trinity!

And Jesus, when he was baptized, went up straightway out of the water: and, lo, the heavens were opened unto him, and he saw the Spirit of God descending like a dove, and lighting upon him: And lo a voice from heaven, saying, This is my beloved Son, in whom I am well pleased.

—Matthew 3:16-17

WORLDLY WISDOM

The Cambridge Dictionary defines Trinity in this way: "A group of three things or people."

The Dictionary of Bible Themes defines Trinity in this way:

> The characteristically Christian doctrine about God; it declares that there is only one true God; that this God is three persons, the Father, the Son and the Holy Spirit, each of whom is distinct from, yet interrelated with, the others; and that all three persons are fully, equally and eternally divine.

Throughout history, scholars have debated whether or not godly wisdom tells us about the Trinity in Scripture. I feel the debate has centered around certain beliefs held, misunderstandings. The first misunderstanding concerns the absence of the word "Trinity" in the Bible. They will say Christians made up this belief in the fourth century. Although the word Trinity is not used in the Bible, it is expressed in many Bible passages to explain the eternal relationship between the Father, the Son, and the Holy Spirit. Many early church fathers defended the doctrine of the Trinity prior to 300 AD, including Clement, Ignatius, Justin Martyr, Theophilus, Athenagoras, Irenaeus, Tertullian, and Gregory Thaumaturgus.

The second misunderstanding occurs because some think Christians believe there are three Gods. Because of this belief, many non-Christians accuse Christians of being polytheists. The Trinity is a concept that must be accepted by faith. The rules of logic used by man cannot be used to explain the concept of the Trinity.

The third misunderstanding occurs because some people believe Jesus is not God. Those who have this belief might accept the fact He was a great prophet, a good man, but not God incarnate. The fourth misunderstanding occurs because some people believe Jesus is a lesser God than the

Father. People with this belief often use the following verses to justify this claim, Colossians 1:14, John 3:16, Proverbs 8:22, John 14:28, 1 Corinthians 15:28, and Mark 13:32.

In Colossians 1:14, they will ask this question, "If Christ is 'the first born of all creation,' was he created?" In John 3:16, they will ask the question, "does only begotten Son mean Jesus had a beginning?" In Proverbs 8:22 they will ask the question, "does this mean that Christ (Wisdom) was created?" In John 14:28, they will ask the question, "if the Father is greater than Jesus, how can Jesus be God?" In 1 Corinthians 15:28, they will ask the question, "if Jesus is God, why will he be subject to the Father?" In Mark 13:32, they will ask the question, "if Jesus is God, how could he not know when he would return?"

I will answer these questions in the Godly Wisdom section of this chapter.

The fifth misunderstanding is some people believe the Father, the Son, and the Holy Spirit are just different titles for Jesus or three different ways that God has revealed Himself.

Although God is the one and only true God, we need to let the Bible define what this means. And in several Bible passages, the Bible makes it clear the Father, the Son, and Holy Spirit are three distinct persons. I will share these passages in the godly wisdom section of this chapter.

The final misunderstanding some people believe is Jesus wasn't really fully God and fully man. Throughout history, many scholars have balked at the notion that Jesus was both man and God. They have tried to resolve this paradox by saying things like Jesus was a mere man through whom God spoke or that He was God and merely appeared to be human.

At least four errors concerning the concept of the Trinity and Jesus arose during the early years of the church. One of these was modalism. In his book *What is the Trinity?* R. C. Sproul gives this account about the idea behind modalism:

> All three persons of the Trinity are the same person, but that
> they behave in unique "modes" at different times. Modalists

held that God was initially the Creator, then became the Redeemer, then became the Spirit at Pentecost. The divine person who came to earth as the incarnate Jesus was the same person who had created all things. When He returned to heaven, He took up His role as the Father again, but then returned to earth as the Holy Spirit. As you can see, the idea here was that there is only one God, but that He acts in different modes, or different expressions, from time to time.

The second error challenging the concept of the Trinity was adoptionism. In her book *Practicing Christian Doctrine: An Introduction to Thinking and Living Theologically*, Beth Jones gives this account about the problem with adoptionism:

> Adoptionism is a form of subordinationism, which would make Jesus and the Spirit less than the Father. The adoptionist understanding of Jesus makes him into an ordinary human being who merited adoption by God, and it was his "moral progress that won for him the title Son of God."

The third error challenging the nature of Christ, was monophysitism. In his book *Open Wide the Doors to Christ: Discovering Catholicism*, Lucas Pollice gives this account about the problem with monophysitism:

> Monophysitism (Greek, meaning "one nature") was a heresy that developed as an overreaction to the heresy of Nestorianism. Monophysitism taught that Jesus' humanity was absorbed by His divinity. Thus, there no longer remained two natures intimately united, but one nature—the divine nature—in which His human nature was lost or absorbed.

The last error challenging the nature of Christ was Nestorianism. In his article "Have We Outmoded Chalcedon," Theodore Mueller gives this

Barry Denzil Haney, MD

account about the problem with Nestorianism:"Nestorianism ultimately denied the reality of the Incarnation, its Christ being a deified man rather than God incarnate (cf. Strong, op. cit., p. 671 f.)."

Jon Weece, Senior Pastor at Southland Christian Church, made this observation during his Easter Sermon in April 2021: "Bad assessments lead to bad assumptions." In my view, many throughout the church history have made bad assessments concerning the concept of the Trinity, leading to bad assumptions and the misunderstandings discussed above.

In his book *Trinity and Reality: An Introduction to the Christian Faith*, Ralph Smith gives us a good insight into the relationship of hell and the Trinity:

> Hell is the rejection of God and therefore the opposite of everything God is. Within the Trinity, each Person is wholly self-realized because each Person is wholly loved and fulfilled in the others. God is also a society in which each Person is fully integrated with the others. To reject God, then, is to reject the ultimate society. Thus hell means psychological and social dis-integration: the ruin of man's heart and the destruction of all his relationships.

Whew! Pretty heady stuff! I hope you survived this brief survey of the Trinity.

ILLUSTRATION

But in a lighter vein, I offer this illustration of the Trinity, taken from Michael P. Green's book *1500 Illustrations for Biblical Preaching*:

> Augustine, while puzzling over the doctrine of the Trinity, was walking along the beach one day when he observed a young boy with a bucket, running back and forth to pour water into a little hole. Augustine asked, "What are you doing?" The boy replied, "I'm trying to put the ocean into this hole." Then Augustine realized that he had been trying to put an infinite God into his finite mind.

GODLY WISDOM

For the Christian, the Trinity is a basic truth. The following Bible passages attest to this fact. The Father sends the Son: "But when the fulness of the time was come, God sent forth his Son, made of a woman, made under the law" (Galatians 4:4).

The Father sends the Spirit: "But the Comforter, which is the Holy Ghost, whom the Father will send in my name, he shall teach you all things, and bring all things to your remembrance, whatsoever I have said unto you" (John 14:26).

The Son speaks, not on his own, but on behalf of the Father: "Then said Jesus unto them, When ye have lifted up the Son of man, then shall ye know that I am he, and that I do nothing of myself; but as my Father hath taught me, I speak these things" (John 8:28).

The Spirit speaks, not on behalf of the Jesus:

Barry Denzil Haney, MD

Howbeit when he, the Spirit of truth, is come, he will guide you into all truth: for he shall not speak of himself; but whatsoever he shall hear, that shall he speak and he will shew you things to come. He shall glorify me: for he shall receive of mine and shall shew it unto you. All things that the Father hath are mine: therefore said I, that he shall take of mine, and shall shew it unto you.

—John 16:13-15

The Father loves the Son, and the Son loves the Father: "The Father loveth the Son, and hath given all things into his hand" (John 3:35).

The Father and the Son count as two witnesses:

If I bear witness of myself, my witness is not true. There is another that beareth witness of me; and I know that the witness which he witnesseth of me is true. Ye sent unto John, and he bare witness unto the truth. But I receive not testimony from man: but these things I say, that ye might be saved. He was a burning and a shining light: and ye were willing for a season to rejoice in his light. But I have greater witness than that of John: for the works which the Father hath given me to finish, the same works that I do, bear witness of me, that the Father hath sent me. And the Father himself, which hath sent me, hath borne witness of me. Ye have neither heard his voice at any time, nor seen his shape.

—John 5:31-37

The Father and the Son glorify one another:

These words spake Jesus, and lifted up his eyes to heaven, and said, Father, the hour is come; glorify thy Son, that thy Son also may glorify thee: As thou hast given him power over all flesh, that he should give eternal life to as many as thou hast given him. And this is life eternal, that they might know thee the only true God, and Jesus Christ, whom thou hast sent. I have glorified thee on the earth: I have finished the work which thou gavest me to do. And now, O Father, glorify thou me with thine own self with the glory which I had with thee before the world was.

—John 17:1-5

The Son is an Advocate for us with the Father: "My little children, these things write I unto you, that ye sin not. And if any man sin, we have an advocate with the Father, Jesus Christ the righteous" (1 John 2:1).

Jesus the Son sent the Holy Spirit, who is another Advocate: "And I will pray the Father, and he shall give you another Comforter, that he may abide with you forever" (John 14:16).

Jesus Christ is not the Father, but the Son of the Father: "Grace be with you, mercy, and peace, from God the Father, and from the Lord Jesus Christ, the Son of the Father, in truth and love" (2 John 3).

I would like to offer this excerpt from Ralph Smiths book *Trinity and Reality: An Introduction to the Christian Faith*: "Nothing in this world or in the world to come can be properly known or appreciated apart from the triune God, whose love and grace sustain, govern, lead, and bring to fulfillment all His works."

In the article "What Are Some Popular Illustrations of the Trinity?" found in the Compelling Truth.org newsletter, the authors discuss the following concepts about the Trinity. Over the centuries, many people have used various illustrations to explain the Trinity. The following is a partial list of the most popular: a clover used by Saint Patrick, an apple; the egg; the sun; and the universe. All of these fall short because they lend themselves to partialism (the belief that each of the persons of the Trinity is only part God, only becoming fully God when they are together).

They go on to share what they feel is the least flawed illustration they have found concerning the Trinity:

Barry Denzil Haney, MD

Perhaps the least flawed illustration we have of God's triune nature is a musical chord of three notes. The three distinct notes work together to make one melodious sound, existing in the same time and space, and unified in purpose while remaining separate and distinct. Each note on its own fills the auditory space and creates a beautiful sound, and yet when combined with the other two notes continues to make a unified melodious sound that fills the auditory space while remaining distinct from the other two. So this example comes close to showing how God's triune nature exists.

PRAYER

Our heavenly Father,

Thank You, Holy Spirit, for teaching us, instructing us, and protecting us. Thank You for being the guiding hand for Handel, who wrote "*The Messiah*," a masterpiece consisting entirely of Scripture, including these words of praise: wonderful, counselor, everlasting Father, mighty God, prince of peace!

Thank You, Father, for Your love, Your mercy, Your kindness, and Your grace. Thank You for Your Son Jesus, through whom we receive Your gift of salvation, the slain Lamb, whose shed blood, saves us from our sin.

Thank You for loving us, even though we don't deserve it. Thank You for allowing us to do Your will, each day, in Your grand scheme of salvation.

Thank You for the Holy Spirit's presence. We can sense the presence of the Holy Spirit, as we read godly wisdom from Your Word.

We accept Jesus as our Lord and Savior. Father, we lift up to You in prayer our needs, and ask for Your continued comfort, peace and encouragement.

In the precious name of Jesus our Lord and Savior,

Amen!

Barry Denzil Haney, MD

CHAPTER 20

The Messiah

I saw in the night visions, and, behold, one like the Son of man came with the clouds of heaven, and came to the Ancient of days, and they brought him near before him. And there was given him dominion, and glory, and a kingdom, that all people, nations, and languages, should serve him: his dominion is an everlasting dominion, which shall not pass away, and his kingdom that which shall not be destroyed...But the judgment shall sit, and they shall take away his dominion, to consume and to destroy it unto the end. And the kingdom and dominion, and the greatness of the kingdom under the whole heaven, shall be given to the people of the saints of the most High, whose kingdom is an everlasting kingdom, and all dominions shall serve and obey him.

—Daniel 7:13-14, 26-27

WORLDLY WISDOM

In this passage, the Holy Spirit is telling me Jesus appears before God, and God grants Jesus kingdom authority, which then leads to the defeat of God's enemies and the saints of God possessing the kingdom of God on Earth.

The Cambridge Dictionary defines Messiah in this way:

> "A person who is expected to come and save the world; in the Christian religion, the Messiah is Jesus; in the Jewish religion, the Messiah has not yet come."

The Dictionary of Bible Themes defines the coming of Messiah in this way:

> The coming of a figure chosen and anointed by God to deliver and redeem his people; anointing was seen as a sign of being chosen by God for a special task of leadership or responsibility; the OT looked ahead to the final coming of such a figure to usher in a new era in the history of the people of God; the NT sees this expectation fulfilled in the person and work of Jesus Christ.

The term "messiah" denotes any redeemer figure. The adjective "messianic" is used in a broad sense to refer to beliefs or theories about an eschatological (relating to death, judgment, and the final destiny of the soul and of humankind) improvement of the state of the humanity of the world. In the Old Testament (OT) of the Bible, no mention is made of an eschatological messiah.

There are passages in the OT containing prophecies of a future golden age under an ideal king. When the historical Israelite kings proved disappointing, "messianic" kingship ideology was projected into the future. Later, after the Babylonian Exile, a prophetic vision of national restoration and universal establishment arose under the leadership of a Davidic heir.

This expectation of a personal messiah increased in prominence during Roman rule and oppression. Some began to believe in a being called the "*Son of Man*" who would descend to save his people. Islam does not have a savior-messiah but did develop the idea of an eschatological restorer of the faith, usually called the Mahdi.

Eschatological figures of a messianic character are known in other religions. The Buddhists believe in the Buddha Maitreya, who will descend from his heavenly abode and bring the faithful to paradise.

In Zoroastrianism, a posthumous son of Zoroaster is expected to effect the final rehabilitation of the world and resurrection of the dead. Atheists do not believe Jesus was a messiah. Here is a quote by Richard Dawkins, an example of what many atheists think about the claim of Christ's deity: "Jesus was a great moral teacher," Richard Dawkins said to The Guardian earlier this week. "Somebody as intelligent as Jesus would have been an atheist if he had known what we know today."

ILLUSTRATION

The following illustration concerning the Messiah is taken from Michael P. Green's book *1500 Illustrations for Biblical Preaching*:

> "Dr. Charles Fineberg, a noted Jewish-Christian scholar, says that in the course of Israel's history since the time of our Lord, sixty-four different individuals have appeared claiming to be the Messiah."

GODLY WISDOM

What does godly wisdom tell us about the concept of messianism?In their book *King and Messiah as Son of God: Diving, Human, and Angelic Messianic Figures in Biblical and Related Literature*, authors Adela Collins and John Collins have this to say about the concept of messianism in ancient times:

Our study shows that the issue is a good deal more complicated than that. The idea of the divinity of the messiah has its roots in the royal ideology of ancient Judah, which in turn was influenced by the Egyptian mythology of kingship.

In their book they go on to say the idea that the king was divine had ancient roots in the Near Eastern world and continued with the Davidic dynasty until the disasters of the Assyrian and Babylonian eras. The concept of the divinity of the messiah reoccurred in ancient Judaism, with the reinterpretation of messianic expectations in Daniel's vision in Daniel 7:13.

In his book *The One Who Is to Come*, Joseph Fitzmyer gives this account of a Jewish scholars definition of the word "Messiah:"

> Furthermore, a Jewish scholar noted for his interpretation of the Hebrew Scriptures and of ancient Near Eastern texts, H. L. Ginsberg, once described the "Messiah" in a noteworthy way: a charismatically endowed descendant of David who the Jews of the Roman period believed would be raised up by God to break the yoke of the heathen and to reign over a restored kingdom of Israel to which all the Jews of the Exile would return. This is a strictly postbiblical concept. Even Haggai and Zechariah, who expected the Davidic kingdom to be renewed with a specific individual, Zerubbabel, at its head, thought of him only as a feature of the new age, not as the author or even agent of its establishment. One can, therefore, only speak of the biblical prehistory of messianism.

Some scholars deny the Old Testament contains any Messianic doctrine. The great body of Jewish and Christian scholars agree on the doctrine of the Messiah; they disagree on the identity of the Messiah; Jews denying Jesus was the Messiah, whereas Christians affirming it.

Barry Denzil Haney, MD

Early rabbis and sages recognized the following passages as referring to the Messiah:

- *Messiah would be from Judah:* "The sceptre shall not depart from Judah, Nor a lawgiver from between his feet, Until Shiloh come; And unto him shall the gathering of the people be" (Genesis 49:10).

- *Messiah would be a descendant of King David:* And when thy days be fulfilled, and thou shalt sleep with thy fathers, I will set up thy seed after thee, which shall proceed out of thy bowels, and I will establish his kingdom. He shall build a house for my name, and I will stablish the throne of his kingdom forever. I will be his father, and he shall be my son. If he commit iniquity, I will chasten him with the rod of men, and with the stripes of the children of men. (2 Samuel 7:12-14)

- *Messiah would be a descendant of King Solomon:* Behold, a son shall be born to thee, who shall be a man of rest; and I will give him rest from all his enemies round about for his name shall be Solomon, and I will give peace and quietness unto Israel in his days. He shall build a house for my name; and he shall be my son, and I will be his father; and I will establish the throne of his kingdom over Israel forever. (1 Chronicles 22:9-10)

- *Messiah was to be born at Bethlehem:* "And it shall come to pass in that day, saith the LORD, That I will cut off thy horses out of the midst of thee, And I will destroy thy chariots" (Micah 5:10).

- *Messiah would arrive before the destruction of the Second Temple:* "Seventy weeks are determined upon thy people and upon thy holy city, to finish the transgression, and to make an end of sins, and to make reconciliation for iniquity, and to bring in everlasting righteousness, and to seal up the vision and prophecy, and to anoint the most Holy. Know therefore and understand, that from the going forth of the commandment to restore and to build Jerusalem unto the Messiah the Prince shall be seven weeks, and threescore and two weeks: the street shall be built again, and the wall, even in troublous times. And after threescore and two weeks shall Messiah be cut off, but not for himself: and the people of the prince that shall come shall destroy the city and the sanctuary; and the end thereof shall be with a flood, and unto the end of the war desolations are determined. And he shall confirm the covenant with many for one week: and in the midst of the week he shall cause the sacrifice and the oblation to cease, and for the overspreading of abominations he shall make it desolate, even until the consummation, and that determined shall be poured upon the desolate." (Daniel 9:24-27)

- *Messiah would present himself by riding on a donkey:* "Rejoice greatly, O daughter of Zion; Shout, O daughter of Jerusalem: Behold, thy King cometh unto thee: He is just, and having salvation; Lowly, and riding upon an ass, And upon a colt the foal of an ass." (Zechariah 9:9)

- *Messiah would be tortured to death:* "My God, my God, why hast thou forsaken me? Why art thou so far from helping me, and from the words of my roaring? O my God, I cry in the daytime, but thou hearest not; And in the night season and am not silent. But thou art holy, O thou that inhabitest the praises of Israel. Our fathers trusted in thee: They trusted, and thou didst deliver them. They cried unto thee, and were delivered: They trusted in thee, and were not confounded. But I am a worm, and no man; A reproach of men, and despised of the people. All they that see me laugh

Barry Denzil Haney, MD

me to scorn: They shoot out the lip, they shake the head, saying, He trusted on the LORD that he would deliver him: Let him deliver him, seeing he delighted in him. But thou art he that took me out of the womb: Thou didst make me hope when I was upon my mother's breasts. I was cast upon thee from the womb: Thou art my God from my mother's belly. Be not far from me; for trouble is near; For there is none to help. Many bulls have compassed me: Strong bulls of Bashan have beset me round. They gaped upon me with their mouths, As a ravening and a roaring lion. I am poured out like water, And all my bones are out of joint: My heart is like wax; It is melted in the midst of my bowels. My strength is dried up like a potsherd; And my tongue cleaveth to my jaws; And thou hast brought me into the dust of death. For dogs have compassed me: The assembly of the wicked have inclosed me: They pierced my hands and my feet. I may tell all my bones: They look and stare upon me. They part my garments among them And cast lots upon my vesture. But be not thou far from me, O LORD: O my strength, haste thee to help me. Deliver my soul from the sword; My darling from the power of the dog. Save me from the lion's mouth: For thou hast heard me from the horns of the unicorns. I will declare thy name unto my brethren: In the midst of the congregation will I praise thee. Ye that fear the LORD, praise him; All ye the seed of Jacob, glorify him; And fear him, all ye the seed of Israel. For he hath not despised nor abhorred the affliction of the afflicted; Neither hath he hid his face from him; But when he cried unto him, he heard. My praise shall be of thee in the great congregation: I will pay my vows before them that fear him. The meek shall eat and be satisfied: They shall praise the LORD that seek him: Your heart shall live forever. All the ends of the world shall remember and turn unto the LORD: And all the kindreds of the nations shall worship before thee. For the kingdom is the LORD's: And he is the governor among the nations. All they that be fat upon earth shall eat and worship: All they that go down to the dust shall bow before him: And none can keep alive his own soul. A seed shall serve him; It shall be accounted to the Lord for a generation. They shall come and shall declare his righteousness Unto a people that shall be born, that he hath done this." (Psalm 22:1-31)

• *Messiah's life would match a particular description, including suffering, silence at his arrest and trial, death and burial in a rich man's tomb, and resurrection:* "Behold, my servant shall deal prudently, He shall be exalted and extolled, and be very high…Therefore will I divide him a portion with the great, And he shall divide the spoil with the strong; Because he hath poured out his soul unto death: And he was numbered with the transgressors; And he bare the sin of many And made intercession for the transgressors." (Isaiah 52:13, 53:12)

In his book *The Messianic Question,* C. I. Scofield lists eleven historical facts that confirm Jesus was the Messiah:

• He is a descendant of Eve—a Man.

• He is the seed of Abraham, nay, the very seed.

• He derives His Abrahamic ancestry through Jacob, not Esau; Isaac, not Ishmael.

• He is of the Tribe of Judah.

• He is David's Son and heir of the Davidic covenant.

• He was miraculously conceived in the womb of a virgin.

Barry Denzil Haney, MD

- He proved His Deity by works beyond the power of man, by superhuman holiness, by the resurrection from the dead, and by His influence upon the world.

- He appeared at precisely the right time according to Daniel's prophecy.

- He was born, against all human probability, in Bethlehem-Ephratah.

- He fulfilled the prophecies of Isaiah concerning His vicarious sacrifice.

- He died in precisely the manner foretold in Psalm 22. His hands and feet were pierced, and His executioners cast lots upon His raiment.

What passages in the New Testament support the claim Jesus is the Messiah?

In John 1:41, Andrew tells Simon Peter he has found the Messiah: "He first findeth his own brother Simon, and saith unto him, We have found the Messias, which is, being interpreted, the Christ."

In John 14:6, Jesus says he is the Messiah: "Jesus saith unto him, I am the way, the truth, and the life: no man cometh unto the Father, but by me." Again, in John 4:25-26, Jesus declares he is the Messiah: "The woman saith unto him, I know that Messias cometh, which is called Christ: when he is come, he will tell us all things. Jesus saith unto her, I that speak unto thee am he."

On November 3, 2003, a few months before he died, Rabbi Yitzhak Kaduri wrote down, on a small note, the name of the Messiah, revealed to him in a vision by the Messiah Himself. As he requested, the note remained sealed until one year after his death. When opened by his disciples, the name they discovered on the note was Yehoshua, or Yeshua (Jesus).

Although many people to this day believe the Messiah has not yet come and are still in search of Him, I think the preponderance of the evidence, in both the Old and New Testament, supports the claim that Jesus was the Messiah!

PRAYER

Our heavenly Father,

We pray the following prayer for Israel.

Protect Israel and her people amidst the brazen and hostile nuclear threats from Iran. Give wisdom and discernment to Israeli leaders as they face a significant prospect for war with Iran and its proxies.

Instill peace in the hearts of the Jewish people in Israel, during this time of uncertainty. Move in the hearts and minds of world leaders, Israel's enemies and the Jewish people, to help them see to the truthfulness of Jesus' Messiahship—the Prince of Peace.

In the precious name of Jesus Christ, our Lord and Savior,

Amen

CHAPTER 21

Attack of The Hornets!

Moreover the Lord thy God will send the hornet among them, until they that are left, and hide themselves from thee, be destroyed. Thou shalt not be affrighted at them: for the Lord thy God is among you, a mighty God and terrible.

—Deuteronomy 7:20-21

WORLDLY WISDOM

In this passage, the Holy Spirit is teaching me God sent the Holy Spirit to instruct, teach and protect the Israelites and was the power of the conquest, just as He is for us, to instruct, teach, and protect us from Satan's lies and deceptions!

The Cambridge Dictionary defines spirit in this way: "The characteristics of a person that are considered as being separate from the body, and that many religions believe continue to exist after the body dies."

The Dictionary of Bible Themes defines Holy Spirit in this way:

> The co-equal and co-eternal Spirit of the Father and the Son, who inspired Scripture and brings new life to the people of God; the Spirit of God is often portrayed in Scripture in terms of "breath," "life" or "wind," indicating his role in sustaining and bringing life to God's creation.

MY PERSONAL EXPERIENCE: ATTACK OF THE HORNETS!

When I was a Boy Scout, I underwent initiation into the *Order of the Arrow*, in the early fall of 1963, at Camp McKee, a Boy Scout Reservation located in Eastern Kentucky. The Order of the Arrow is a Scouting's National Honor Society to recognize those scouts who best exemplify the Scout Oath and Law in their daily lives.

The induction ceremony is called the Ordeal. During the experience, I was required to maintain silence, and I received small amounts of food during the weekend initiation ceremony. On Saturday morning after sleeping overnight, terrified, by myself, in the dark, under the stars, all the while, maintaining silence, I was awoken by my guide, "a fully garbed Indian," and in silence, taken to my assigned work area, given a hand ax, and given the task to clear brush from the lakeshore.

Excited to begin this task, I quickly began chopping brush down, anticipating the end of the workday, when I would be rewarded for my hard work, with a large, luscious, extravagant, awe-inspiring, splendiferous feast in the camp's chow hall!

Barry Denzil Haney, MD

While I was chopping into a large, rotting tree limb located on the ground, I heard a strange sound coming from the center of the log, and then, with the last blow from my ax, I realized the sound was coming from a hornet's nest.

In my panic to get away, I tripped on spiny vines. I was immediately surrounded by what seemed like hundreds of swarming, stinging hornets. Screaming, trying to protect my face from the relentless hornets, I ran toward the lake and jumped into the cold, clear, deep water!

When I surfaced, the horde of swarming hornets circled the water above me, with the intent, I'm sure, to stink me over and over again! After several minutes of dunking myself back under the surface of the water, then resurfacing, the mob of mad, swarming hornets finally left.

I crawled out of the lake, soaking wet, and ran as fast as I could to the first aid station, where a panic-stricken nurse frantically began providing me with first aid treatment; I'm sure scared to death, I would die from this "attack of the hornets."

Although I did not know it then, I believe the Holy Spirit was with me that day, protecting me from this attack!

What do non-Christians believe about the concept of the "Holy Spirit?"

The three other Abrahamic religions, Judaism, Islam, and Bahá'í Faith, have differing viewpoints concerning the Holy Spirit.

The Holy Spirit in Judaism generally refers to the divine aspect of prophecy and wisdom.

In Islam, the "holy spirit" is mentioned four times in the Qur'an, who acts as an agent of divine action or communication.

The Bahá'í Faith has the concept of the *Most Great Spirit,* seen as the bounty of God.

Other religions reference a spirit that has a name resembling the Holy Spirit found in the Christian and Jewish faiths, but similar to Islam, a different spirit with a different purpose is unique to each religion.

What are the other spirits present in this world?

The Bible tells us, spiritual warfare is occurring around us during our daily life.

Michael Heiser, in his book *The Unseen Realm: Recovering the Supernatural Worldview of the Bible,* refers to this as the "unseen realm." The spirits in the "unseen realm" are at war with God's angels, led by Satan.

In his book *The Holy Spirit and Other Spirits,* D. O. Teasley describes the work of Satan in this following excerpt from his book:

> This is the plan that Satan is working on today; he has ceased to use force and seeks to deceive. This scheme has worked and is working much better than martyrdom. Deception and spiritual lethargy have slain more souls than ever were slain by martyrdom. Satan now arrays himself in the robes of hypocrisy, spiritualism, hypnotism, mesmerism, sectarianism, and thousands of other deceptive attires, and "walks about" as "an angel of light," "seeking whom he may" deceive.

GODLY WISDOM

What does godly wisdom tell us about the Holy Spirit? In Genesis 1:2, we are told the Holy Spirit was one of the authors of the universe: "And the earth was without form, and void; and darkness was upon the face of the deep. And the Spirit of God moved upon the face of the waters." In Job 26:13, we are told the Holy Spirit "garnished the heavens:" "By his spirit he hath garnished the heavens; His hand hath formed the crooked serpent." In Ezekiel 37:14, we are told the Holy Spirit gives life to those who are physically dead: "And shall put my spirit in you, and ye shall live, and I shall place you in your own land: then shall ye know that I the LORD have spoken it, and performed it, saith the LORD."

In Isaiah 40:7, we are told the Holy Spirit brings life to an end: "The grass withereth, the flower fadeth: Because the spirit of the LORD bloweth upon it: Surely the people is grass." In John 14:16-17, Jesus made clear statements about the coming of the Spirit:

> And I will pray the Father, and he shall give you another
> Comforter, that he may abide with you forever; Even the
> Spirit of truth; whom the world cannot receive, because it
> seeth him not, neither knoweth him: but ye know him; for
> he dwelleth with you and shall be in you.

In Acts 2:1-4, we find the first record of the appearance of the Holy Spirit, the wonderful event which completed the church and endowed it with that mysterious power which has given it the source of its life and success:

> And when the day of Pentecost was fully come, they were
> all with one accord in one place. And suddenly there came
> a sound from heaven as of a rushing mighty wind, and
> it filled all the house where they were sitting. And there
> appeared unto them cloven tongues like as of fire, and it sat
> upon each of them. And they were all filled with the Holy
> Ghost, and began to speak with other tongues, as the Spirit
> gave them utterance.

Four characteristics are attributed to the Holy Spirit in Scripture, eternity, omnipresence, omniscience, and omnipotence. "How much more shall the blood of Christ, who through the eternal Spirit offered himself without spot to God, purge your conscience from dead works to serve the living God?" (Hebrews 9:14).

> Whither shall I go from thy spirit? Or whither shall I flee from thy presence? If I ascend up into heaven, thou art there: If I make my bed in hell, behold, thou art there. If I take the wings of the morning, And dwell in the uttermost parts of the sea; Even there shall thy hand lead me, And thy right hand shall hold me.
>
> —Psalm 139:7-10

> But God hath revealed them unto us by his Spirit: for the Spirit searcheth all things, yea, the deep things of God. For what man knoweth the things of a man, save the spirit of man which is in him? even so the things of God knoweth no man, but the Spirit of God.
>
> —1 Corinthians 2:10-11

> And the angel answered and said unto her, The Holy Ghost shall come upon thee, and the power of the Highest shall overshadow thee: therefore also that holy thing which shall be born of thee shall be called the Son of God.
>
> —Luke 1:35

Three works are attributed to the Holy Spirit, creation, the impartation of life, and prophecy. "I would order my cause before him and fill my mouth with arguments" (Job 23:4). "And this he said to prove him: for he himself knew what he would do" (John 6:6). "For the prophecy came not in old time by the will of man: but holy men of God spake as they were moved by the Holy Ghost" (2 Peter 1:21). In the New Testament, the Holy

Barry Denzil Haney, MD

Spirit is given the position of Deity in Acts 28:25-27:

> And when they agreed not among themselves, they
> departed, after that Paul had spoken one word, Well spake
> the Holy Ghost by Esaias the prophet unto our fathers,
> Saying, Go unto this people, and say, Hearing ye shall
> hear, and shall not understand; and seeing ye shall see, and
> not perceive: For the heart of this people is waxed gross,
> and their ears are dull of hearing, and their eyes have they
> closed; lest they should see with their eyes, and hear with
> their ears, and understand with their heart, and should be
> converted, and I should heal them.

In the New Testament, the Holy Spirit is connected with God in 1
Corinthians 12:4-6:

> Now there are diversities of gifts, but the same Spirit. And
> there are differences of administrations, but the same Lord.
> And there are diversities of operations, but it is the same
> God which worketh all in all.

In the New Testament, the Holy Spirit is called God in Acts 5:3,4:

> But Peter said, Ananias, why hath Satan filled thine heart
> to lie to the Holy Ghost, and to keep back part of the price
> of the land? Whiles it remained, was it not thine own? and
> after it was sold, was it not in thine own power? why hast
> thou conceived this thing in thine heart? thou hast not lied
> unto men, but unto God.

Why is the Holy Spirit so important to a Christian during their journey
to salvation?

The Holy Spirit wants to live in our hearts. He wants to speak to us through the Bible. He wants to teach us, instruct us, and protect us from the wily Satan. He wants to be the "hornet" to attack Satan, defeat the one who is trying to separate us from God, and drag us to hell with him!

———————

ILLUSTRATION

The following illustration concerning the Holy Spirit is taken from Michael P. Green's book *1500 Illustrations for Biblical Preaching*:

> Many people ask, "How do I know the Holy Spirit is living in me?" I know in the same way that I know there is music on a cassette tape, even though I don't see the music on the tape. I can know that in either of two ways. I can believe the label that says there is music, or I can play the tape and hear it. We can know the Holy Spirit indwells us by believing God, who tells us in His Word, or by seeing His results in our lives when we are obedient to Him.

———————

PRAYER

Our heavenly Father,

You have told us before our body dies, we will undergo progressive sanctification, progressive holiness. But You have warned us, our soul will continue to be tempted, and we will fall. But You have promised us because our spirit is

Barry Denzil Haney, MD

saved, our sin will not be held against us. Thank You, for that promise!

However, You have also told us, with that comes a responsibility. We must repent of our transgressions and strive to do those things which please You. To help us, You sent the Holy Spirit to work in our hearts, to protect us from Satan's wily ways!

You have promised us, if we honestly do this, if we honestly have faith in Jesus, if we have honestly repented, then we will become more holy each day of our lives, and we will find it easier to resist temptation.

Thank You, our Father, for Your unending love! Thank You for imagining us in Your dreams! Thank You for creating us in Your image! Thank You for not quitting on us! Thank You for providing us with hope! The hope of spending an eternity, with such a marvelous, loving Father!

In the precious name of Jesus Christ our Lord and Savior,

Amen!

CHAPTER 22

In God's Plan, What Comes First: Redemption or Righteousness?

But when the fulness of the time was come, God sent forth his Son, made of a woman, made under the law, To redeem them that were under the law, that we might receive the adoption of sons. And because ye are sons, God hath sent forth the Spirit of his Son into your hearts, crying, Abba, Father. Wherefore thou art no more a servant, but a son; and if a son, then an heir of God through Christ. Howbeit then, when ye knew not God, ye did service unto them which by nature are no gods.

—Galatians 4:4-8

I have fought a good fight, I have finished my course, I have kept the faith: Henceforth there is laid up for me a crown of righteousness, which the Lord, the righteous judge, shall give me at that day: and not to me only, but unto all them also that love his appearing. Do thy diligence to come shortly unto me.

—2 Timothy 4:7-9

In the passage in Galatians, the Holy Spirit is teaching me, all of us are children of God only because of God's grace, God's gift to us, not by our own power, not by our works adhering to the law, but by the redeeming work of Jesus on the cross at Calvary. We cannot earn it, and we do not deserve it.

In the second passage in 2 Timothy, the Holy Spirit is teaching me when we have faith in Jesus; it is possible for us to be righteous because of Christ's righteousness, who now lives in us.

The Holy Spirit is also providing us with Paul's example of how to conduct our life journey: to preserve the teachings of the Gospel and to maintain our faith in Jesus throughout our life journey.

The Cambridge Dictionary defines redemption in this way: "The state of being kept from evil or of improving morally."

The Merriam-Webster dictionary defines righteous in this way: "Acting in accord with divine or moral law: free from guilt or sin: morally right or justifiable; arising from an outraged sense of justice or morality."

Humanly speaking, we could understand and interpret the question, "What comes first, redemption or righteousness?" in a myriad of ways. However, the Holy Spirit does not mean for these concepts to be discussed as ideals but to be acted on. Because of sin, our human mind is naturally limited to accept the truth of godly wisdom. Satan prevents us from seeing the truth by "blinders," he places on our awareness, our perception.

According to worldly wisdom, our perception is limited by two problems. The first problem has to do with limitations on our sensory ability, secondary to a number of factors, including the aging process, the limitation of our vision when compared with a deer's or turkey's vision, and the limitation of our hearing compared with a dog's, who can hear frequency levels we don't hear. In order to counter this problem with perception, we have created elaborate tools to enhance our perception, such as electron microscopy to see the smallest things, the Hubble telescope to see the largest things, and the Large Hadron Collider to study the subatomic world.

The second problem for perception is we influence our perception by adding or subtracting information from the true reality. Our mind tends to distort reality, a problem men such as Kant, Hume, and other philosophers have wrestled and still do wrestle with. Do our perceptions correspond to reality?

Because of this problem with perception, in the history of Christian theology, philosophy has sometimes been seen as a natural complement to theological reflection, but at other times practitioners of the two disciplines have viewed each other as enemies.

At this point in my life journey, my struggle with the concepts of redemption and righteousness, which comes first, is like the struggle of others throughout history, the struggle of men like Augustine of Hippo, Martin Luther, John Wesley, C. H. Spurgeon, and C. S. Lewis. Who struggled with their perception, their philosophical worldview, until the Holy Spirit was able to convict them, and through godly wisdom, were converted, then realized the answer to the question I have posed in this chapter!

Augustine's conversion came about under a fig tree, in a garden outside his home, when he heard a voice saying, "Take and read," which led him to read Romans 13:13-14,

> Let us walk honestly, as in the day; not in rioting and
> drunkenness, not in chambering and wantonness, not in
> strife and envying. But put ye on the Lord Jesus Christ, and
> make not provision for the flesh, to fulfil the lusts thereof.

When he read this passage, the "blinders" of his perception were removed, and his doubts and fears about leaving his old life were removed, leading to a decisive change in his life. Martin Luther's conversion in 1519 occurs when the "blinders" of his perception are removed by the Holy Spirit and occurred only after he meditated day and night about the words of Paul in his epistles to the Romans, to the Galatians, and to the Hebrews.

According to him, after hours and days of meditation, he finally understood as he tells us in his own words:

> The righteousness of God is revealed by the gospel, namely, the passive righteousness with which merciful God justifies us by faith, as it is written, *"He who through faith is righteous shall live."* Here I felt that I was altogether born again and had entered paradise itself through open gates. There a totally other face of the entire Scripture showed itself to me. Thereupon I ran through the Scripture from memory. I also found in other terms an analogy, as, the work of God, that is what God does in us, the power of God, with which he makes us wise, the strength of God, the salvation of God, the glory of God. And I extolled my sweetest word with a love as great as the hatred with which I had before hated the word *"righteousness of God."* Thus that place in Paul was for me truly the gate to paradise. And I extolled my sweetest word with a love as great as the hatred with which I had before hated the word *"righteousness of God."* Thus that place in Paul was for me truly the gate to paradise.

A reluctant John Wesley finally had the "blinders" of perception removed by the Holy Spirit, on May 24, 1738, when depressed, he unwillingly attended a Christian meeting in Aldersgate, London. There, he heard a reading from the reformer Martin Luther's preface to the epistle to Romans. As he heard Luther's words, the "blinders" of perception were lifted by the Holy Spirit; as Wesley tells us in his own words,

> While he was describing the change in which God works in the heart through faith in Christ, I felt my heart strangely warmed. I felt I did trust in Christ, Christ alone for salvation; and an assurance was given me that He had taken

Barry Denzil Haney, MD

away my sins, even mine, and saved me from the law of sin and death.

John Wesley went on with his brother, Charles, to found the movement of Methodism, spreading evangelical revival throughout this country and the world. The story is similar for Charles Spurgeon, who admits his eternal destiny was changed from hell to heaven, through God's grace, when the "blinders" of perception were removed by the Holy Spirit, as told in his own *lengthy* but, I think, timeless, instructive words:

> In my conversion, the very point lay in making the discovery that I had nothing to do but to look to Christ, and I should be saved. I believe that I had been a very good, attentive hearer; my own impression about myself was that nobody ever listened much better than I did. For years, as a child, I tried to learn the way of salvation; and either I did not hear it set forth, which I think cannot quite have been the case, or else I was spiritually blind and deaf and could not see it and could not hear it; but the good news that I was, as a sinner, to look away from myself to Christ, as much startled me, and came as fresh to me, as any news I ever heard in my life.
>
> Had I never read my Bible? Yes, and I read it earnestly.
>
> Had I never been taught by Christian people? Yes, I had, by mother, and father, and others.
>
> Had I not heard the Gospel? Yes, I think I had, and yet, somehow, it was like a new revelation to me that I was to "*believe and live.*" I confess to have been tutored in piety, put into my cradle by prayerful hands, and lulled to sleep by songs concerning Jesus; but after having heard the Gospel continually, with line upon line, precept upon precept, here much and there much, yet, when the Word of

the Lord came to me with power, it was as new as if I had lived among the unvisited tribes of Central Africa, and had never heard the tidings of the cleansing fountain filled with blood, drawn from the Savior's veins.

When, for the first time, I received the Gospel to my soul's salvation, I thought that I had never really heard it before, and I began to think that the preachers to whom I had listened had not truly preached it. But, on looking back, I am inclined to believe that I had heard the Gospel fully preached many hundreds of times before and that this was the difference—that I then heard it as though I heard it not; and when I did hear it, the message may not have been any more clear in itself than it had been at former times, but the power of the Holy Spirit was present to open my ear and to guide the message to my heart.

I sometimes think I might have been in darkness and despair until now had it not been for the goodness of God in sending a snowstorm one Sunday morning while I was going to a certain place of worship. When I could go no further, I turned down a side street and came to a little Primitive Methodist Chapel. In that chapel, there may have been a dozen or fifteen people. I had heard of the Primitive Methodists, how they sang so loudly that they made people's heads ache, but that did not matter to me. I wanted to know how I might be saved, and if they could tell me that, I did not care how much they made my head ache. The minister did not come that morning; he was snowed up, I suppose. At last, a very thin-looking man, a shoemaker, or tailor, or something of that sort, went up into the pulpit to preach. Now, it is well that preachers should be instructed; but this man was really stupid. He was obliged

Barry Denzil Haney, MD

to stick to his text for the simple reason that he had little else to say. The text was—

"Look unto me, and be ye saved, all the ends of the earth." —Isaiah 45:22

He did not even pronounce the words rightly, but that did not matter. There was, I thought, a glimpse of hope for me in that text. The preacher began thus:

"My dear friends, this is a very simple text indeed. It says, 'Look.' Now lookin' don't take a deal of pains. It ain't liftin' your foot or your finger; it is just, 'Look.' Well, a man needn't go to College to learn to look. You may be the biggest fool, and yet you can look. A man needn't be worth a thousand a year to be able to look. Anyone can look; even a child can look. But then the text says, 'Look unto Me.' Ay!" said he, in broad Essex, *"Many on ye are lookin' to yourselves, but it's no use lookin' there. You'll never find any comfort in yourselves. Some look to God the Father. No, look to Him by-and-by. Jesus Christ says, 'Look unto Me.' Some on ye say, 'We must wait for the Spirit's working.' 'You have no business with that just now. Look to Christ. The text says, 'Look unto Me.'"*

Then the good man followed up his text in this way—

"Look unto Me; I am sweatin' great drops of blood. Look unto Me; I am hangin' on the cross. Look unto Me; I am dead and buried. Look unto Me; I rise again. Look unto Me; I ascend to heaven. Look unto Me; I am sittin' at the Father's right hand. O poor sinner, look unto Me! Look unto Me!"

When he had gone to about that length and managed to spin out ten minutes or so, he was at the end of his tether. Then he looked at me under the gallery, and I daresay, with so few present, he knew me to be a stranger. Just fixing his eyes on me, as if he knew all my heart, he said,

"Young man, you look very miserable."

Well, I did; but I had not been accustomed to have remarks made from the pulpit on my personal appearance before. However, it was a good blow, struck right home. He continued,

"And you always will be miserable—miserable in life, and miserable in death—if you don't obey my text, but if you obey now, this moment, you will be saved."

Then, lifting up his hands, he shouted, as only a Primitive Methodist could do, *"You man, look to Jesus Christ. Look! Look! Look! You have nothin' to do but to look and live."* I saw at once the way of salvation.

I know not what else he said—I did not take much notice of it—I was so possessed with that one thought. Like as when the brazen serpent was lifted up, the people only looked and were healed, so it was with me. I had been waiting to do fifty things, but when I heard that word, "Look!" what a charming word it seemed to me!

Oh! I looked until I could almost have looked my eyes away. There and then the cloud was gone, the darkness had rolled away, and that moment I saw the sun; and I could have risen that instant, and sung with the most enthusiastic of them, of the precious blood of Christ, and simple faith which looks alone to Him.

Oh, that somebody had told me this before, "Trust Christ, and you shall be saved."

It is not everyone who can remember the very day and hour of his deliverance, but, as Richard Knill said, "At such a time of the day, clang went every harp in heaven, for Richard Knil was born again," it was even so with me.

Barry Denzil Haney, MD

The clock of mercy struck in heaven the hour and moment of my emancipation, for the time had come. Between half-past ten o'clock, when I entered that chapel, and half-past twelve o'clock, when I was back again at home, what a change had taken place in me! I had passed from darkness into marvelous light, from death to life.

Simply by looking to Jesus, I had been delivered from despair, and I was brought into such a joyous state of mind that, when they saw me at home, they said to me, "Something wonderful has happened to you;" and I was eager to tell them all about it...I have always considered, with Luther and Calvin, that the sum and substance of the Gospel lie in that word "substitution"—Christ standing in the stead of man. If I understand the Gospel, it is this: I deserve to be lost forever; the only reason why I should not be damned is that Christ was punished in my stead, and there is no need to execute a sentence twice for sin.

On the other hand, I know I cannot enter heaven unless I have perfect righteousness; I am absolutely certain I shall never have one of my own, for I find I sin every day; but then Christ had perfect righteousness, and He said,

"There, poor sinner, take My garment, and put it on; you shall stand before God as if you were Christ, and I will stand before God as if I had been the sinner; I will suffer in the sinner's stead, and you shall be rewarded for works which you did not do, but which I did for you."

I find it very convenient every day to come to Christ as a sinner, as I came as the first. "You are no saint," says the devil. Well, if I am not, I am a sinner, and Jesus Christ came into the world to save sinners.

Sink or swim, I go to Him; other hope I have none. By looking to Him, I received all the faith which inspired me with confidence in His grace; and the word that first drew my soul—"Look unto Me"—still rings its clarion note in my ears.

There I once found conversion, and there I shall ever find refreshing and renewal.

After years of being an atheist, C. S. Lewis had his "blinders" of perception removed by the Holy Spirit only after an unusually long spiritual journey, much like the Apostle Paul. Although his conversion was not a "Damascus road" conversion, it took him fifteen years to change his mind from this statement he made to a friend at age seventeen, "I believe in no religion. There is absolutely no proof for any of them, and from a philosophical standpoint, Christianity is not even the best."

He returned to Christianity, influenced by arguments with his Oxford colleague and Christian friend J. R. R. Tolkien. Lewis vigorously resisted conversion, noting that he was brought into Christianity like a prodigal, "kicking, struggling, resentful, and darting his eyes in every direction for a chance to escape." He described his last struggle in *"Surprised by Joy"*:

You must picture me alone in that room in Magdalen [College, Oxford], night after night, feeling, whenever my mind lifted even for a second from my work, the steady, unrelenting approach of Him whom I so earnestly desired not to meet. That which I greatly feared had at last come upon me. In the Trinity Term of 1929 I gave in, and admitted that God was God, and knelt and prayed: perhaps, that night, the most dejected and reluctant convert in all England.

Barry Denzil Haney, MD

C. S. Lewis converted to Christianity in 1931, following a long discussion and late-night walk with his close friends Tolkien and Hugo Dyson. He records making a specific commitment to Christian belief while on his way to the zoo with his brother. My long spiritual journey finally ended during my Emmaus walk, when I laid at the foot of the cross, the one thing I had failed to surrender to God, preventing me from having complete trust in God. Then, the "blinders" of my perception were lifted by the Holy Spirit. Now, I know the answer to the question I posed in this chapter.

GODLY WISDOM

"Look unto Me, and be ye saved, all the ends of the earth: for I am God, and there is none else" (Isaiah 45:22). The Holy Spirit used this scripture to convert C.H Spurgeon. What does godly wisdom tell us about the answer to the question posed in this chapter's title, "In God's Plan, What Comes First, Redemption or Righteousness?"

In Lee Strobel's book *The Case for Faith: A Journalist Investigates the Toughest Objections to Christianity*, Ravi Zacharias claims redemption is the most important step toward righteousness; it comes first. According to him, God's pattern of salvation can be found in the book of Exodus:

> God brought the people out of Egypt, he gave them moral
> law, and then he gave them the tabernacle. In other words,
> redemption, righteousness, worship. You can never violate
> that sequence. Unless you are redeemed, you cannot be
> righteous. Unless you are redeemed and righteous, you
> cannot worship, *"for who shall ascend unto the hill of the
> Lord,"* says the Bible, *"but he who has clean hand and a pure
> heart?"*

According to godly wisdom, where did redemption originate? The origin of redemption, the object of redemption, the plan of redemption, the purpose of redemption, the extent of redemption, and the result of redemption is found in the teaching of the Holy Spirit found in John 3:16: "For God so loved the world, that he gave his only begotten Son, that whosoever believeth in him should not perish, but have everlasting life."

Godly wisdom tells us in Philippians 3:9, once redemption has been accomplished through faith in Jesus, righteousness is possible because of Christ, who now resides in our heart, and our spirit becomes righteous, because of Christ's righteousness: "And be found in him, not having mine own righteousness, which is of the law, but that which is through the faith of Christ, the righteousness which is of God by faith."

What is the righteousness which God will judge us on judgment day? It will be the righteousness based on God's creative justice, as Jurgen Moltmann describes in the following excerpt from his book *Sun of Righteousness, Arise!*:

> Will not be the justice that establishes what is good and
> what is evil; nor will it be the retributive justice which
> rewards the good and punishes the wicked. It will be God's
> creative justice, which brings justice for the victims and puts
> the perpetrators right.

ILLUSTRATION

The following illustration concerning religious conversion is taken from Michael P. Green's book *1500 Illustrations for Biblical Preaching*:

> When many people are converted, they make the mistake of
> thinking that the battle was already theirs, that the victory

Barry Denzil Haney, MD

is now won. But, after serving Christ for a few months, we realize that conversion is like enlisting in the army: there is a battle at hand and many more in the future.

PRAYER

Our heavenly Father,

Thank You for being our Creator God. Thank You for Your unconditional love and mercy. Thank You for imagining us in Your dreams. Thank You for Your free gift of salvation. Thank You for being the Lion of Judah & the slain Lamb, whose shed blood saves the world from sin. We bow down before You this morning, in worship and praise.

Lord, thank You for the Holy Spirit, who guided me this past week during my daily reading and study of Your Word, and also led me to other saints and their divine-inspired thoughts concerning their study of Your Word. Help us not to be Christians who are known more for being judgmental than for our gentleness and respect.

Help us be seen as people filled with living hope and inexpressible joy, not as boring, irrelevant, and lacking vitality. Help us not have a life of what C. S. Lewis called "negative spirituality" but instead a vibrant, hopeful life in Christ.

Help us not believe that holiness is turning away from the miraculous capacity to enjoy the delights of taste, touch, sound, sight, and smell—gifts You have given us—and retreating into the world of abstract, theological ideas.

Help us to imagine being in the presence of God at whose "right hand are pleasures forevermore."

Help us to be centered on the expansion of consciousness and agency, by which we become ever more aware of ourselves, others, and God, allowing us to act more and more out of free choice. Help us to take in physical pleasure and beauty, and with our minds connect those sensations to the God who gave them to us.

We ask for Your continued comfort, peace, and divine healing presence in all of the prayer requests both spoken and unspoken this morning.

We ask that You be the guiding hand for the doctors, nurses, other health care providers, and others You have placed in the lives of those with needs.

We ask for You guidance for the leaders of Your Church, as they plan ways for Your Church to fulfill of Your plan of salvation for this world.

In the precious name of Jesus Christ, our Lord and Savior,

Amen

Barry Denzil Haney, MD

CHAPTER 23

The Pool of Unbelief!

After this there was a feast of the Jews; and Jesus went up to Jerusalem. Now there is at Jerusalem by the sheep market a pool, which is called in the Hebrew tongue Bethesda, having five porches. In these lay a great multitude of impotent folk, of blind, halt, withered, waiting for the moving of the water. For an angel went down at a certain season into the pool and troubled the water: whosoever then first after the troubling of the water stepped in was made whole of whatsoever disease he had. And a certain man was there, which had an infirmity thirty and eight years. When Jesus saw him lie, and knew that he had been now a long time in that case, he saith unto him, Wilt thou be made whole? The impotent man answered him, Sir, I have no man, when the water is troubled, to put me into the pool: but while I am coming, another steppeth down before me. Jesus saith unto him, Rise, take up thy bed, and walk. And immediately the man was made whole, and took up his bed, and walked: and on the same day was the sabbath.

—John 5:1-9

———————

WORLDLY WISDOM

The setting for this narrative is the pool of Bethesda, a place where many invalids are gathered. Jesus sees a man who had been ill for thirty-eight years at the pool and asks him if he wants to be made well. Instead of answering yes, the man offers a complaint.

In this passage, the Holy Spirit is teaching me; there are worse things than not obeying the law, breaking the Sabbath. The man is guilty of the sin of unbelief and risks incurring the judgment of God, eternal separation from Him.

The Cambridge Dictionary defines unbelief in this way: "The fact of not having religious belief."

The Dictionary of Biblical Themes defines unbelief in this way: "The lack of faith and trust in God that challenges his truthfulness and finds expression in disobedience and rebellion."

Before discussing the problem of unbelief, I would first like to talk about the pool of Bethesda and the importance of pools to mankind now and in the past. The Merriam-Webster Dictionary defines the word pool in these ways:

> A small and rather deep body of usually freshwater; a quiet place in a stream; a body of water forming above a dam; something resembling a pool, a pool of light; a small body of standing liquid; a continuous area of porous sedimentary rock that yields petroleum or gas.

The setting of the meeting between God and the man in the Gospel of John is a pool called Bethesda, located near the Sheep's Gate in Jerusalem. Lying on the porches around the pool are many invalids, the blind, the lame, and paralyzed. In the earliest manuscripts of John, why they are there is not revealed, but later scribes added an explanation that the people believed an angel of the Lord would come and stir the waters and that whoever was the first to enter the pool after the waters were stirred, would be healed of their affliction.

From the beginning, man knew the importance of water; he knew "water is life." Through the ages, because of dependence on water, mankind has lived their lives, with water at the center. In the article "A Brief History of Water and Health from Ancient Civilizations to Modern Times," the authors discuss the importance of water to early humans:

> Some 10,000 years ago, when people adopted an agrarian way of life, mankind established permanent settlements. This new type of livelihood spread everywhere and the population began to expand faster than ever before. Sedentary agricultural life made it possible to construct villages, cities and eventually states, all of which were highly dependent on water. This created a brand-new relation between humans and water. Pathogens transmitted by contaminated water became a very serious health risk for the sedentary agriculturists. In this world guaranteeing pure water for people became a prerequisite for successful urbanization and state formation.

The "Great Bath" at the site of Mohenjo-Daro, in modern-day Pakistan, was probably the first swimming pool dug during the third millennium BC. Most scholars believe this structure was used for special religious functions, to purify and renew the well-being of bathers.

Ancient Greeks and Romans built pools for athletic training and for nautical games, preparing for military battles. Roman emperors had private swimming pools, where fish were also kept. The first heated swimming pool was built by Gaius Maecenas on the Esquiline Hill of Rome between thirty-eight and eight BC. The ancient Sinhalese built pairs of pools called "Kuttam Pokuna" in the kingdom of Anuradhapura, Sri Lanka, in the fourth century.

Over the centuries, mankind has recognized the healing powers of pools of water, both for physical and emotional healing. Because of the amniotic qualities of water when swimming in seawater or hot mineral springs, many describe a sense of well-being, relaxation.

MY PERSONAL EXPERIENCE: SWIMMING WITH GOD!

I have been an avid swimmer for most of my life. I discovered the meditative quality of swimming early on. When I swim laps in a pool, I always have a wonderful sense of wellbeing, contentment, and being connected to nature, to my Creator God.

While swimming, it is just me, my mind, and the Holy Spirit rhythmically gliding through the serene water of life. With each stroke, I imagine the angels in heaven appearing in the air bubbles caused by my hand entering the water, as the bubbles rise, quickly to the surface; I imagine Jesus at the transfiguration, as the light shimmers, and dances, moving through the depths of the pool; I sense being held in the arms of God, as I glide gracefully through the water of life!

GODLY WISDOM

In the book *Where Is Your God? Responding to the Challenge of Unbelief and Religious Indifference Today*, the following statement is made concerning new and old causes of unbelief:

> It would be naïve to blame the spread of unbelief and the
> new forms of religiosity on a single cause, all the more
> so since this cultural phenomenon is more tied to group
> behavior than individual choice. Some affirm that the
> problem of unbelief is more a question of negligence than

Barry Denzil Haney, MD

malice. Others are firmly convinced that, behind this phenomenon, there are organized movements, associations, and deliberately orchestrated campaigns.

The Holy Spirit is teaching us about the problem of unbelief in the story told in the Gospel of Luke about the healing of the man at the pool of Bethesda. He is reminding us we risk eternal separation from God if we do not have faith in Jesus.

In his book *Gems from Martin Lloyd-Jones: An Anthology of Quotations from "the Doctor,"* Tony Sargent offers this quote about the word unbelief:

> The problem of unbelief is the same today as it was in the first century, and as it was before that. Unbelief has been a universal problem ever since the Fall. Unbelief is not the consequence of modern knowledge, but neither is it based upon reason, intelligence and understanding.

William R. Newell, pastor, evangelist, Bible teacher, author, speaker, and writer of the beloved hymn "At Calvary," says this about unbelief: "Satan hates active faith in a believer's heart and opposes it with all his power. The world, of course, is unbelieving and despises those who claim only 'the righteousness of faith.'"

In the passage found in Isaiah 59:1-2, the Holy Spirit teaches us unbelief produces spiritual paralysis:

> Behold, the LORD's hand is not shortened, that it cannot save; Neither his ear heavy, that it cannot hear: But your iniquities have separated between you and your God, And your sins have hid his face from you, that he will not hear.

In Luke 1:20, the Holy Spirit is instructing us about the unacceptableness and offensiveness of unbelief to God: "And, behold, thou shalt be dumb, and not able to speak, until the day that these things shall be performed, because thou believest not my words, which shall be fulfilled in their season."

Finally, a key text of the whole subject of unbelief is found in Hebrews 3:12: "Take heed, brethren, lest there be in any of you an evil heart of unbelief, in departing from the living God." The Holy Spirit is telling us the sin of unbelief is very important to God. Although man tends to think little of the sin of unbelief, God makes much of it.

A. T. Pierson, in his book *A Spiritual Clinique: Four Bible Readings Given at Keswick* in 1907, gives us this insight concerning habitual unbelief:

> "This great sin lies at the basis of every other, partly because
> it is the one sin that damns the soul, and partly because
> its removal means the relief of all other forms of spiritual
> difficulty."

The reason unbelief is the "great sin" is because it will lead to eternal separation from God! Remember, Jesus tells us this in John 14:6, "Jesus saith unto him, I am the way, the truth, and the life: no man cometh unto the Father, but by me."

PRAYER

Our heavenly Father,

Great are You, Lord! It's Your breath in our lungs. We pour out our praise; we glorify Your name; we love You!

We lift up to You in prayer all of those with needs this day. Thank You for providing Your healing power, comfort, peace, and love to them and their families.

Thank You for blessing and guiding the doctors, nurses, other health care providers, and others You have placed in their lives. Thank You for providing comfort, encouragement, peace, and love to them and their loved ones.

In the precious name of Jesus Christ our Lord and Savior,

Amen.

CHAPTER 24

What to Do With All Those... isms?

Beware lest any man spoil you through philosophy and vain deceit, after the tradition of men, after the rudiments of the world, and not after Christ. For in him dwelleth all the fulness of the Godhead bodily. And ye are complete in him, which is the head of all principality and power.

—Colossians 2:8-10

WORLDLY WISDOM

In this passage, the Holy Spirit is telling me, beware of the guesses and conclusions of the inadequate mind of man, because they represent the basic principles of this world, worldly wisdom, not godly wisdom and claim Jesus was nothing but a good man, not God Himself, who died for our sins.

The Cambridge Dictionary defines "ism" in this way: "A set of beliefs, especially ones that you disapprove of; a set of beliefs, especially ones that you disapprove of."

In preparation for this chapter, I did a google search for the suffix "ism." In 0.69 seconds, I received 118,0000,000 results. On a site called *The Phrontistery*, two hundred thirty-four philosophical "isms" are listed.

You can put the suffix "ism" on any word. For example, if you add "ism" to my name, you would have the word "*barryism*," a belief in Barry, something my wife would disapprove of when she is angry with me!

So, what is the problem with all those "isms"?

As Paul tells us, we need to watch out for those people who try to convince us with their intellectual double-talk, who try to confuse us with endless nonsensical arguments and spread their ideas through human tradition and superstition. The worldly wisdom they have pushed over the centuries has contributed to the shift away from biblical authority. The basic problem with the "isms" has to do with the source of truth. Where does genuine truth come from? How do we know what is actually true? The answer to these questions comes under the area of study called epistemology, an attempt to answer the question of ultimate authority. Most agree there are three ways to analyze competing claims to truth: human reason, ecclesiastical authority, divine revelation.

According to the secular worldview, human reason and human conscience are all we need to arrive at the truth. They believe it is possible for human beings to know the truth without God. This worldview leads to a plethora of "isms" including but not limited to moral relativism, perennialism, traditionalism, ecumenism, and religious pluralism.

Religious pluralists believe in toleration, the acceptance of all religious paths as equally valid, promoting coexistence. They believe in moral relativism, which is a view that moral judgments are true or false only relative to some particular standpoint, that there is no absolute truth, only the truths that a particular individual or culture happen to believe.

Paul warns us to beware of philosophy, of "isms." These beliefs have led to what some call the problem of "theological pluralism." In his article "Man and Knowledge: The Search for Truth in a Pluralistic Age," Winfried Vogel argues theological pluralism is not a viable option for Christians because of the following reasons:

- Its relativistic and nihilistic underpinnings set it in dia-metrical opposition to the biblical understanding of truth, which is presented as absolute and universal in time and space.

- Theological pluralism neglects to a large extent the miracu-lous working of the Holy Spirit, Who indeed can lead into all truth, and Who can unite human minds in one under-standing of truth.

- Theological pluralism does not honor the authority of Scripture as the final arbiter of all doctrine.

- Theological pluralism deprives any given community of faith the ability or willingness to differentiate between orthodoxy and heresy.

Worldly wisdom also tells us another way to determine what is true is ecclesiastical authority, a belief that my church is the ultimate authority, again, dangerously, based on human reason. All of the "isms" found today in our culture are man's attempt to understand the meaning of life. Each "ism" is an attempt by a human to explain the world around them. Because of each person's pride and arrogance, the "truths" espoused are suspect. If we are honest with ourselves, the meaning of life cannot be explained.

The complexity of life, the universe we see around us, is mind-boggling. Our brain cannot in any way perceive or answer the question, "How can this be?" Science tries to explain what we experience of our world through our five senses, but this experience is limited by our brain. What we expe-rience with our five senses is what God allows us to see of His creation. If we are truly honest with ourselves, we will admit this.

We need to remember He is all-powerful Creator God, who created us in His image. Our brains were not designed to comprehend the omni-science, omnipresence, and omnipotence of our triune God. Once we rec-ognize and admit this truth, then we will be able to praise Him, worship Him, and serve Him. It is through daily prayer, meditation, and study of

His Word, led by the Holy Spirit, that we learn how to do these things. God, because of His gifts to individuals and through His grace, allows scientists to learn some of the details of His creation, so they can make our temporary time on Earth better.

Postmodernism (secularism) has allowed human philosophy to infiltrate biblical truth, allowing Satan to deceive many in the world today. These human philosophies have corrupted many people's understanding of God's truth, causing many to doubt the validity and reliability of the Bible. Human philosophy doesn't even require you to know the truth.

A person with a secular worldview would say, "There is no such thing as absolute truth." To them, truth is viewed as being relative. They would say, "you have your truth, and I have mine, and neither of us has the right to declare our truth is the absolute truth."

Apathy is a stronger challenge to evangelism than atheism is. According to Kyle Idleman, "The nonchalant attitude toward God from many in today's world is probably more challenging to evangelism than religious pluralism, agnosticism, and atheism."

As Christians, how do we navigate our path to salvation through the chaotic, treacherous waters of our world in this age of science, tolerance, and compromise?

ILLUSTRATION

The following illustration concerning unbelief/atheism, is taken from Michael P. Green's book *1500 Illustrations for Biblical Preaching*:

> The atheist's dilemma is that when he feels very grateful and wants to give thanks, he has no one to give it to.

Barry Denzil Haney, MD

GODLY WISDOM

Godly wisdom tells us absolute truth can only be known from God through general revelation, found in His creation and special revelation, found in the Bible.

In the New Testament, Jesus is asked by Pilate, *"What is truth?"* from the very man who was truth, in the following passage found in John 18:37-38:

> Art thou a king then? Jesus answered, Thou sayest that I am a king. To this end was I born, and for this cause came I into the world, that I should bear witness unto the truth. Every one that is of the truth heareth my voice. Pilate saith unto him, What is truth? And when he had said this, he went out again unto the Jews, and saith unto them, I find in him no fault at all.

The following verses give us godly wisdom about absolute truth, written through John's quill, in the Gospel of John: "And the Word was made flesh, and dwelt among us, (and we beheld his glory, the glory as of the only begotten of the Father,) full of grace and truth" (John 1:14). "Jesus saith unto him, I am the way, the truth, and the life: no man cometh unto the Father, but by me" (John 14:6). "And ye shall know the truth, and the truth shall make you free" (John 8:32).

> Howbeit when he, the Spirit of truth, is come, he will guide you into all truth: for he shall not speak of himself; but whatsoever he shall hear, that shall he speak and he will shew you things to come.
>
> —John 16:13

Then spake Jesus again unto them, saying, I am the light of the world: he that followeth me shall not walk in darkness, but shall have the light of life. The Pharisees therefore said unto him, Thou bearest record of thyself; thy record is not true. Jesus answered and said unto them, Though I bear record of myself, yet my record is true: for I know whence I came, and whither I go; but ye cannot tell whence I come, and whither I go.

—John 8:12-14

And this is the condemnation, that light is come into the world, and men loved darkness rather than light, because their deeds were evil. For everyone that doeth evil hateth the light, neither cometh to the light, lest his deeds should be reproved. But he that doeth truth cometh to the light, that his deeds may be made manifest, that they are wrought in God.

—John 3:19-21

For God so loved the world, that he gave his only begotten Son, that whosoever believeth in him should not perish, but have everlasting life.For God sent not his Son into the world to condemn the world; but that the world through him might be saved.

—John 3:16-17

In these verses, the Bible tells us absolute truth can only be found in Jesus. Jesus is the subject. Scripture tells us that there is no other way to eternal salvation but through Jesus Christ, our Lord and Savior. We need to begin meditating daily on the Word of God.

Meditation means to allow the Holy Spirit to have control over our minds so that the Word will dominate our thinking. Time spent meditating on God's Word is time spent with Jesus. Many feel, and I do too; we are in the last days of this age. Jesus is coming soon, and we should be grateful, but we need to be vigilant because these are dangerous times. John tells us that Jesus is the Word. It is not sufficient to profess to be a recipient of Christ's saving work; our life should show it in what we do.

In today's world, many people are more than happy to tell you their interpretation of worldly events. But remember, that's just their interpretation. We do not have to believe what we read on the Internet. What we should be doing is reading the Bible daily and meditating about what we read daily.

Absolute truth is in the Bible. We need to remember, man's attempt to understand what the meaning of life is in a vain attempt to explain what is true, a human perspective marred by our pride and arrogance. If we want absolute truth, we need to study God's Word!

PRAYER

Our heavenly Father,

Thank You for being our Creator, for imagining us in Your dreams, then creating us in Your image. Thank You for allowing us to live in Your dreams, and help us to live our lives according to Your will. Thank You for the Holy Spirit who helps us understand and discover absolute truth found in the Bible.

Thank You for Your unchanging love. Thank You for Your mercy! Thank You for providing for us all our daily physical and spiritual needs.

Thank You for Your total provision in our walk to salvation You have planned for us. Thank You for protecting us.

Thank You for sending Your Son to walk among us, to show us how to live in holiness.

Thank You for Your free gift of salvation, granted to those who have faith in Your Son Jesus, who shed his blood on the cross at Calvary, to pay the penalty for our sins.

Thank You for Your immutable promise to us, that whoever believes in Your Son, will not perish, but have everlasting, eternal life, in a loving relationship with You.

Thank You for giving us Your wisdom, through Your inspired Word contained in the Bible, to teach us how to please You and to become more Holy while we reside here on Earth.

Thank You for the Holy Spirit, to guide us, to instruct us, and to protect us, and for giving us strength to withstand temptation as we travel along the road of salvation while we are here on Earth.

Thank You for the assurance that You will deliver us from our enemies. We honor as holy and sacred, Your name.

We ask that Your perfect will take place on Earth. We ask You forgive the wrong things we Have done, as we forgive those who have injured us.

We pray for protection, from all the things that trip us up and undo us. We thank You for, and ask for Your continual comfort, peace, and divine healing power, for those with both spoken and unspoken physical and spiritual needs.

In the precious name of Jesus Christ our Lord and Savior,

Amen.

CHAPTER 25

Beware of False Prophets!

This know also, that in the last days perilous times shall come. For men shall be lovers of their own selves, covetous, boasters, proud, blasphemers, disobedient to parents, unthankful, unholy, Without natural affection, trucebreakers, false accusers, incontinent, fierce, despisers of those that are good, Traitors, heady, highminded, lovers of pleasures more than lovers of God; Having a form of godliness but denying the power thereof: from such turn away. For of this sort are they which creep into houses, and lead captive silly women laden with sins, led away with divers lusts, Ever learning, and never able to come to the knowledge of the truth. Now as Jannes and Jambres withstood Moses, so do these also resist the truth: men of corrupt minds, reprobate concerning the faith.

—2 Timothy 3:1-8

WORLDLY WISDOM

In this passage, the Holy Spirit is teaching me, all of us will encounter religious imposters, false teachers, and when we do, we should flee from them!

The Cambridge Dictionary defines imposters in this way: "A person who pretends to be someone else in order to deceive others."

The Dictionary of Bible Themes defines false teachers in this way: "Those who teach error and in so doing lead others astray. They are to be distinguished from false prophets who are equally condemned in Scripture."

Many false prophets are found in the pages of the Bible.

In the Old Testament, the false prophets described include the pagan prophets claiming to speak on behalf of pagan gods such as the four hundred fifty prophets of Baal and the four hundred prophets of Asherah who served King Ahab and Queen Jezebel of Israel:

> Now therefore send, and gather to me all Israel unto mount
> Carmel, and the prophets of Baal four hundred and fifty,
> and the prophets of the groves four hundred, which eat at
> Jezebel's table. So Ahab sent unto all the children of Israel
> and gathered the prophets together unto mount Carmel.
>
> —1 Kings 18:19-20 (NKJV)

In 1 Kings 22:5-8, the Bible tells us about false prophets from Israel who claimed to speak on behalf of the true God, such as Zedekiah and the 400 prophets with him:

> And Jehoshaphat said unto the king of Israel, Inquire, I
> pray thee, at the word of the LORD today. Then the king
> of Israel gathered the prophets together, about four hundred
> men, and said unto them, Shall I go against Ramoth-gil-
> ead to battle, or shall I forbear? And they said, Go up; for
> the Lord shall deliver it into the hand of the king. And
> Jehoshaphat said, Is there not here a prophet of the LORD
> besides, that we might inquire of him? And the king of
> Israel said unto Jehoshaphat, There is yet one man, Micaiah
> the son of Imlah, by whom we may inquire of the LORD:
> but I hate him; for he doth not prophesy good concerning
> me, but evil. And the king of Israel said unto Jehoshaphat,

Barry Denzil Haney, MD

There is yet one man, Micaiah the son of Imlah, by whom
we may inquire of the LORD: but I hate him; for he
doth not prophesy good concerning me, but evil. And
Jehoshaphat said, Let not the king say so.

Other unnamed false prophets of Israel were condemned by the true
prophets Isaiah, Jeremiah, Ezekiel, and Micah.

False prophets are also found in the New Testament. In Matthew 7:15,
Matthew 24:11, and Matthew 24:24, Jesus warned about false prophets,
that false prophets would be numerous, and they would perform deceptive
miracles:

Beware of false prophets, which come to you in sheep's
clothing, but inwardly they are ravening wolves...And
many false prophets shall rise and shall deceive many...For
there shall arise false Christs, and false prophets, and shall
shew great signs and wonders; insomuch that, if it were
possible, they shall deceive the very elect.

The New Testament identifies three false prophets: Elymas the
magician (Acts 13:6-8); a woman called Jezebel (Revelation 2:20); and a
miracle-working false prophet (Revelation 13:11-18). John warned Christians that "many false prophets are gone out into the world" (1John 4:1).

In his book *Prophet Arise*, John Eckhardt compared false prophets to
true prophets in this way:

A part of the prophet's ministry is to discern the true from
the false. Prophets hate lies and deception.

- False prophets are greedy. True prophets hate greed.

- False prophets are covetous. True prophets hate covetousness.

- False prophets are abusive. True prophets hate abuse.

- False prophets are controlling. True prophets hate control.

- False prophets are arrogant. True prophets are humble.

- False prophets cannot produce good fruit. True prophets look for fruit.

- False prophets are deceptive. True prophets discern deception.

How do we recognize false prophets?

The best passage concerning false prophets in the Bible can be found in Jude 4-19 (MSG):

> What has happened is that some people have infiltrated our ranks (our Scriptures warned us this would happen), who beneath their pious skin are shameless scoundrels. Their design is to replace the sheer grace of our God with sheer license—which means doing away with Jesus Christ, our one and only Master. I'm laying this out as clearly as I can, even though you once knew all this well enough and shouldn't need reminding. Here it is in brief: The Master saved a people out of the land of Egypt. Later he destroyed those who defected.
>
> And you know the story of the angels who didn't stick to their post, abandoning it for other, darker missions. But they are now chained and jailed in a black hole until the great Judgment Day. Sodom and Gomorrah, which went to sexual rack and ruin along with the surrounding cities that acted just like them, are another example. Burning and burning and never burning up, they serve still as a stock warning. This is exactly the same program of these latest infiltrators: dirty sex, rule and rulers thrown out; glory dragged in the mud. The Archangel Michael, who went

Barry Denzil Haney, MD

to the mat with the Devil as they fought over the body of Moses, wouldn't have dared level him with a blasphemous curse, but said simply, "No you don't. God will take care of you!" But these people sneer at anything they can't understand, and by doing whatever they feel like doing—living by animal instinct only—they participate in their own destruction. I'm fed up with them! They've gone down Cain's road; they've been sucked into Balaam's error by greed; they're canceled out in Korah's rebellion. These people are warts on your love feasts as you worship and eat together. They're giving you a black eye—carousing shamelessly, grabbing anything that isn't nailed down. They're —Puffs of smoke pushed by gusts of wind; late autumn trees stripped clean of leaf and fruit, Doubly dead, pulled up by the roots; wild ocean waves leaving nothing on the beach but the foam of their shame; Lost stars in outer space on their way to the black hole. Enoch, the seventh after Adam, prophesied of them: "Look! The Master comes with thousands of holy angels to bring judgment against them all, convicting each person of every defiling act of shameless sacrilege, of every dirty word they have spewed of their pious filth." These are the "grumpers," the bellyachers, grabbing for the biggest piece of the pie, talking big, saying anything they think will get them ahead. But remember, dear friends, that the apostles of our Master, Jesus Christ, told us this would happen: "In the last days there will be people who don't take these things seriously anymore. They'll treat them like a joke and make a religion of their own whims and lusts." These are the ones who split churches, thinking only of themselves. There's nothing to them, no sign of the Spirit!

ILLUSTRATION

The following illustration concerning false doctrine, is taken from Michael P. Green's book *1500 Illustrations for Biblical Preaching*:

> In an examination at a Christian school, the teacher asked the following question: "What is false doctrine?"
>
> Up went a little boy's hand, and there came this answer: "It's when the doctor gives the wrong stuff to people who are sick."
>
> Although the little boy had obviously confused *doctrine* with *doctorin'*, he arrived at the correct definition.

GODLY WISDOM

What information does godly wisdom in the Bible give us about religious imposters?

In the passage 2 Timothy 3:1-9, Paul is warning us to avoid the religious imposters who were already infecting the church. He is warning believers to guard their hearts and home.

According to Paul, they are religious imposters whose primary identifying feature is misplaced love. He tells us they have the following characteristics: they love themselves; they love money; they are unloving; they love pleasure.

There are things we need to look for to identify false prophets: religious appearance without character; religious words without consent.

Paul warns us to turn away from them when we find them.

In the Life Commentary Application Bible, the authors list the following issues surrounding false teachers in 1 Timothy 1:3-11:

Barry Denzil Haney, MD

- False teachers taught what was wrong (1:3).

- False teachers engaged in trivial but divisive arguments (1:4)

- False teachers were more interested in controversy than in faithfully spreading the Gospel (1:4).

- False teachers had turned away from the personal evidence of God's presence in their lives and had taken up "meaning-less talk" instead (1:6).

- False teachers desired the position and prestige of teachers, but they had nothing of value to communicate (1:7).

- False teachers set the law and the Gospel against each other, although each has its own place in the plan of God (1:8-11).

In 2 Peter 2:1-3, Peter mentions the false teachers for the first time and describes their evil ways:

> But there were false prophets also among the people, even as there shall be false teachers among you, who privily shall bring in damnable heresies, even denying the Lord that bought them, and bring upon themselves swift destruction. And many shall follow their pernicious ways; by reason of whom the way of truth shall be evil spoken of. And through covetousness shall they with feigned words make merchandise of you: whose judgment now of a long time lingereth not, and their damnation slumbereth not.

In closing, The Bible warns us about false teachings in the last days in 1 Timothy 4:1-5 (NLV):

> The Holy Spirit tells us in plain words that in the last days some people will turn away from the faith. They will listen

to what is said about spirits and follow the teaching about demons. Those who teach this tell it as the truth when they know it is a lie. They do it so much that their own hearts no longer say it is wrong. They will say, "Do not get married. Do not eat some kinds of food." But God gave these things to Christians who know the truth. We are to thank God for them. Everything God made is good. We should not put anything aside if we can take it and thank God for it. It is made holy by the Word of God and prayer.

———————

PRAYER

Our heavenly Father,

God turned away from Jesus, when He took on the sins of the world, just as He turns away from us because we are sinners. But the good news is, because He loves us so much, and through His grace, He gave His only begotten Son, to shed His blood on the cross, to die to pay the penalty for our sins, so we can receive the free gift of salvation, and spend an eternity, in a loving relationship with our Creator. As He intended it to be when He created us.

Martin Lloyd Jones said it most simply when he defined revival as, "…days of Heaven upon the earth." Father, we ask for continued revival in each of us, renew our minds so we can do Your will. We ask for continued revival in Your Church, so we as a church can participate in the works of Your church to make disciples of all men by spreading the Good News of the Gospel! We ask for an outpouring of the

Holy Spirit in Your church, so Your will may be done on earth.

We ask that the heart of each member of Your church be touched by the Holy Spirit about the financial needs of your Church, needed to complete Your plan of salvation for the world.

We pray each of us might serve as a beacon of light to the world and provide a means for the Holy Spirit to work in the hearts of the unsaved, so they too might have an eternal relationship with You, in heaven.

In the precious name of Jesus Christ our Lord and Savior,

Amen.

CHAPTER 26

What Causes Cruelty?

"For from within, out of the heart of men, proceed evil thoughts, adulteries, fornications, murders, Thefts, covetousness, wickedness, deceit, lasciviousness, an evil eye, blasphemy, pride, foolishness: All these evil things come from within, and defile the man."

—Mark 7:21-23

———————

WORLDLY WISDOM

In this passage, the Holy Spirit is teaching me about things that can hurt us, things that come from us, not from outside us. The Holy Spirit is warning all of us we choose what to let into our hearts and what we let come back out of us. This defines us. The Holy Spirit is warning us to be careful, so who we become will be the person we want to present to God on judgment day!

The Cambridge Dictionary defines cruelty in this way: "The act of being extremely unkind and unpleasant and causing pain to people or animals intentionally."

The Merriam-Webster Dictionary defines cruelty in the following ways: "The quality or state of being cruel; a cruel action; inhuman treatment; marital conduct held (as in a divorce action) to endanger life or health or to cause mental suffering or fear."

MY PERSONAL EXPERIENCE: FIRECRACKERS & BABY BIRDS!

The word cruelty reminds me of this *tragic* childhood story:

When I was around eight years old, my father bought firecrackers on the fourth of July. I can vividly remember my dad lighting the fuse on the pack of firecrackers, watching the sparking fuse move rapidly toward the bundled firecrackers, then the glorious bombardment as the firecrackers ignited. Their powder sparking bright, their machine-gun burst; the loudest noise I had ever heard!

I remember my father's warning not to light the fuse on a pack of firecrackers without his supervision, but, somehow, as I slipped a pack of firecrackers into my pants pocket, the temptation to be my own man, buried that warning deep in my subconscious brain.

The next morning, after my father went to work, I asked my mother if I could go outside to play. She said okay, but not to wander too far from the house. Before I left my bedroom, I had put the pack of firecrackers in my pants pocket, along with a book of matches I found in a kitchen drawer. I ran to a group of trees in the backyard.

In a low-lying tree, I heard the sound of chirping birds. On a low-lying branch, I saw a small nest containing two small baby birds, chirping frantically, moving their heads from side to side, with their mouths wide open, waiting for their mother to bring them food! I remember thinking how helpless they seemed.

But then, I'm not sure what happened!

My thoughts seemed to be controlled as I started thinking about the glorious bombardment of the firecrackers I witnessed the day before.

I slowly reached into my pants pocket, took out the firecrackers, lit the fuse—remembered the warning of my father not to light the firecrackers without his supervision—and quickly threw the bundle of lit firecrackers toward the branch of the tree. The bundle of firecrackers exploded, their powder sparking bright, their machine-gun burst, the second loudest noise I had ever heard—but to my horror, the two little birds in the nest were motionless and bloody; the firecrackers had hit the nest!

In shock, I remember trying to revive the little birds, then running home to my house, sobbing in my bedroom. For many days, I was sad and wondered why I could have been so stupid to have thrown that bundle of firecrackers toward the nest, why I lit that bundle of firecrackers without my father's supervision. I never told my parents or anyone else about this incident.

I buried it in my memory, only to surface now, as I write this chapter about cruelty. I hope these birds are now in heaven, and I am given a chance to tell them; I'm so sorry!

How can man be so cruel? Can we discover a "cruel center" in our brain, then surgically remove that center to eliminate cruelty in this world?

Isn't it funny, the human brain? We can study the brain using tools such as microscopy, gross anatomy, MRI, intra-operative electrode manipulation, EEG, and other man-made tools. Through histology, pathology, MRI studies, and other means, we think we understand the human brain or at least in the future will understand the human brain.

Non-believers think the human brain is an organic representation of a supercomputer. They think the human brain, the small human brain, can comprehend the omniscience and omnipotence of the creator God. How vain we are! How proud and arrogant we are. Because no matter how much we study the human brain, we will never be able to scientifically explain why cruelty exists in the world.

Sigmund Freud believed cruelty is the result of a mix of sexual desire and aggression, which have biological bases and are part of human nature. He thought we all have the possibility of acting on the impulses to cause pain to other human beings, and it was the responsibility of parents to teach their children to control these natural impulses.

Heinz Kohut, in the 1970s, developed a theory called "Self-Psychology." He believed aggression against another person is always psychologically motivated. He thought anger, hate, and rage happens when a person feels he or she is not being understood or accepted by someone important to them. When this happens, a person becomes unglued; they lose themselves.

Christopher Bollas, a British psychoanalyst, believes beneath hatred and hateful behavior lies a sense of emptiness, a void.

Ruth Stein has written about terrorists who kill others in the name of their god. She theorizes these people idealize a supreme being in order to undo their own self-hatred.

In November 2011, Robert Champion, a Florida A&M band student, died after his fellow band members allegedly beat him brutally as part of a tradition of hazing.

In an issue of *The Chronicle of Higher Education* dated February 17, 2012, the headline of the article "After a Death, A Question: Are Students Hard-wired for Hazing?" Implied students, in fact, all humans are hard-wired for acts of cruelty toward our fellow man.

In *Zero Degrees of Empathy: A New Theory of Human Cruelty,* Baron-Cohen tells us brain science can help us understand why some people are evil. He believes cruelty is due to lack of empathy, empathy exists in a measurable quantity, and empathy is due to a state of the "empathy circuit" in the brain.

Some in today's world promote the idea human nature is hard-wired by evolution into the human brain and, like Baron-Cohen, in the "empathy circuit." Those who promote this idea use this for both acts of kindness and cruelty, depending on who's doing the writing.

I do not believe human nature is impervious to change or that human nature is genetically set to make us behave in certain ways.

GODLY WISDOM

What does God say about cruelty and how we can conquer cruelty while we are here on earth? In his book *Evil and the Justice of God,* N. T. Wright says this:

> The heady combination of technological achievement, medical advances, Romantic pantheism, Hegelian progressive Idealism, and social Darwinism created a climate of thought...certain things are now to be expected... we envisage a steady march towards freedom and justice, conceived...in Western-style liberal democracy and soft versions of socialism...now that we're living in the twenty-first century...progress has become the single most important measuring rod in society and culture.

Since worldly wisdom seems to promote the doctrine of progress, moving towards a better, fuller, more perfect end, and this justifies the suffering, the cruelty humans inflict on others along the way, then what right do we have to demand the end of evil, cruelty in our world today?

Godly wisdom gives us this right!

The entire book of Job tells a story about what God is doing about evil. Twentieth-century Christian thought concerns the role of faith in Jesus, rescuing people from the evil world, ensuring them forgiveness, and promising them the reward of an eternal relationship with God in heaven.

In the passage John 7:19-24, Jesus talks about cruelty and how it is dishonoring:

> Did not Moses give you the law, and yet none of you
> keepeth the law? Why go ye about to kill me? The people
> answered and said, Thou hast a devil: who goeth about to
> kill thee? Jesus answered and said unto them, I have done
> one work, and ye all marvel. Moses therefore gave unto
> you circumcision; (not because it is of Moses, but of the
> fathers;) and ye on the sabbath day circumcise a man. If a
> man on the sabbath day receive circumcision, that the law
> of Moses should not be broken; are ye angry at me, because
> I have made a man every whit whole on the sabbath day?
> Judge not according to the appearance but judge righteous
> judgment.

In this encounter, Jesus knew the evil intentions of those who not only wanted to stop His ministry but wanted to kill Him. He answers quickly the veiled cruelty of the people and their dishonoring of Him. The Holy Spirit is telling us that sin, when unchecked, leads to cruelty. Cruel words lead to cruel, sinful deeds. I have spent my entire life trying to control, understand and make sense of the universe I experience through my five senses. I have filled my senses and my brain with knowledge gained through study.

I have studied the greatest philosophers, great religious leaders, great political leaders, and others in university settings. The knowledge I have gained has been substantial. Although I cannot remember many of the things I have learned, I am still searching for what life is all about. My search ended when I finally realized that worldly wisdom cannot answer questions of evil, questions of sin, like cruelty.

Barry Denzil Haney, MD

Because we were created by God to have a relationship with him, sin has created a separation from God which we experience as a void in our heart. We spend most of our lives trying to fill this void, this emptiness in our heart, with earthly pleasures.

Moral relativism teaches, whatever is good for you is good. Moral relativism does not believe in absolute truth. However, we are born with a sense of right and wrong, the absolute truth of God, placed in us by God at our conception.

I will conclude this chapter on cruelty with the following illustration taken from a sermon by Adrian Rogers *The Sixth Commandment: Thou Shall Not Kill*:

> The Chinese used to have a torture, the Chinese water torture. They would put an individual, tie him beneath a reservoir where there would be a constant dropping of water—constant, constant, constant—until, finally, the nervous system would explode with a devastating explosion. And death would result, not from one severe blow, but from the constant, constant, constant, constant drip, drip, drip, drip. Murder by cruelty—murder by cruelty.

PRAYER

Our heavenly Father,

Why do evil thoughts proceed out of men's hearts? Do we have a cruelty center in our brain where Satan resides? My God, some atheists believe the human brain is hard-wired with an "empathy circuit" where both acts of kindness and cruelty are imagined! But the Holy Spirit has instructed me this is not true. We are not genetically set to behave in certain ways, instead, we have free choice!

Father, thank You for giving us the gift of free will! You have offered us hope through faith in Your son Jesus! By faith in Jesus, we are rescued from the evil world. Because You are immutable, You have promised us forgiveness! You have promised us the reward of Eternal relationship with God in heaven!

In the precious name of Jesus Christ our Lord and Savior,

Amen!

Barry Denzil Haney, MD

CHAPTER 27

Greed!

"For the love of money is the root of all evil: which while some coveted after, they have erred from the faith, and pierced themselves through with many sorrows."

—1 Timothy 6:10

WORLDLY WISDOM

In this passage, the Holy Spirit is telling me to beware of placing anything above Jesus in our everyday lives. He is telling us once we have faith in

Jesus, He will help us remove all forms of evil, keeping us from doing His will for our life.

The Cambridge Dictionary defines greed in this way: "A strong desire to continually get more of something, especially money."

The Dictionary of Bible Themes defines greed in this way: "An excessive appetite for further goods or food, often linked to selfishness and gluttony."

Man's obsession with money has been recorded in many volumes of text. Even today, those who would call themselves Christians, those who minister to others in the name of Jesus, have been tempted by the lure of money.

For instance, the media has asked the following questions about prominent evangelists: was it not greed that caused a prominent evangelist to recently give an expensive car to his wife as an anniversary present?; was it not greed when a prominent evangelist ask his supporters to give money to buy another multimillion-dollar jet in the pretense to reach the unsaved?; was it not greed when a prominent evangelist, allegedly spent and acquired, according to the St. Louis Post-Dispatch in 2003, a multimillion-dollar corporate jet, a six-figure silver-gray Mercedes sedan, her two million dollar home and houses worth another two million for her four children, a twenty million dollar headquarters, furnished with over five million dollars worth of furniture, artwork, glassware, and the latest equipment and machinery, while still asking her viewers for their support?; was it not greed, when another prominent evangelist, asked for donations from his supporters, to buy a another multimillion-dollar jet in the pretense to reach the unsaved?

Although I don't know the answer to these questions, each person will have to justify what decisions they make concerning monetary matters during their lifetime, during the Great White Throne Judgement.

I would say this; when discussing questions concerning money, each person needs to pray to God and ask for protection by the Holy Spirit from Satan's deception. Satan can insert his tentacles into the soul of each man or woman, Christian and non-Christian alike, convincing them it is okay to give in to the temptation of the lure of money. For Christians, if the secular world perceives that you might be misusing money, Satan will allow this information to discredit you in the eyes of the unsaved, Satan convincing them to turn away from God and follow him!

According to worldly wisdom, money is a big thing! Throughout history, man has lusted after money. Whatever the other reasons for war might be, there is almost always an economic motive underlying most conflicts, usually based on one country's wish to take control of another's wealth. Since ancient times, man has lusted after another man's possessions, especially any money or wealth he has accumulated.

Not much has changed over the years. Today, people have different attitudes about money based on their personal interests and societal influences. Nevertheless, money, for many in today's secular world, is a personal "god" they worship. Money is something to seek out, to accumulate with the end goal to become more and more wealthy and to use the money accumulated for personal pleasure and enjoyment. This lure of money has its root in mankind's natural state of selfishness. In the *Workers Bulletin*, dated 1902, the following insightful, applicable quote about selfishness can be found:

> The sowing of seeds of selfishness in the human heart was the first result of the entrance of sin into the world. God desires everyone to understand the evil of selfishness, and to cooperate with Him in guarding the human family against its terrible, deceptive powers.

In his book *Systematic Theology*, Augustus Strong says this about sin as selfishness:

> We hold the essential principle of sin to be selfishness. By selfishness we mean not simply the exaggerated self-love which constitutes the antithesis of benevolence, but that choice of self as the supreme end which constitutes the antithesis of supreme love to God.

In today's world, many times selfishness raises its ugly head in marriages. In his article "Counseling Hispanics," Luis Villareal makes this observation about selfishness in marriage:

> Allegations of selfishness within marriage usually arise when one partner feels neglected or not listened to. If his spouse constantly insists on having her own way and refuses to allow the offended spouse to express his viewpoint, accusations of selfishness will soon emerge.

In the final analysis, selfishness is "the lack or opposite of biblical love" (Lou Priolo, *"Selfishness: Helping People with the Mother of All Sins"*).

The attitude of many in today's world can be summed up in this verse from Abba's hit tune in the '70s "Money Money Money."

> *In my dreams I have a plan*
> *If I got me a wealthy man*
> *I wouldn't have to work at all*
> *I'd fool around and have a ball*
>
> *Money, money, money*
> *Must be funny*
> *In the rich man's world*
>
> *Money, money, money*
> *Always sunny*
> *In the rich man's world*

Modern man has believed Satan's lies concerning money. Satan tells us money will give us security, power, privilege, social standing, success, love, attention, peace of mind, freedom from consequences, and happiness. Man falls for Satan's deception because many of these things seem true at first glance, but they are fleeting and, in the long run, unsatisfying.

Barry Denzil Haney, MD

ILLUSTRATION

The following illustration concerning greed is taken from Michael P. Green's book *1500 Illustrations for Biblical Preaching*:

> A little girl accompanied her mother to the country store where, after the mother had made a purchase, the clerk invited the child to help herself to a handful of candy. The youngster held back. "What's the matter? Don't you like candy?" asked the clerk.
>
> The child nodded, and the clerk smilingly put his hand into the jar and dropped a generous portion into the little girl's handbag.
>
> Afterward, the mother asked her daughter why she had not taken the candy when the clerk first offered some to her. "Because his hand was bigger than mine," replied the little girl.

GODLY WISDOM

What does godly wisdom tell us about money?

Money is a small thing to God. What concerns God is what we do with money. Despite what we might think, money is a gift from God. God is concerned with our stewardship of what he has entrusted to us.

In Matthew 6:19-21, Jesus tells us to invest in the kingdom of God:

Lay not up for yourselves treasures upon earth, where moth
and rust doth corrupt, and where thieves break through and
steal: But lay up for yourselves treasures in heaven, where
neither moth nor rust doth corrupt, and where thieves do
not break through nor steal: For where your treasure is,
there will your heart be also.

When we consider what to do with God's gift of money, we need to
base it on what the Bible says. In general, the Bible tells us the guidelines
about money: money is a corrupting influence; we should avoid it; money
should be given away; possessions should be minimal; spending on yourself
should be only for basic needs; a sign of holiness is poverty.

Although God is the owner of money, he has made us managers. The
Bible gives us this instruction, in Proverbs 3:9-10, concerning the manage-
ment of money: "Honour the LORD with thy substance, And with the
first fruits of all thine increase: So shall thy barns be filled with plenty, And
thy presses shall burst out with new wine."

In Matthew 25:23, the Holy Spirit tells us God will reward us if we
manage the money God has given us wisely: "His lord said unto him, Well
done, good and faithful servant; thou hast been faithful over a few things, I
will make thee ruler over many things: enter thou into the joy of thy lord."

The Holy Spirit also tells us God will bless those who give to the needy,
in Deuteronomy 15:10: "Thou shalt surely give him, and thine heart shall
not be grieved when thou givest unto him: because that for this thing the
LORD thy God shall bless thee in all thy works, and in all that thou puttest
thine hand unto."

Billy Graham said, "Give me five minutes with a person's checkbook,
and I will tell you where their heart is."

In Luke 12:48, the Bible tells us this:

But he that knew not, and did commit things worthy of
stripes, shall be beaten with few stripes. For unto whomso-
ever much is given, of him shall be much required: and to

Barry Denzil Haney, MD

whom men have committed much, of him they will ask the more.

God has entrusted us to manage money, and if we do this wisely, he will bless us as the Bible tells us in 2 Corinthians 9:6-11:

> But this I say, He which soweth sparingly shall reap also sparingly; and he which soweth bountifully shall reap also bountifully. Every man according as he purposeth in his heart, so let him give; not grudgingly, or of necessity: for God loveth a cheerful giver. And God is able to make all grace abound toward you; that ye, always having all sufficiency in all things, may abound to every good work: (As it is written, He hath dispersed abroad; he hath given to the poor: his righteousness remaineth forever. Now he that ministereth seed to the sower both minister bread for your food, and multiply your seed sown, and increase the fruits of your righteousness;) Being enriched in everything to all bountifulness, which causeth through us thanksgiving to God.

When we allow money to become an idol, our lives are corrupted. When this happens, greed enters the picture. Greed is condemned by Scripture as contrary to the purposes of God. Greed is a feature of the fallen world seen in the following passages: "For the wicked boasteth of his heart's desire, And blesseth the covetous, whom the LORD abhorreth" (Psalm 10:3).

> Being filled with all unrighteousness, fornication, wickedness, covetousness, maliciousness; full of envy, murder, debate, deceit, malignity; whisperers, Backbiters, haters of God, despiteful, proud, boasters, inventors of evil things, disobedient to parents, Without understanding, covenant

breakers, without natural affection, implacable, unmerciful: Who knowing the judgment of God, that they which commit such things are worthy of death, not only do the same, but have pleasure in them that do them.

—Romans 1:29-32

Greed is also an expression of a sinful human nature, as seen in the following passages:

For from within, out of the heart of men, proceed evil thoughts, adulteries, fornications, murders, Thefts, covetousness, wickedness, deceit, lasciviousness, an evil eye, blasphemy, pride, foolishness: All these evil things come from within, and defile the man.

—Mark 7:21-23

"For tout of the heart proceed evil thoughts, murders, adulteries, fornications, thefts, false witness, blasphemies: These are the things which defile a man: but to eat with unwashen hands defileth not a man."

—Matthew 15:19-20

The lure of money ultimately leads to destruction. The Bible gives us this warning about the love of money in this passage, 1 Timothy 6:9-10:

But they that will be rich fall into temptation and a snare, and into many foolish and hurtful lusts, which drown men in destruction and perdition. For the love of money is the root of all evil: which while some coveted after, they have erred from the faith, and pierced themselves through with many sorrows.

Barry Denzil Haney, MD

In conclusion, what should we do with the money God has entrusted to us to manage?

In 1 John 3:16-18, John tells us we should give, and that giving comes from love:

> Hereby perceive we the love of God, because he laid down his life for us: and we ought to lay down our lives for the brethren. But whoso hath this world's good, and seeth his brother have need, and shutteth up his bowels of compassion from him, how dwelleth the love of God in him? My little children, let us not love in word, neither in tongue; but in deed and in truth.

PRAYER

Our heavenly Father,

I pray for a great revival, an outpouring of the Holy Spirit throughout the world! I pray for all those who are unsaved, will be saved; I pray for an outpouring of God's unconditional love throughout the world!

I pray for an acknowledgment by all God's people, what they are really searching for is an intimate, personal relationship with our Creator God; I pray for the presence of God in their hearts!

I pray the absolute truths of God would flow through each of us, and be instilled in us, and be brought forth into our conscious mind; I pray for an outpouring of the Holy Spirit, to allow the unsaved to accept Jesus Christ as their personal Savior!

Then, by doing this, they too, might spend an eternity with God! Then, they too, will have hope, because of the promise of an eternal relationship with You! I pray for the Holy Spirit's presence in the daily lives of each believer!

To guide, instruct, teach, and protect each believer, helping them during their walk of progressive sanctification, during their walk of being made more Christ-like, during their walk of being made more holy, while here on Earth!

In the precious name of Jesus Christ our Lord and Savior,

Amen!

Barry Denzil Haney, MD

CHAPTER 28

One Day...
Making Memories!

And I said, This is my infirmity: But I will remember the years of the right hand of the most High. I will remember the works of the LORD: Surely I will remember thy wonders of old. I will meditate also of all thy work and talk of thy doings. Thy way, O God, is in the sanctuary: Who is so great a God as our God? Thou art the God that doest wonders: Thou hast declared thy strength among the people.

—Psalm 77:10-14

WORLDLY WISDOM

In Psalm 77, the Holy Spirit is teaching me not to let our emotions govern how we think because our feelings often can narrow our thinking, limiting all the facts we consider when making choices.

Instead, if we let godly wisdom govern how we think, our vision is no longer restricted by our emotions, and we will see things based on absolute truths instead of worldly truths.

The Cambridge Dictionary defines memory in this way:

The ability to remember things; something that you remember from the past; the ability to remember information, experiences, and people; the part of a computer in which information or programs are stored either permanently or temporarily, or the amount of space available on it for storying information.

MY PERSONAL EXPERIENCE: LOST MEMORIES!

In the summer of 2019, Judy and I planned three trips for December 2019, January 2020, and June 2020, with the intention of creating "memories." Unfortunately, in December 2019, Judy and I were forced to cancel the trips to Israel and Germany because of my health concerns. In addition, the pandemic caused by the Covid virus wreaked havoc on travel.

On that same day, we decided, even though we were going to Breckenridge, Colorado for Christmas, to spend the holiday with our three daughters, our three sons-in-law, and our six grandchildren, we decided to put up the Christmas decorations in our home, so our two grandchildren living in Georgetown, could enjoy the ambiance of Christmas, through the decorations displayed in our home, creating another "precious memory."

While putting up the decorations, I realized the joy I had missed over the years, not sharing this experience of putting up the decorations with my wife during past Christmases. In the past, I normally would get the boxes out of storage, then let her do most of the decorating. Oh, how much I miss not sharing these precious moments with my wife in the past!

The events of the day brought back both good and bad memories about past Christmases, bad memories concerning those times I didn't decorate with Judy. I hope this is the start of a new relationship we will carry into the future. During our Breckinridge vacation, we created many special memories the family will share for years.

What does science tell us about memory?

Neuroscientists tell us memory is a physical fact of the brain. They describe memory as a complex multistep, multifactorial process that involves the entire brain. This complex process cannot be explained in this short book, but I will give you a short "mini-course" about this topic.

Most neuroanatomists describe the brain as having four outer lobes, called the frontal, parietal, occipital, and temporal lobes. The cerebellum is located at the base of the brain and is responsible for the regulation and control of coordinated movement, posture, and balance.

Deep inside the brain is a fifth lobe, known by some as the limbic system. There are two important structures in the limbic system that help the brain process information and develop memory. One structure is called the hippocampus, a structure like a library, where information the brain receives and learns is collected, cataloged, and filed. The second structure is called the amygdala, a structure, like a relay station, responsible for screening information received to determine if it is emotionally important for long-term storage. Think of the hippocampus as the place telling you who someone is, and the amygdala as the place telling you how to feel about the person.

How do we receive information the brain uses to process information and develop memory?

We receive information into our brains through our five senses. The information obtained from four of these (visual, taste, touch, and hearing) is connected via neural pathways, first filtered through the brainstem, then relayed to the thalamus. The thalamus is located centrally and plays a significant role acting as a relay station for many sensory and motor signals. In addition, the thalamus acts as a detection center for pain and has an important role in sleep.

The fifth sense of smell differs anatomically from the rest. The sense of smell's neural connection is direct, through receptors located in the nose, to the olfactory nerve, which directly connects to the amygdala and olfactory cortex, bypassing the thalamus.

How is this sensory information transmitted to the appropriate parts of the brain where it can be processed?

This information is transmitted through specialized nerve cells called neurons. A neuron is an electrically excitable cell. It transmits information by electrochemical signals via connections with other cells. Neuroanatomists estimate this transmission takes place approximately two hundred times a second. Neuroanatomists also estimate the human brain has more than one hundred billion neurons and between five hundred trillion and one quadrillion synapses.

Although transmission within the neuron is electrical, transmission between neurons is chemical. The chemicals involved are called neurotransmitters. Over sixty neurotransmitters have been identified. Neurotransmitters allow information to cross the synaptic gap between neurons, measuring approximately .02 microns.

Other important concepts, too lengthy to discuss in this chapter, include the following:

- Neurotransmitters can be affected negatively by external stimuli; stress, especially chronic stress, can affect the entire process of learning and memory through the production of neurotransmitters like cortisol, which inhibit neurotransmitters in the brain, resulting in a vicious cycle, negatively affecting learning and memory;
- Learning appears to rewire the brain; the frontal cortex is involved in the interaction of emotions with memory;

- There are two aspects of memory, retrieval, and storage;

- There are five pathways our brains use to locate memory stored in our brain;

- There are three different types of memory, sensory memory, short term memory, and long term memory;

- Sensory and short-term memory are fleeting, lasting less than a minute; long-term memory lasts a lifetime.

In her article "How the Brain Works," Holly Inglis, Joseph LeDoux, a researcher at the State University of New York at Stony Brook, believes this about how the brain processes information and stores it as memory:

> The frontal cortex is involved in the process of feelings and actually does a detailed analysis of the information, bringing in information from many parts of the brain to make an "informed" decision, which is then sent back to the amygdala, either affirming or quelling the initial response called for by the amygdala. Once the situation has been assessed and your brain figures out that it is indeed a stick and not a snake, then the amygdala is informed to stand down; no running is necessary.

In her article "How the Brain Works," Holly Inglis tells us this about the brain's pathway to store long term memory:

> Information about events, experiences, facts, and concepts is received by different parts of the brain. These bits of information, decoded by the various sensory areas of the cortex, get routed through the hippocampus, the reference librarian, which triggers the search for prior matching information. The hippocampus knows where the previously stored information is located, retrieves it, and shuttles

it, along with the new information, back into temporary storage areas in each lobe to be examined. If the prior information connects to the new information, it is sent to the working memory in the prefrontal cortex. Unless it gets distracted, working memory will continue to sort and sift the old and new material, provided the prefrontal cortex judges it to be relevant, interesting, significant, and worth our attention. Because of our prior knowledge, our attention, or interest, the new information may be added to the old and form a stronger memory. Every time this process is repeated, the hippocampus strengthens the associations. With enough repetitions, it no longer has to work as hard to solidify the connection because the synaptic connections have been reinforced. The cortex, where the hippocampus sends the strengthened information, has "learned" to make its own associations. This process may have to be repeated several times before long-term memory is actually formed. If emotion or feelings are associated with the sensory input, then the amygdala declares that the information will definitely be remembered and trumps all other forms of memory. Just remember, if something distracts you in the midst of this process, or you lose interest or are doing too many things at one time, the information can disappear from working memory, and you will need to start all over again. It's a wonder we ever remember anything at all!

She goes on to say, according to studies at Northwestern University, your memories change each and every time you recall them, implying serious legal implications.

So, what does this rather lengthy neurosciences review of memory tell us?

Worldly wisdom, based on human memory, is flawed and limited. As humans, we will never be able to fully comprehend the mind of God. But, because we were created in His image, we can use godly wisdom to help us during our life journey.

GODLY WISDOM

God gave us the beautiful gift of memory! I often find myself reminiscing about the good times, the good memories I created with families and friends. But, sometimes, the memories are about the bad times, about the times I would rather not remember, because of mistakes I had made.

What does the Bible say about memory?

In Luke 2:41-51, Luke tells us Mary kept this particular story about Jesus in her heart:

> Now his parents went to Jerusalem every year at the feast of
> the Passover. And when he was twelve years old, they went
> up to Jerusalem after the custom of the feast. And when
> they had fulfilled the days, as they returned, the child Jesus
> tarried behind in Jerusalem; and Joseph and his mother
> knew not of it. But they, supposing him to have been in the
> company, went a day's journey; and they sought him among
> their kinsfolk and acquaintance. And when they found him
> not, they turned back again to Jerusalem, seeking him. And
> it came to pass, that after three days they found him in the

temple, sitting in the midst of the doctors, both hearing them, and asking them questions. And all that heard him were astonished at his understanding and answers. And when they saw him, they were amazed: and his mother said unto him, Son, why hast thou thus dealt with us? behold, thy father and I have sought thee sorrowing. And he said unto them, How is it that ye sought me? wist ye not that I must be about my Father's business?

And they understood not the saying which he spake unto them. And he went down with them, and came to Nazareth, and was subject unto them: but his mother kept all these sayings in her heart.

The Bible is hinting; we should treasure the events that take place during our walk with Jesus, not only the good times but the bad because the bad times can also be used by God to glorify His kingdom.

I am so thankful each day when I remember what God has done for me. Because of His grace, I am saved through my faith in Jesus, reminding me of His love, His faithfulness, and His goodness.

In 1 Peter 1:10-12, Peter is confirming this concept by referring that salvation is available only by God's grace through the faith of those who believe, found in Paul's writings in Ephesians 2:8-9:

Of which salvation the prophets have inquired and searched diligently, who prophesied of the grace that should come unto you: Searching what, or what manner of time the Spirit of Christ, which was in them did signify, when it testified beforehand the sufferings of Christ, and the glory that should follow. Unto whom it was revealed, that not unto themselves, but unto us they did minister the things, which are now reported unto you by them that have preached the gospel unto you with the Holy Ghost sent down from heaven; which things the angels desire to look into.

Barry Denzil Haney, MD

In the final analysis, we should always remember, we will be just a memory. Therefore, we should strive to be the best we can be, always trying to please Jesus in everything we do. Then, we will be an encouragement and inspiration to others.

In Philippians 3:13-14, Paul says this:

> Brethren, I count not myself to have apprehended: but this one thing I do, forgetting those things which are behind, and reaching forth unto those things which are before, I press toward the mark for the prize of the high calling of God in Christ Jesus.

Finally, Jesus tells us in John 14:16, Jesus is all we need! "Jesus saith unto him, I am the way, the truth, and the life: no man cometh unto the Father, but by me."

PRAYER

Our heavenly Father,

We look forward to the day when You come back, and we are gathered up into the cloud with You, to be united with You, to sit at the right hand of God in heaven.

We also realize that day will be a sad day for You, because as You have told us in Your Word, many will choose not to follow You, but will instead choose to be eternally separated from You.

Oh, I pray that each person will have a renewal of their mind and see the light. I pray You will become the light in the darkness, so they will not spend an eternity in the dark, cold, place of nothingness, called hell.

I pray they will not be the baby crying out in the dark for help in a black place of nothingness, where no relationship is possible, no intimacy exists, no stimulation exists, nothingness prevails for an eternity.

Thank You for the hope that You have given me. I know my spirit will be with You in heaven for an eternity. I bow down before You in praise and worship; You are the Alpha and the Omega. Thank You for imagining me in Your dreams.

In the precious name of Jesus Christ, our Lord and Savior,

Amen.

CHAPTER 29

Sweet, Sweet Music!

Praise ye the Lord. Praise God in his sanctuary: Praise him in the firmament of his power. Praise him for his mighty acts: Praise him according to his excellent greatness. Praise him with the sound of the trumpet: Praise him with the psaltery and harp. Praise him with the timbrel and dance: Praise him with stringed instruments and organs. Praise him upon the loud cymbals: Praise him upon the high-sounding cymbals. Let everything that hath breath praise the Lord. Praise ye the Lord.

—Psalm 150:1-6

"For the time past of our life may suffice us to have wrought the will of the Gentiles, when we walked in lasciviousness,

lusts, excess of wine, revellings, banquetings, and abomina-
ble idolatries."

—1 Peter 4:3

WORLDLY WISDOM

Psalm 150 has been called "the shortest possible primer on what it means
to praise God."

In six short verses, the Holy Spirit tells us where to praise the Lord, why
to praise the Lord, how to praise the Lord, and finally, who should praise
the Lord.

The Holy Spirit is describing both earthly and heavenly praise and is
worthy of praise every single day!

Psalm 150 also implies it doesn't matter what we use to praise God;
we are free to praise Him in any way we want and commands all of God's
creation to praise the Lord, including the creatures He created.

The Cambridge Dictionary defines praise in this way: "To honor,
worship, and express admiration for (God or a god)."

Although David in Psalm 150 is describing praising God through
mediums such as music, in this section of worldly wisdom, I will concentrate on the concept of idolatry, used by many in the secular world as a
poor substitute for the praise to God David speaks of.

In 1 Peter 4:3, the Holy Spirit is telling me in order to walk the narrow
path with Jesus as our focus, we must suffer and reject those things in
the past we used to fill the void in our heart, those things we worshiped,
idolized as our god. Only then will we be able to stay on the narrow path
to heaven to spend an eternity with God!

The Dictionary of Bible themes defines idolatry in this way: "The
worship or adoration of anyone or anything other than the LORD God;

idolatry includes the worship of other gods, such as those of the nation's surrounding Israel, images or idols and the creation itself."

IDOLATRY

Before discussing music, I will discuss idolatry and its importance to non-Christians.

When did idolatry begin? When did humankind begin to honor, worship, and express admiration for a god or object?

The first signs of religious practices date back to the Upper Paleolithic Period (about 40,000 years ago).

During that period, archaeological digs have uncovered burial sites containing carved figurines, suggesting that early man worshipped idols.

The earliest, so-called Venus figurine, is a statuette portraying a woman. They have been unearthed in Europe but have been found as far away as Siberia, distributed across much of Eurasia.

Archaeological evidence from the islands of the Aegean Sea has yielded Cycladic figures from the fourth and third millennium BC. Cycladic figures were produced by the Cycladic culture, which flourished in the islands of the Aegean Sea from 3300 to 1100 BCE.

Idols from the Indus Valley Civilization have been unearthed, with the figures in the namaste posture, a customary Hindu greeting, given in a slight bow, hands pressed together, palms touching and fingers pointing upwards, thumbs close to the chest.

Older petroglyphs (images created by removing part of a rock surface by incising, picking, carving, or abrading, as a form of rock art) have been discovered, some dating back 40,000 years.

The ancient philosophy and religious practices of the Greeks and Romans included polytheistic idolatry.Earliest historical records confirm cult images from the ancient Egyptian civilization. By the second millennium BC, two forms of cult images have been identified: the zoomorphic (god in the image of animal or animal-human fusion), more commonly found in ancient Egyptian influenced beliefs; anthropomorphic (god in the image of man), more commonly found in Indo-European cultures. Symbols of nature, useful animals, or feared animals may also be included by both.

Plato suggested images can be a remedy or poison to the human experience. According to Paul Kugler, an image is an appropriate intermediary that "bridges between the inner world of the mind and the outer world of material reality. The image is a vehicle between sensation and reason."

With the rise of Christianity and later Islam, opposition to the idolatry of the Greeks and Romans led to widespread desecration and defacement of ancient Greek and Roman sculptures that have survived into the modern era.

Before we see what godly wisdom can teach us about what is appropriate and inappropriate for a Christian to praise and worship, I want to explore with you the word music.

———————

MUSIC

Why does the Bible mention music as a way for us to praise God?

Music is found in every known culture. Anthropologists have discovered, even the most isolated tribal groups have some form of music, suggesting music was present in the ancestral population prior to the dispersal of humans around the world. The first music may have been invented in

Barry Denzil Haney, MD

Africa and then evolved to become an important part of human life.

The origin of Prehistoric music (includes all of the world's music that has existed before the advent of any currently extant historical sources concerning that music) is unknown, but some suggest the origin of music likely stems from naturally occurring sounds and rhythms.

The first musical instrument was probably the human voice.

Some archaeologists believe the Dive Babe Flute to be the world's oldest musical instrument (although contested by alternative theories), produced 50,000 to 60,000 years ago by the Neanderthals.

In 2008, archaeologists discovered a bone flute in the Hole Felt cave near Ulm, Germany, considered to be about 35,000 years old.

The oldest known wooden pipe was discovered near Greystone, Ireland, in 2004.

The oldest known written song was written in cuneiform, dating to 3400 years ago from Ugarit in Syria.

The oldest surviving example of a complete musical composition is the Seikilos epitaph, dated to be either from the first or second century AD. The song, although short, is engraved on a tombstone from the Hellenistic town Tralles near present-day Aydin, Turkey, not far from Ephesus.

The following is a transliteration of the words written on the tombstone, which excludes the musical notation:

> *While you live, shine*
> *have no grief at all*
> *life exists only for a short while*
> *and time demands his due.*

According to Easton's Bible Dictionary, Jubal was named by the Bible as the inventor of musical instruments. The Hebrews cultivated music. The Hebrew history and literature contain abundant evidence of this, which I will discuss in Godly Wisdom.

ILLUSTRATION

The following illustration concerning praise is taken from Michael P. Green's book *1500 Illustrations for Biblical Preaching*:

> One Sunday morning after the service, a woman came up to the pastor and thanked him for the encouraging sermon he had preached.
>
> In response, he said, "Why? Don't thank me, thank the Lord."
>
> She said, "Well, I thought of that, but it wasn't quite that good."

GODLY WISDOM

What does godly wisdom teach us about what is appropriate and what is inappropriate for a Christian to praise and worship? There were a lot of different pagan religions in the ancient world, and most of them were polytheistic, and it was very common in ancient Greece and Rome. Some believe the word pagan was first used by Christians in regard to non-believers.

The Jewish people identified pagans as people who worshiped idols with elaborate rituals, ceremonies, and other practices that involved worship of their god or gods.

Even though this word is rarely used today, in ancient times, for Christians, it was a derogatory term used to describe a religious group or community of unbelievers.

Although pagan worship of other gods is not mentioned specifically in the book of Genesis, Jon Garvey, in his article "Where are all the Pagans in

Barry Denzil Haney, MD

Genesis," suggests in Genesis, chapters 2-11, "a story of increasing evil," we might infer "the perversion of religion into paganism."

In Exodus 12:12, Yahweh predicts he will execute judgments on other gods: "For I will pass through the land of Egypt this night and will smite all the firstborn in the land of Egypt, both man and beast; and against all the gods of Egypt I will execute judgment: I am the LORD."

In Exodus 20:3, when God gives the people the Ten Commandments, the first commandment implies the existence of other gods: "Thou shalt have no other gods before me."

In Deuteronomy 4:19, God tells the Israelites not to worship objects in the heavens:

> And lest thou lift up thine eyes unto heaven, and when
> thou seest the sun, and the moon, and the stars, even all the
> host of heaven, shouldest be driven to worship them, and
> serve them, which the LORD thy God hath divided unto
> all nations under the whole heaven.

Many scholars believe Psalm 82 speaks both of weak "gods," possibly fallen angels, and hints of spiritual warfare, a cosmos at war, both spiritually and politically. If true, this would indicate a cosmic rebellion against Yahweh.

In 1 Corinthians 5:1 (ESV), Apostle Paul angrily wrote to the church at Corinth: "It is actually reported that there is sexual immorality among you, and of a kind that is not tolerated even among pagans, for a man has his father's wife."

Paul's point is that even the pagans or unbelievers know better than to do what this man was doing, so we shouldn't be too hard on non-believers.

What Godly wisdom does the Bible give Christians to appropriately worship God?

In Psalm 98:4-6, the Bible tells us to "praise and worship God using musical instruments and singing:"

> Make a joyful noise unto the LORD, all the earth: Make
> a loud noise, and rejoice, and sing praise. Sing unto the
> LORD with the harp; With the harp, and the voice of a
> psalm. With trumpets and sound of cornet make a joyful
> noise before the LORD, the King.

In Psalm 47:1-2, the Bible tells us to "praise and worship with shouts of joy and clapping of hand:" "O clap your hands, all ye people; Shout unto God with the voice of triumph. For the LORD most high is terrible; He is a great King over all the earth."

In 2 Chronicles 29:8, the Bible tells us to "praise and worship in the assembly and by ourselves." "Wherefore the wrath of the LORD was upon Judah and Jerusalem, and he hath delivered them to trouble, to astonishment, and to hissing, as ye see with your eyes."

Godly wisdom suggests God especially enjoys music as a way to praise Him, as revealed in Revelation 5:8-10:

> And when he had taken the book, the four beasts and four
> and twenty elders fell down before the Lamb, having every
> one of them harps, and golden vials full of odours, which
> are the prayers of saints. And they sung a new song, saying,
> Thou art worthy to take the book, and to open the seals
> thereof: for thou wast slain, and hast redeemed us to God
> by thy blood out of every kindred, and tongue, and people,
> and nation; And hast made us unto our God kings and
> priests: and we shall reign on the earth.

Whenever the heavenly hosts sing a song, I imagine God sits on His throne, humming, "Oh, the sweet, sweet music!"

MY PERSONAL EXPERIENCE: THE BEAUTIFUL SINGING OF SONGBIRDS!

Did you know, often, the smallest songbirds have the most interesting songs because of their loud voices and many complex songs. I think God created them in this way.

On my farm, I would sit on my cabin porch on an early summer morning, and the surrounding hills would be alive with the beautiful sound of birds singing!

PRAYER

Our heavenly Father

Sometimes I hear someone say, "I have Jesus!" But, if you think about it, that is not a true statement, because, in fact, Jesus has us!

Jesus owns us because of the price He paid for our sin. It's only through His grace we will be allowed to stand before You on judgment day. Otherwise, because of our sin, we will not be allowed to bear the sight of the pure loving God, the perfect God, the wonderful counselor, the mighty God, the everlasting Father, the prince of peace!

I now love Your Word and enjoy my times of meditation and prayer with You. Although I don't hear a conversational voice, I do hear Your voice. I see You working in my life; I sense the Holy Spirit working in my life. I feel the nudges, feel the displeasure each time I displease You, and I am quicker to recognize when I displease You, quicker to repent, quicker to ask for forgiveness, not only from those I offend or hurt here on Earth, but also You, whom I displease. Thank You, Jesus.

Because of my daily walk with Jesus, highs are even higher, and my lows are much lower! I have so much more joy, the highs and lows are more exciting and more bearable.

In the Bible, if we listen, we will hear Your words whispered in our ears and we will feel the inexpressible joy and love, through the Holy Spirit's instruction.

Thank You for each day You give us, to please You and do Your will for our lives while here on earth. Thank You, Father God!

In the precious name of Jesus our Lord and Savior,

Amen!

CHAPTER 30

My Narrow, Rocky Road to Salvation!

Enter ye in at the strait gate: for wide is the gate, and broad is the way, that leadeth to destruction, and many there be which go in There'at: Because strait is the gate, and narrow is the way, which leadeth unto life, and few there be that find it.

—Matthew 7:13-14

WORLDLY WISDOM

In this passage, the Holy Spirit is telling me, the wide gate is the world, and it is very easy to enter; nothing prevents you from entering it.

All that is required to enter it is to follow your natural, sinful nature. The narrow gate represents the kingdom of heaven, and it is difficult to enter, as Paul tells us in Ephesians 2:8: "For by grace are ye saved through faith; and that not of yourselves: it is the gift of God."

The Cambridge Dictionary defines salvation in this way: "In some religions, salvation is the state of complete belief in God that will save those who believe from the punishment of God for evil or immoral acts."

The Dictionary of Bible Themes defines salvation in this way: "The transformation of a person's individual nature and relationship with God as a result of repentance and faith in the atoning death of Jesus Christ on the cross; all humanity stands in need of salvation, which is only possible through faith in Jesus Christ."

What are the current beliefs among the American public about salvation?

According to the Pew Research Center article "Many Americans Say Other Faiths Can Lead to Eternal Life," a national survey conducted by the Pew Forum on Religion and Public Life in 2008 found the following:

> Fifty-two percent of American Christians think at least some non-Christian faiths can lead to eternal life... among Christians who believe many religions can lead to eternal life, eighty percent name at least one non-Christian faith that can do so roughly one-third of Americans (thirty percent) believe that whether one achieves eternal life is determined by what a person believes, with nearly as many (twenty-nine percent) saying eternal life depends on one's actions... one-in-ten Americans say the key to obtaining eternal life lies in a combination of belief and actions... the remaining one-third of the public says that something else is the key to eternal life, they don't know what leads to eternal life or they don't believe in eternal life.

Barry Denzil Haney, MD

Some Christians believe in universalism. They believe every human will be saved in a religious or spiritual sense. In his article "A Practical Theology of Salvation for a Multi-Faith World," Wayne Morris says this about universalism:

> At least two approaches to understanding a universalist theology of salvation: 'pluralist universalism' and 'particularist universalism… pluralist universalism suggests that salvation is possible for all, and can be realized through many different means, including it being open to those who do not experience transformation… particularist universalism argues that salvation is for everyone, indeed, some will argue that it is for the entire cosmos… salvation is only possible because of and through Christ… not concerned, in the main, with making any claims about the possibility of salvation through any other faiths.

In the article "Salvation: Can Non-Christians Be Saved," the authors make this claim:

> Most Americans believe that anyone who leads a good life will eventually spend eternity in Heaven. They hold beliefs that are more related to the religion of Zoroastrianism than to historical Christianity. They frequently believe in some form of final judgment at which one's good and bad deeds are evaluated and compared. Those who receive a passing grade are sent to Heaven; those who fail to end up in hell.

What do the other non-Christian religions believe about salvation?

In his article "What Other Religions Teach About Salvation," Mike Mazzalongo makes this claim about the other thirteen major religions or systems in the world:

> First of all, they all have some form or idea of salvation. Every group aspires to a better life somehow, either a better life here through the practice of their quote, religion, or belief, or a better life in another world, the spirit world after this life is over. But every single one of them has this idea in their religion, which is actually the thing that moves their religion. Take that element out; the religion is useless. And secondly, and this is the important one, every one of these, except Christianity, is a works or law-based system for achieving salvation or heaven or the good life or whatever it is. All of them are work-based concepts.

Christianity is the only religion where God Himself became fully human, became both God and man, then paid the penalty for our sins on the cross at Calvary, providing us a way to spend eternity with Him in heaven.

ILLUSTRATION

The following illustration concerning salvation is taken from Michael P. Green's book *1500 Illustrations for Biblical Preaching*:

> A certain atheistic barber was conversing with a minister as they rode through the slums of a large city. Said the unbeliever, "If there is a loving God, how can he permit all this poverty, suffering, and violence among these people? Why doesn't he save them from all this?"

Just then, a disheveled bum crossed the street. He was unshaven and filthy, with long scraggly hair hanging down his neck. The minister pointed to him and said, "You are a barber and claim to be a good one, so why do you allow that man to go unkempt and unshaven?"

"Why, why…" the barber stuttered, "he never gave me a chance to fix him up."

"Exactly," said the minister. "Men are what they are because they reject God's help."

GODLY WISDOM

In the Bible, what does godly wisdom tell us about salvation? The Bible tells us we must follow God's road to heaven and go through the narrow gate. The following verses give us godly wisdom, written through Paul's quill, in the book of Romans: "For all have sinned and come short of the glory of God" (Romans 3:23). "For the wages of sin is death; but the gift of God is eternal life through Jesus Christ our Lord" (Romans 6:23). "But God commendeth his love toward us, in that, while we were yet sinners, Christ died for us" (Romans 5:8). "That if thou shalt confess with thy mouth the Lord Jesus, and shalt believe in thine heart that God hath raised him from the dead, thou shalt be saved" (Romans 10:9).

In his book *My Favorite Illustrations*, Herschel Hobbs offers the following illustration about the choices we need to make concerning our salvation.

A man stands at a fork in the road trying to decide which way to go. One road has a sign which says "law." The other has a sign reading "grace." If he chooses to travel the law road, he falls away from the grace road. It is not a matter of being in grace and falling out of it. It is a matter of never having been in grace. One cannot travel both roads. For law and grace negate each other. If it is by works it cannot be by grace or as a gift. If it is by grace, then it cannot be by law. Christ is in the grace road. So if you travel the law road, you are cut off from Him and His saving power. To depend upon legalism in any form or degree for salvation is to turn your back upon Christ.

Paul addresses the relationship between Salvation by Faith, Salvation by Works, and Salvation by Grace, at great length in Romans 3:20-4:25. Because I feel this is so important to understanding godly wisdom concerning salvation, I am including it here, in its entirety.

Therefore by the deeds of the law there shall no flesh be justified in his sight: for by the law is the knowledge of sin. But now the righteousness of God without the law is manifested, being witnessed by the law and the prophets; Even the righteousness of God which is by faith of Jesus Christ unto all and upon all them that believe: for there is no difference: For all have sinned, and come short of the glory of God; Being justified freely by his grace through the redemption that is in Christ Jesus: Whom God hath set forth to be a propitiation through faith in his blood, to declare his righteousness for the remission of sins that are past, through the forbearance of God; To declare, I say, at this time his righteousness: that he might be just, and the justifier of him which believeth in Jesus. Where is boasting then? It is excluded. By what law? of works? Nay: but by the law of faith. Therefore we conclude that a man is justified by faith without the deeds of the law. Is he the God of the Jews only? is he not also of the Gentiles? Yes, of the Gentiles also: Seeing it is one God, which shall justify the circum-

Barry Denzil Haney, MD

cision by faith, and uncircumcision through faith. Do we then make void the law through faith? God forbid: yea, we establish the law. What shall we say then that Abraham our father, as pertaining to the flesh, hath found? For if Abraham were justified by works, he hath whereof to glory; but not before God. For what saith the scripture? Abraham believed God, and it was counted unto him for righteousness. Now to him that worketh is the reward not reckoned of grace, but of debt. But to him that worketh not, but believeth on him that justifieth the ungodly, his faith is counted for righteousness. Even as David also describeth the blessedness of the man, unto whom God imputeth righteousness without works, Saying, Blessed are they whose iniquities are forgiven, and whose sins are covered. Blessed is the man to whom the Lord will not impute sin. Cometh this blessedness then upon the circumcision only, or upon the uncircumcision also? for we say that faith was reckoned to Abraham for righteousness. How was it then reckoned? when he was in circumcision, or in uncircumcision? Not in circumcision, but in uncircumcision. And he received the sign of circumcision, a seal of the righteousness of the faith which he had yet being uncircumcised: that he might be the father of all them that believe, though they be not circumcised; that righteousness might be imputed unto them also: And the father of circumcision to them who are not of the circumcision only, but who also walk in the steps of that faith of our father Abraham, which he had being yet uncircumcised. For the promise, that he should be the heir of the world, was not to Abraham, or to his seed, through the law, but through the righteousness of faith. For if they which are of the law be heirs, faith is made void, and the promise made of none effect: Because the law worketh wrath: for where no law is, there is no transgression. Therefore it is of faith, that it might be by grace; to the end the promise might be sure to all the seed; not to that only which is of the law, but to that also which is of the faith of Abraham; who is the father of us all, (As it is written, I have made thee a father of many nations,) before him whom he believed, even God, who quickeneth the dead, and calleth those things which be not as though they were. Who against hope believed in hope, that he might become the father of many nations; according to that which was spoken, So shall thy seed be. And being not weak in faith, he considered not his own body now dead, when he was about a hundred years old, neither yet the deadness of Sara's womb: He staggered not at the promise of God through unbelief; but was strong in faith, giving glory to God; And being fully persuaded that, what he had promised, he was able also to perform. And therefore it was imputed to him for righteousness. Now it was not written for his sake alone, that it was imputed to him; But for us also, to whom it shall be imputed, if we believe on him that raised up Jesus our Lord from the dead; Who was delivered for our offences and was raised again for our justification.

MY PERSONAL EXPERIENCE: WHERE ARE YOU GOING?

As I lay here in bed, hearing the distant sounds of people traveling on the interstate near my home, I wonder, where are they going right now, where are they in their walk with Jesus? Are they struggling with the same things I am struggling with during my journey along the rocky road to salvation? Are pride and arrogance also stumbling blocks for them doing Your will in their lives?

I realize I have no control over anyone's salvation. I cannot save anyone! I know I can only serve as a beacon of light by the work of the Holy Spirit flowing through me, and through this light, they will see the fruits of the spirit: love, joy, peace, patience, kindness, goodness, faithfulness, gentleness, and self-control.

But, it is still hard not to try convincing them; they are blinded by Satan's lies and deceptions! I want to convince them that by trusting You, by having faith in Jesus, the Holy Spirit will convict them, He will remove the blinders of deception.

Heavenly Father, even now, as I think and say these words, I can feel the wily presence of Satan and his minions, creeping, searching, looking for any crack in my full armor of God, to deceive me. As You have instructed me in James 4:7, I submit to you my heavenly Father, I resist the devil, now flee from me Satan!

PRAYER

Our heavenly Father,

As Jim Lyon says, "Allow us to become supernatural instruments—daring, radical, world-changing, life-altering, risk-assuming way of Jesus. Help us answer Your call to a kingdom life of transformational passion empowered by the Holy Spirit."

Jim Lyon continues, "Help us to see like Jesus, hear like Jesus, act like Jesus, love like Jesus, risk like Jesus, and be like Jesus."

Thank You for Your continued guidance during our journey of holiness while we are here on earth. We ask for Your continued guidance to the leadership and to each member of Your church as we prepare the secular world for Your second coming.

We lift up to You in prayer all of our spoken and unspoken prayer requests.

In the precious name of Jesus Christ, our Lord and Savior,

Amen.

CHAPTER 31

Don't Procrastinate!

For after all these things do the Gentiles seek:) for your heavenly Father knoweth that ye have need of all these things. But seek ye first the kingdom of God, and his righteousness; and all these things shall be added unto you. Take therefore no thought for the morrow: for the morrow shall take thought for the things of itself. Sufficient unto the day is the evil thereof.

—Matthew 6:32-34

WORLDLY WISDOM

In this passage, the Holy Spirit is teaching me not to bother God to give us worldly things that, in the end, won't make us happy—don't procrastinate!

Instead our goal should be to seek God Himself and try to discover what His will is for our life and trust God to provide the worldly things we need.

The Cambridge Dictionary defines procrastination in this way: "The act of delaying something that must be done, often because it is unpleasant or boring; implying putting things off until the future."

The Dictionary of Bible Themes defines future in this way: "God's promises about the future are certain because it is under God's control;

Christians should live on the basis that these promises, which focus on the return of Jesus Christ, will be fulfilled."

For many years I put off asking people to forgive me, who I had harmed because of my self-centeredness. We are reminded by Jesus of the importance God places on faith and forgiveness in Mark 11:25-26:

> And when ye stand praying, forgive, if ye have ought against
> any: that your Father also which is in heaven may forgive
> you your trespasses. But if ye do not forgive, neither will
> your Father which is in heaven forgive your trespasses.

As I matured, I began asking for forgiveness, even before I asked God to forgive my sins, repented, and was born again three years ago. During this forty-day journey, I finally stopped procrastinating and asked two very important people in my life's journey to forgive me.

People have struggled with putting things off, going back to ancient civilization.

The first instance of procrastination probably occurred when the first task was assigned. One of the earliest recorded proclamations against procrastination came from the Greek poet Hesiod. In his poem *Work and Days*, Hesiod says this to his brother, Perses:

> Do not put your work off till to-morrow and the day after;
> for a sluggish worker does not fill his barn, nor one who
> puts off his work: industry makes work go well, but a man
> who puts off work is always at hand-grips with ruin.

Cicero, in a series of speeches known as the Philippics, called procrastination "detestable in the conduct of most affairs." In Geoffrey Chaucer's book *In the Canterbury Tales*, Dame Prudence advises Melibee and his friends, "…The goodness you may do this day, do it; and delay it not until the morrow."

In his article "Why Wait? The Science Behind Procrastination," Eric Jaffe states this:

> Psychological researchers now recognize true procrastination is a complicated failure of self-regulation...a voluntary delay of some important task that we intend to do, despite knowing that we'll suffer as a result. "He further states" people who procrastinate have higher levels of stress and lower well-being.

In a study published in *Psychological Science* back in 1997, Diane Tice and Roy Baumeister found the costs of procrastination far outweighed the temporary benefits. According to them, "Procrastinators earned lower grades than other students and reported higher cumulative amounts of stress and illness."

Neuropsychology researchers have found a link between procrastination and the domain of executive functioning found in the frontal systems of the brain. Procrastination is internally troubling, leading to problems of insomnia, immune system, and gastrointestinal disturbances, leading to problems with personal relationships. In a vicious cycle, these problems may result in increasing procrastination because of preoccupation with the ailments.

Benjamin Franklin put it this way: "Dost thou love life. Then do not squander time; for that's the stuff life is made of."

ILLUSTRATION

The following illustration concerning procrastination is taken from Michael P. Green's book *1500 Illustrations for Biblical Preaching*:

While cleaning out his desk, a man found a shoe repair ticket that was ten years old. Figuring that he had nothing to lose, he went to the shop and gave the ticket to the repairman, who began to search the backroom for the unclaimed shoes. After several minutes, he reappeared and gave the ticket back to the man.

"What's wrong?" asked the man. "Couldn't you find my shoes?"

"Oh, I found them," replied the repairman, "and they'll be ready next Friday."

Procrastination is not the result of lack of time to complete a task. It is an attitude and must be dealt with as such.

GODLY WISDOM

In the Bible, godly wisdom tells us to stop procrastinating, don't wait till it is too late!

In 1 Peter 1:17-19, the Holy Spirit is warning to be careful how we spend our time here on earth:

> And if ye call on the Father, who without respect of persons judgeth according to every man's work, pass the time of your sojourning here in fear: Forasmuch as ye know that ye were not redeemed with corruptible things, as silver and gold, from your vain conversation received by tradition from your fathers; But with the precious blood of Christ, as of a lamb without blemish and without spot.

Barry Denzil Haney, MD

Paul advises us in Ephesians 5:15-16 to watch our time on earth prudently and deliberately, not to procrastinate: "See then that ye walk circumspectly, not as fools, but as wise, Redeeming the time, because the days are evil."

Two of the most common causes of procrastination are laziness and avoiding negative feelings. Godly wisdom addresses this issue in Proverbs 24:30-34:

> I went by the field of the slothful, And by the vineyard of the man void of understanding; And, lo, it was all grown over with thorns, And nettles had covered the face thereof, And the stone wall thereof was broken down. Then I saw, and considered it well: I looked upon it, and received instruction. Yet a little sleep, a little slumber, A little folding of the hands to sleep: So shall thy poverty come as one that traveleth; And thy want as an armed man.

In Proverb 27:1, the Holy Spirit is telling me we do not know if tomorrow will come, so today, we need to make sure we have a right relationship with God: "Boast not thyself of tomorrow; For thou knowest not what a day may bring forth."

Finally, in James 4:13-14, the Holy Spirit is warning not to worry about tomorrow:

> Go to now, ye that say, Today or tomorrow we will go into such a city, and continue there a year, and buy and sell, and get gain: Whereas ye know not what shall be on the morrow. For what is your life? It is even a vapour, that appeareth for a little time, and then vanisheth away.

We cannot be sure about tomorrow. Don't procrastinate and be like the person who says, "I'm too busy today to think of godly things; I will do it tomorrow when the chaos of my daily life calms down!" The problem with this attitude is, someday may never come.

As the saying goes, "Don't put off until tomorrow what you can do today." Godly wisdom in the Bible tells us this in 1 Thessalonians 5:2: "For yourselves know perfectly that the day of the Lord so cometh as a thief in the night."

For Christians, procrastination will undermine our attempts to do God's will for our lives. It is the best tool Satan uses to sabotage God's plan for our life. We need to be vigilant, guarding against Satan's use of procrastination in our thought processes! Anything that causes us to waste our time on earth is a spiritual issue, one we must take seriously!

In his article entitled "Procrastination: Conquering the Time Killer," Steve Cable offers these five steps to reduce the impact of procrastination in your life:

- Probing your problem
- Praying for perspective
- Proper priorities
- Perspective-based planning
- Proactive partnering

Don't procrastinate about your eternity. Beware of your sin today! Today, turn from sin!

PRAYER

Our heavenly Father,

Thank You for Your unlimited grace and mercy, which are more than enough to cover all our sins. Thank You for making available to us Your free gift of salvation through this grace and mercy.

Barry Denzil Haney, MD

By faith, we believe in this gift of salvation You have given us, through the shed blood of Your Son Jesus Christ on the cross at Calvary, who paid the penalty for our sins, so we might enjoy an eternal relationship with You in heaven.

Faith is the victory because works without faith are dead. You have told us it is dead as dead can get. You have told us Faith is designed to always spur us on to obedience in Christ and to be like he was. As You told us in Hebrews 11:1, faith is the "evidence of things that we do not see."

Jesus, You have told us in John 14:13-14, "You can ask for anything in my name, and I will do it, because the work of the Son brings glory to the Father. Yes, ask anything in my name, and I will do it!" Jesus also told us in Matthew 18:20 "For where two or three gather in my name, there am I with them."

Father, we ask for continued revival in each of us, renew our minds so we can do Your will. We ask for continued revival in Your Church, so we as a church can participate in the works of Your church to make disciples of all men by spreading the Good News of the Gospel.

In the precious name of Jesus Christ our Lord and Savior,

Amen.

CHAPTER 32

Saving Grace, How Sweet Thou Art!

For the grace of God that bringeth salvation hath appeared to all men, Teaching us that, denying ungodliness and worldly lusts, we should live soberly, righteously, and godly, in this present world; Looking for that blessed hope, and the glorious appearing of the great God and our Saviour Jesus Christ; Who gave himself for us, that he might redeem us from all iniquity, and purify unto himself a peculiar people, zealous of good works.

—Titus 2:11-14

—————

WORLDLY WISDOM

In this passage, the Holy Spirit is teaching me to be active and faithful in our service in Him while we wait for His coming.

He is also teaching us there is no salvation outside of Jesus and grace is about the incarnation of Jesus, who redeemed mankind through his work on the cross at Calvary.

The Merriam-Webster Dictionary defines grace in this way: "Unmerited divine assistance given to humans for their regeneration or sanctification."

The Dictionary of Bible Themes defines grace in this way: "The unmerited favor of God, made known through Jesus Christ, and expressed supremely in the redemption and full forgiveness of sinners through faith in Jesus Christ."

Saving grace, how sweet thou art! This phrase brings to mind the song *Amazing Grace*, written by John Newton, a former slave trader. I read that "Amazing Grace" has been recorded more than six thousand times. Jerry Bailey, an executive at Broadcast Music, Incorporated, says it may be the most recorded song on the planet.

What makes this song so appealing? Perhaps, because it tells us because of hope, no matter what sin we commit, forgiveness and redemption are possible.

All of us, who profess to be Christians, should take time to stop and smell the roses! Actually, interact with the people we come into contact with on a daily basis in our community and in our church, recognize those who appear worn out, and ask them, "Are you okay? Is something wrong? Can I help you?"

We need to be willing to take time to tell them our story of healing and hope. We need to be willing to talk about Jesus and the hope we have because of the work He did on the cross at Calvary. We need to share our story to show God's grace and mercy in our life.

We also must remember, words can sometimes be cheap, but as John tells us in 1 John 3:18, "My little children, let us not love in word, neither in tongue; but in deed and in truth."

MY PERSONAL EXPERIENCE: THE KITCHEN!

This reminds me of a story about my mother's kitchen and my grandmother's kitchen, special places in my memory, places where I experienced their grace. I remember both kitchens being very warm, cozy, inviting spaces, where food was prepared with love. Every prepared meal was delicious. I couldn't wait to eat the pies, cakes, and cookies I would smell baking in the oven, especially the cherry cobbler pie and chocolate meringue pie. I can still remember the smell of the bacon frying early in the morning, homemade biscuits in the oven, fried chicken sizzling in the frying pan, the ice-cold Kool-Aid, and the warm smile I received, but what I remember most is the love I felt in their presence.

Over the centuries, mankind has struggled with the concept of grace. Many have noted an inconsistency in the concept of the unconditional free gift of grace. How can you say grace is a free gift, requiring nothing on our part, while at the same time require that you do something to earn it?

Some find it hard to accept a deathbed conversion—a person who lives a despicable life can be forgiven on their death bed by saying they have faith in Jesus and then go to heaven. They have a difficult time accepting the declaration Paul makes in Romans 3:24-28,

> Being justified freely by his grace through the redemption
> that is in Christ Jesus: Whom God hath set forth to be
> a propitiation through faith in his blood, to declare his
> righteousness for the remission of sins that are past, through
> the forbearance of God; To declare, I say, at this time his
> righteousness: that he might be just, and the justifier of
> him which believeth in Jesus. Where is boasting then? It is
> excluded. By what law? of works? Nay: but by the law of
> faith. Therefore we conclude that a man is justified by faith
> without the deeds of the law.

In order to reconcile this apparent contradiction, early Christians developed the concept of universalism, still believed by many in today's culture, also a concept believed by many to support their secular worldview.

These early Christians strongly believed in grace, a grace with no requirements. However, they also believed, because God is a loving God, everyone is saved, past, present, future, whether they lived a good life or not, whether they have ever heard of God. Universalism is still alive and well in religious circles today, now called Christian Universalism.

Although *lengthy*, I want to share with you the thinking of a modern-day universalist, David Green, concerning grace from a humanist perspective:

> What does (grace) mean from an interfaith or humanist perspective? Basically, we can take "grace," crack the religious shell away, and we're still left with the same essential concept. A free, unearned gift. And with that shell removed, here's what we have from a humanist perspective. A humanist grace does not require a belief in God, nor does it deny a belief in God. What it does require is a belief in one another: the belief that our world, our lives, and our relationships, are gifts. They're gifts because we simply can't take any credit for them. Even looking at the origins of human life from a purely scientific standpoint, we had nothing to do with it. We can't earn or buy the fact that we live and breathe on a beautiful planet. Or any other good thing that we've never earned but received just the same. Those are gifts. The cost to us is zero. And that is gracious. Most importantly, from a humanist perspective, grace has to do with each other. For what we give and receive in our relationships. The most significant way we encounter grace is one-on-one. It happens when we've done wrong by someone and they forgive us anyway.

Wow! Amazing how the human mind works! How the human mind can deny the evidence of a Creator God despite the evidence, he can easily detect through the senses God has given him! Satan is truly a wily deceiver, whose deception and lies have blinded the unsaved!

Barry Denzil Haney, MD

GODLY WISDOM

In his book *Provocations*, Søren Kierkegaard says this about grace:

> Christ says: Do according to what I say—then you shall
> know. Consequently, decisive action first of all. By acting,
> your life will come into collision with existence, and then
> you will know the reality of grace. Nowadays, we have
> turned the whole thing around. Christianity has become a
> worldview. Thus, before I get involved, I must first justify it.
> Good night to Christianity!

Apostle Paul tells us we are saved by faith in Jesus, not by our works.
Church fathers have wrestled with the apparent contradiction between Paul
and James on the question of whether salvation is by faith or by works, this
notion of working our way to heaven versus faith alone.

Paul in Romans 5:1-2 writes,

> Therefore being justified by faith, we have peace with God
> through our Lord Jesus Christ: By whom also we have
> access by faith into this grace wherein we stand and rejoice
> in hope of the glory of God.

Paul goes on to say in Ephesians 2:8-10, our salvation is not through
our works but is because of God's grace, the gift of God:

> For by grace are ye saved through faith; and that not of
> yourselves: it is the gift of God: Not of works, lest any man
> should boast. For we are his workmanship, created in Christ
> Jesus unto good works, which God hath before ordained
> that we should walk in them.

James seems to say just the opposite in James 2:24-28, where he writes,

> Ye see then how that by works a man is justified, and not by
> faith only. Likewise also was not Rahab the harlot justified
> by works, when she had received the messengers, and had
> sent them out another way? For as the body without the
> spirit is dead, so faith without works is dead also.

Is it sufficient to just have faith, then proceed to satisfy one's hunger for earthly pleasures? Or does our salvation require more from us? If God expects us to do certain things in order to please Him, aren't we doing works?

How do we reconcile this apparent contradiction about faith and works?

If you look at the entire passage in James 14-26, you discover James makes it clear the relationship between faith and works. In this passage, James is comparing genuine faith, which leads to good works, and empty faith, which is not really faith at all.

The Holy Spirit is telling us faith and works are important in salvation; however, believers are justified solely by faith in Jesus Christ, and we are saved by God's grace, through faith alone.

Works are evidence of genuine salvation. Works are the visible proof of our saving faith! God expects those who believe in Jesus to demonstrate our faith by a sanctified life through the renewing work of the Holy Spirit.

Dr. Paul Elliott defines this reconciliation in this way:

> On October 31, 1517, the great reformer Martin Luther
> nailed his famous 95 theses to the church door at Wit-
> tenberg in Germany. Why did Luther do this? He did it
> because, as he studied the Scriptures for himself, he had a
> growing certainty that the church and the Pope were wrong.
> He had a growing certainty that a man is made right with
> God by being justified by grace through faith in the finished

work of Jesus Christ alone as full and final atonement for
sin.

In Ephesians 2:10, Paul tells us that we are God's workmanship, we
were created in Christ Jesus, and God planned all these things out for us,
so we could do good works. Paul also warns us we are under the bondage
of *"the lust of the flesh."* Had it not been for the love and grace of God, we
would be without hope! Although we deserve hell, eternal separation from
God, it is only through God's grace that we are given access to heaven.

In the hymn *Grace Enough For Me*, the songwriter E. O. Excell was
right, "Grace is flowing from Calvary!"

I think this beautiful description by Paul Zahl, found in his book *Grace
in Practice: A Theology of Everyday Life,* sums up the meaning of God's
grace:

> God's grace exists in relation to the human world only
> because of the substitutionary defeat of Christ's final love
> on the cross. If God had not been defeated in a moment
> of time, then our own defeats would have implied the
> possibility of victory. But the beginning of wisdom comes
> when individual human beings put an end to the possibil-
> ity of overcoming. Only then are they able to deliver their
> life over to God. If there is the slightest chance of a person
> doing it for himself or herself, God's grace is made null.
> And the death of human hope in the death of God makes it
> possible for a person to trust the Outsider.

Finally we should heed this warning of Paul in 2 Corinthians 6:1-2:

> We then, as workers together with him, beseech you also
> that ye receive not the grace of God in vain. For he saith,
> I have heard thee in a time accepted, and in the day of

salvation have I succoured thee: behold, now is the accepted time; behold, now is the day of salvation.

ILLUSTRATION

The following illustration concerning grace is taken from Michael P. Green's book *1500 Illustrations for Biblical Preaching*:

> During the Spanish-American War, Theodore Roosevelt came to Clara Barton of the Red Cross to buy some supplies for his sick and wounded men. His request was refused. Roosevelt was troubled and asked, "How can I get these things? I must have proper food for my sick men."
>
> "Just ask for them, Colonel," said Barton.
>
> "Oh," said Roosevelt, "then I do ask for them." He got them at once through grace, not through purchase.

PRAYER

Our heavenly Father,

Thank You for Your saving grace! The saving grace that offers us hope, regardless of sins committed, the hope that forgiveness and redemption are possible, no matter how horrendous our sin might be!

Thank You for giving us the opportunity, to play a part in Your grand plan of salvation for the world!

Thank You for allowing us to be disciples, to spread the good news of the Gospel, the teachings of Jesus to the unsaved, the broken-hearted. Thank You, Father, God, for making us right with God, for making us justified by grace through faith in the finished work of Jesus Christ, alone as the full and final atonement for sin. We will strive to demonstrate our faith by a sanctified life, through the renewing work of the Holy Spirit!

In the precious name of Jesus our Lord and Savior,

Amen!

CHAPTER 33

Freedom From Captivity!

The Spirit of the Lord is upon me, because he hath anointed me to preach the gospel to the poor; he hath sent me to heal the brokenhearted, to preach deliverance to the captives, and recovering of sight to the blind, to set at liberty them that are bruised, To preach the acceptable year of the Lord.

—Luke 4:18-19

WORLDLY WISDOM

In this passage, the Holy Spirit is teaching me, through Jesus, we can be rescued from captivity, whatever is separating us from God.

He can rescue us from spiritual and moral poverty, temptation, sin, Satan, tradition, legalism, physical suffering, mental suffering, and all forms of oppression. He is telling us Jesus is the way, the only way to the Father!

The Cambridge Dictionary defines captivity in this way: "The situation in which a person or animal is kept somewhere and is not allowed to leave."

The Dictionary of Bible Themes defines captivity in this way:

> The state of individuals, communities or nations held in bondage by a foreign power; such captivity may be punishment from God who, nevertheless, hears the cry of his captive people; god will punish those who, in their arrogance, take others captive; the term is sometimes used metaphorically of the bondage of sin. Jesus Christ alone can free people from such a state.

I like to think of captivity in terms of physical and mental enslavement. Slavery, the condition of being legally owned by someone else, is one form of physical enslavement. But people in prison or people in the military can be thought of as being physically enslaved. People who are physically enslaved are freed from their enslavement through legal remedies.

Mental enslavement can take place in a variety of ways. People can be emotionally imprisoned by guilt, self-hatred, financial obligations, and addictions. Worldly wisdom tells people they can be freed from emotional and mental causes of "captivity," but not freed from addictions—once an alcoholic, always an alcoholic; once addicted to pornography, always addicted to pornography!

Psychologists will tell you, one of our basic human needs is a sense of control. Psychologists use the term locus of control. The more internal our locus of control (LOC), the more we feel in control of our lives; the more external our LOC, the more we feel our lives are controlled by outside forces. In her article "How Much Control Do You Have In Your Life," Dian Dreher says this: "Research has linked external LOC with poor mental and physical health, passivity, anxiety, depression, and learned helplessness; and internal LOC with greater happiness, health, success, and the ability to cope with challenges."

Psychologists also talk about psychological slavery in homes where highly abusive relationships exist. According to some psychologists, psychological slavery is a legacy from slavery and human exploitation, still existing today.

Psychologists have observed that patients who have undergone physical and/or emotional abuse, such as children who have been abused, battered women, prisoners of war, or victims of incest, may develop positive feelings toward the abuser, the so-called Stockholm syndrome.

The Stockholm syndrome is defined as a condition in which hostages develop a psychological alliance with their captors during captivity because of an inherent survival instinct.

In her article "Psychological Slavery," Ana Nogales says researchers studies have found four situations necessary for psychological slavery to occur:

- Perception of a threat, physical or psychological, and the conviction that misfortune can really occur;

- Appreciation of small acts of kindness by the abuser towards the victim;

- Isolation from others;

- Conviction that one is unable to escape the situation.

But people can also be imprisoned by such things as guilt, self-hatred, or financial obligations. This self-imposed captivity can be just as debilitating.

Scientific consensus recognizes addiction, enslavement as a chronic disease that changes both brain structure and function. Researchers have identified the brain's reward center.

The brain recognizes all pleasures, whether originating from alcohol, a drug, a sexual encounter, an enjoyable meal, in the same way. When the brain detects pleasure, the neurotransmitter dopamine is released from the brain's reward center, the nucleus accumbens, a cluster of nerves lying underneath the cerebral cortex of the brain. Whatever a person is addicted to, food, drugs, alcohol, sex, causes a powerful surge of dopamine from the brain's reward center. Another part of the brain, called the hippocampus, lays down memories of this rapid sense of satisfaction, and the amygdala creates a conditioned response to certain stimuli.

In the article "How Addiction Hijacks The Brain," the authors talk about how complex the brain's learning process is in addiction:

> Recent research suggests that the situation is more complicated. Dopamine not only contributes to the experience of pleasure, but also plays a role in learning and memory—two key elements in the transition from liking something to becoming addicted to it...dopamine interacts with another neurotransmitter, glutamate, to take over the brain's system of reward-related learning...has an important role in sustaining life because it links activities needed for human survival (such as eating and sex) with pleasure and reward... reward circuit in the brain includes areas involved with motivation and memory as well as with pleasure. Addictive substances and behaviors stimulate the same circuit— and then overload it...repeated exposure to an addictive substance or behavior causes nerve cells in the nucleus accumbens and the prefrontal cortex (the area of the brain involved in planning and executing tasks) to communicate in a way that couples liking something with wanting it, in turn driving us to go after it...this process motivates us to take action to seek out the source of pleasure.

Neuroimaging technologies and recent research have shown other activities such as gambling, shopping, and sexual addiction affect the brain's reward center in the same way. Because of the complexity of the addictive process, most mental health professionals believe overcoming addiction requires multiple strategies, including psychotherapy, medication, and self-care.

Barry Denzil Haney, MD

ILLUSTRATION

The following illustration concerning spiritual slavery is taken from Michael P. Green's book *1500 Illustrations for Biblical Preaching*:

> Some years ago in Los Angeles, a man was walking down the street with a sign on his shoulders. The front of it said, *"I'm a slave for Christ."* The back of it read, *"Whose slave are you?"*

That is a good question because all of us are slaves to one or the other of two masters—sin or righteousness. We have no other choices. By the very nature of our humanity, we are made to serve and to be controlled by forces beyond our power.[12901]

GODLY WISDOM

In Genesis 1:26-28, the Bible tells us, even from the beginning, Adam and Eve were created in God's image, dependent upon Him for everything, and given stewardship of the Earth:

> And God said, Let us make man in our image, after our likeness: and let them have dominion over the fish of the sea, and over the fowl of the air, and over the cattle, and over all the earth, and over every creeping thing that creepeth upon the earth. So God created man in his own image, in the image of God created he him; male and

female created he them. And God blessed them, and God said unto them, Be fruitful, and multiply, and replenish the earth, and subdue it: and have dominion over the fish of the sea, and over the fowl of the air, and over every living thing that moveth upon the earth.

Because God is our Creator, we are instructed to praise Him in Psalm 66:4:

"All the earth shall worship thee and shall sing unto thee; they shall sing to thy name."

In John 15:4-5, the Bible makes it clear we are dependent upon God:

Abide in me, and I in you. As the branch cannot bear fruit of itself, except it abide in the vine; no more can ye, except ye abide in me. I am the vine, ye are the branches: He that abideth in me, and I in him, the same bringeth forth much fruit: for without me ye can do nothing.

Although man was created dependent on God, because of sin, he wants to be independent; he wants to be a god. Those with a secular worldview believe you do whatever you want to do, whatever feels right for you, whenever you want to. Because, according to them, it is all up to you! However, those who try to live their lives in this way, who strive for autonomy and self-sufficiency, fail at some point.

Because, no matter what we think or who we listen to, we will always be missing something; we will always be searching for something to soothe the emptiness we experience inside. Since what we are missing is the God we have rejected, we turn to other things to fill the void in our hearts. We allow other things to be the idols we worship. We learn to escape reality by worshipping whatever idol gives us pleasure that fills the void in our hearts.

Barry Denzil Haney, MD

Enslavement is not caused by the substance. Enslavement is conceived in the heart from temptations we receive from Satan.

We become enslaved when we act on the temptation; when we don't resist temptation.

In Luke 9:23-24, Jesus tells us this:

> And he said to them all, If any man will come after me, let him deny himself, and take up his cross daily, and follow me. For whosoever will save his life shall lose it: but whosoever will lose his life for my sake, the same shall save it.

I spent most of my life in bondage to sin. Thank God, the Holy Spirit came to my rescue, convicted me of my sin, and the chains of my captivity were broken, as the Bible tells us in Luke 4:18-19:

> The Spirit of the Lord is upon me, because he hath anointed me to preach the gospel to the poor; he hath sent me to heal the brokenhearted, to preach deliverance to the captives, and recovering of sight to the blind, to set at liberty them that are bruised, to preach the acceptable year of the Lord.

In his book *Making The Most of Life*, Charles Ryrie makes this point:

> The fact of the matter is, our Lord said we cannot be independent of Him except at the expense of life itself. And without life, of what use are we? So life and usefulness depend on dependence on Christ. Furthermore, He said on another occasion, *"Take my yoke upon you, and learn of me"* (Matthew 11:29).

Finally, in Romans 6:17-23, Paul gives us hope, encouraging us when he tells us we may as well serve God, rather than be slaves to our sin:

But God be thanked, that ye were the servants of sin, but ye have obeyed from the heart that form of doctrine which was delivered you. Being then made free from sin, ye became the servants of righteousness. I speak after the manner of men because of the infirmity of your flesh: for as ye have yielded your members servants to uncleanness and to iniquity unto iniquity; even so now yield your members servants to righteousness unto holiness. For when ye were the servants of sin, ye were free from righteousness. What fruit had ye then in those things whereof ye are now ashamed? for the end of those things is death. But now being made free from sin, and become servants to God, ye have your fruit unto holiness, and the end everlasting life. For the wages of sin is death; but the gift of God is eternal life through Jesus Christ our Lord.

PRAYER

Our heavenly Father,

Because of Jesus' work on the cross, my spirit man has been saved, and made righteous because of His righteousness! My spirit man is holy because of Christ's holiness! Now, the void, the chasm, the separation from You has been removed because of His shed blood on the cross at Calvary! Now, my sins have been forgiven!

I've been made right in Your eyes! I've been justified in Your sight! Sin no longer separates me from You! I know, I was created in Your image, to spend an eternity with You! I know this search throughout my life, to fill this void, this empty godly container in my heart with earthly pleasures was an unsuccessful attempt to remove that separation, to satisfy that unquenchable hunger, for a relationship with You, my Creator God!

Thank You for Your immutability! Thank You for Your omnipotence! Thank You for Your omnipresence! Thank You for Your omniscience! Thank You for Your inexpressible joy! Thank You for Your endless unconditional love!

In the precious name of Jesus Christ, our Lord and Savior,

Amen!

CHAPTER 34

The Gideons!

"Then saith he unto his disciples, The harvest truly is plenteous, but the labourers are few; Pray ye therefore the Lord of the harvest, that he will send forth labourers into his harvest."

—Matthew 9:37-38

WORLDLY WISDOM

Missions statistics tell us there are over seven and one-half billion people in the world today, and over three billion of these people are among the unreached, who have never heard the name of Jesus.

The above passage found in the Gospel of Matthew gives us two ways for us to reach the unsaved: by praying earnestly for God to give us the compassion and concern for those separated from God; to be involved financially in sending out those workers to spread the good news of the Gospel, and for some to answer God's call to go, to witness to others, which may allow the Holy Spirit to convict them of their sins, so they too, might be saved.

The Merriam-Webster dictionary defines *gideon* in this way: "An early Hebrew hero noted for his defeat of the Midianites"; and *Gideon* in this way: "a member of an interdenominational organization whose activities include the placing of Bibles in hotel rooms."

What is Gideons?

Gideons International is an organization whose purpose has been sharing the Gospel with the world since 1899.

The vision of Samuel Hill, John Nicholson, and Will Knights at a meeting, July 1, 1899, in a YMCA in Janesville, Wisconsin, was to create an association of born-again Christian business and professional men to share the gospel with the world.

Little did these three men know, from the humble beginnings of the association of three members, the organization would grow today to a membership of over two hundred sixty-nine thousand Gideons and Auxiliary.

From the first twenty-five Bibles placed on November 10, 1908, at the Superior Hotel, located in Superior (now called Iron Mountain), Montana, distribution has grown to placement today, of over two billion Bibles and New Testaments, at a staggering rate of two copies of God's Word distributed per second.

I am proud to be a member of Gideons International. I look forward each day to obeying the instruction of the Great Commission located in Matthew 28:16-20 to spread His teachings to all the nations of the world.

I look forward to bringing the good news of the Gospel to those who have not heard it, and to be a beacon of light for the unsaved, allowing the Holy Spirit to convict them, so they too might enjoy eternal salvation. As Paul tells us in Ephesians 2:8, "For by grace are ye saved through faith; and that not of yourselves: it is the gift of God."

Remember, the subject is Jesus. Thank You, Jesus. God bless You.

ILLUSTRATION

The following illustration concerning witness is taken from Michael P. Green's book *1500 Illustrations for Biblical Preaching*:

> A minister was making a wooden trellis to support a climbing vine. As he was pounding away, he noticed that a little boy was watching him. The youngster didn't say a word, so the preacher kept on working, thinking the lad would leave. But he didn't. Pleased at the thought that his work was being admired, the pastor said, "Well, son, trying to pick up some pointers on gardening?"
>
> "No," replied the boy, "I'm just waiting to hear what a preacher says when he hits his thumb with a hammer."

GODLY WISDOM

I truly believe, once we have asked Jesus into our lives, once we have faith in Jesus, once we have turned complete control of our lives to him, then we begin to do His will for our lives. I feel at that moment; we begin to fulfill God's plan for our life.

Thank You, Lord Jesus, for leading me to the Gideons! I thank God for helping me to wake up each morning, trying to please Him. I know by pleasing Him, I will be fulfilling His plan for my life in His grand scheme, His grand plan for the salvation of the world.

PERSONAL EXPERIENCE: DIVINE APPOINTMENT!

At a morning breakfast in November 2019, I met a group of Christ-followers, brothers in Christ, to meet under the umbrella of Gideons International. I discovered the men are truly God's disciples, following God's commandment to make disciples of all men and to witness to all the nations, to spread the good news of the Gospel, in the name of the Father, the Son, and the Holy Spirit. I truly feel my meeting with them that morning was a divine appointment. I believe God, in His omniscience and omnipotence, planned this day for me as I continue my journey to salvation. I feel the Holy Spirit led me to that meeting place in order to do God's will, to further the kingdom of God, while I am here on earth. Thank You, Lord Jesus. Thank You, Holy Spirit. Thank You, Father.

It is an honor for me to serve Jesus. I know when I please Him, I am doing His will, and through the work of the Holy Spirit in me, the fruits of the spirit will flow through my heart, my heart will be a conduit for God's unconditional love, and others will see in me, God's love, God's joy, God's peace, God's patience, God's kindness, God's goodness, God's faithfulness, God's gentleness, and God's self-control.

These attributes of the Holy Spirit will serve as a light, a beacon of light to those who are unsaved. They will serve as a way for the Holy Spirit to convict the unsaved, so they too might spend an eternity with our father God when they die. As Jesus tells us, there's only "one way to the Father, and that is through me."

When we become Christian, we begin to work for Jesus. In Matthew 28:16-20, Jesus tells us what we are to do:

> Then the eleven disciples went away into Galilee, into a
> mountain where Jesus had appointed them. And when they
> saw him, they worshipped him: but some doubted. And

Jesus came and spake unto them, saying, All power is given unto me in heaven and in earth. Go ye therefore, and teach all nations, baptizing them in the name of the Father, and of the Son, and of the Holy Ghost: Teaching them to observe all things whatsoever I have commanded you: and, lo, I am with you always, even unto the end of the world. Amen.

We are to become fishers of men. Every Christians duty is to do as God commands us to do, witness to those around us!

What does it mean to witness?

Since I was "born again," nothing has been more exciting and spiritually rewarding than witnessing the good news of the Gospel! However, I must admit, in the beginning, I was afraid to witness to others.

During my journey to salvation, I have met many who make a claim I do not witness; I leave that up to the pastors and evangelists. When I have dug deeper into why they believe that, many in the end would admit they don't witness to others because they are afraid to. In his article entitled "I'm Afraid to Share My Faith," Trevin Wax offers these reasons why they don't witness:

- I might not do it right, and this will turn them away from the Gospel.
- I don't witness to my family because it might lead to family dysfunction.
- I don't want to be rejected.
- If they ask me questions, I might not have the right answers.

Jesus does not offer a loophole in Matthew 28:16-20. In this passage, he does not say if you are afraid, you don't have to witness.

Although, as Christian, God commands us to be fishers of men, I'm afraid many Christians do not. I do believe you can witness to others by becoming a conduit for the Holy Spirit, so others see in you the fruits of the Spirit, allowing the Holy Spirit to convict others.

For those who don't believe they need to share the Gospel through prayer and meditation in God's Word, I believe God will give each person an answer to how they can best participate in the Great Commission.

How do I witness?

I will not attempt to answer this question in this book. For those interested in pursuing this topic further, a good starting point is to study the Bible. Talk with your pastor or ask a Gideon for more information.

However, I will give the following pointers as a starting point for those interested in witnessing, taken from a Gideons International publication, entitled *Conversations: A Simple Approach to Sharing the Gospel:*

- No one can come to Jesus unless the Holy Spirit draws them.
- Pray for reception to the Holy Spirit's conviction.
- Pray for open doors.
- Pray for boldness.

———

PERSONAL EXPERIENCE: TWO OF THE SADDEST MOMENTS IN MY LIFE!

At a recent Gideon Meeting in April 2021, Brother Randall shared the following:

"What are two of the saddest moments in your life that you can remember? For me, the following would be the two saddest moments. First, to arrive at heaven's gate, stand in front of God at the Great White Throne Judgement, and hear Jesus say He does not know me. The second saddest moment would be after being given passage to Heaven, standing at the right hand of God, watching a friend, acquaintance, or family member condemned to hell, and as they are escorted away to begin their journey to hell, have them turn to me and say why didn't you tell me about Jesus!"

So, Jesus is the subject. As Jim Lyon tells us in his book *Jesus B: The Calling of Every Christian,*

The Holy Spirit will help us to see like Jesus, here like Jesus, act like Jesus, love like Jesus, risk like Jesus, and be like Jesus. Thank you, our heavenly father, for loving us so much you became flesh. You as God incarnate, became the man known as Jesus and walked among us on earth. You showed us that it is possible to live without sin because Jesus did. You gave us a small glimpse of what it will be like when we get to heaven, a glimpse of what it is to live without sin and to have an eternal relationship with the Father in Heaven.

Because He loved us so much, He decided the only way He could have a human family, to spend an eternity with humans who have a sinful nature, was to pay the penalty for our sin and die on the cross at Calvary. By doing this, we could be justified, made right, in His sight.

Because of God's grace and kindness, He has provided a way for us to spend an eternity with Him, and there is only one way, and that is through faith in Jesus. Thank You for this gift of salvation, our heavenly Father!

PRAYER

Our heavenly Father,

You are beautiful, and we know You are the great *I am.* We give all the glory to You and thank You for Your love that abounds in us.

We need a touch from You, and God, help us to trust the fact You are always present. Lord, we know You will stand by us during our darkest moments.

We know that true faith will conquer the darkness and by the cross, we are saved. We want to take Your Word and shine it all around but first, help us to live according to Your Word.

When time has surrendered, and Earth is no more, we know we will be rejoicing with You in heaven. Therefore, with angels and archangels, and with all the company of heaven, we laud and magnify Your glorious name.

Evermore praising You and saying, *Holy, holy, holy, Lord God of hosts, heaven, and Earth are full of Your glory. Glory be to You, O Lord most high.*

In the precious name of Jesus name, we pray,

Amen.

CHAPTER 35

Precious Mother!

Strength and honour are her clothing; And she shall rejoice in time to come. She openeth her mouth with wisdom; And in her tongue is the law of kindness. She looketh well to the ways of her household, And eateth not the bread of idleness. Her children arise up, and call her blessed; Her husband also, and he praiseth her. Many daughters have done virtuously, But thou excellest them all. Favour is deceitful, and beauty is vain: But a woman that feareth the Lord, she shall be praised. Give her of the fruit of her hands; And let her own works praise her in the gates.

—Proverbs 31:25-31

WORLDLY WISDOM

In this passage, the Holy Spirit is describing a godly woman and faithful things she might do during her lifetime. He tells us she fears the Lord, she is trustworthy, she is hardworking, she is strong, and she is kind and caring,

The Cambridge Dictionary defines mother in this way: "A female parent; to treat someone with kindness and affection and try to protect that person from danger or difficulty."

The Dictionary of Bible Themes defines mothers in this way: "The female parent of children. The role and influence of mothers are frequently stressed in Scripture, and their care for children is used as a picture of God's care for his people."

In today's world, many women might cringe at this description of the "perfect woman" in Proverbs. Some might feel guilty because, in this day of the hustle and bustle, where women are asked to multitask, they may feel, even on their best day, they lack the ability to measure up to this woman.

According to worldly wisdom, humans can have a biological and/or a non-biological mother. Biological motherhood occurs when a female gestates a fertilized ovum after sexual intercourse. A fetus develops from the viable zygote in the woman's uterus. This process of gestation is around nine months in duration. Non-biological motherhood can occur through adoption, surrogate mother relationship, and same-sex relationships.

A woman becomes a mother when she has a child. As a mother, she is expected to care for and love her children. Role expectations can change over time and depend on the culture and the woman's social class. Traditionally, many cultures expect women to be both a mother and wife, spending most of their time in these roles. Traditionally, in most parts of the world, a mother was expected to be a married woman, with birth outside marriage highly frowned upon. However, in many Western countries, single motherhood is more socially acceptable.

Nearly all religions define tasks or roles for mothers through their religious laws or through the glorification of mothers. Major religions which have scriptural canon regarding mothers include Christianity, Judaism, and Islam.

History records many instances of mother-offspring violence. In modern history, matricide, the killing of one's mother, and filicide, the killing of one's son or daughter, have been studied but remain poorly understood. Causes for these morally reprehensible acts of violence include psychosis, schizophrenia, and domestic abuse.

Throughout history, mothers with their children have often been the subject of artistic works, such as paintings, sculptures, or writings. Most people believe in the universality of mother love. However, before discussing godly wisdom concerning motherhood, the elephant in the room needs to be addressed, the "bad mother."

In her article "What Is A Toxic Mother and How Does She Affect Relationships?" Sarah Fader lists these eight characteristics or traits of an abusive or toxic mother:

- Constant criticism
- Controlling behavior
- Guilt-tripping and manipulation
- Humiliation
- Invalidation of your emotions
- Passive aggression
- Disrespectful of personal boundaries
- One-sided relationship

Why do some mothers become abusive or toxic mothers? Many psychologists think these characteristics are due to "dysfunctional coping mechanisms" in patriarchal cultures, leading to an inner sense of disempowerment and worthlessness, factors that determine all relationships in a person's life.

Psychologists recommend mothers struggling with these problems seek professional help. I would agree, but strongly from a Christian counselor.

ILLUSTRATION

The following illustration concerning motherhood is taken from Michael P. Green's book *1500 Illustrations for Biblical Preaching*:

A small boy invaded the lingerie section of a large department store and shyly presented his problem to a woman clerk in the lingerie department. "I want to buy a slip as a present for my mom," he said. "But, I don't know what size she wears."

"Is she tall or short, fat or skinny?" asked the clerk.

"She's just perfect," beamed the small boy. So the clerk wrapped up a size thirty-four for him.

Two days later, mom came to the store by herself and changed the slip to a size fifty-two.

GODLY WISDOM

In Psalm 127 and Psalm 128, the Holy Spirit gives us a beautiful description of mothers and children in the home:

> Except the LORD build the house, they labour in vain that build it: Except the LORD keep the city, the watchman waketh but in vain. It is vain for you to rise up early, to sit up late, To eat the bread of sorrows: For so he giveth his beloved sleep. Lo, children are a heritage of the LORD: And the fruit of the womb is his reward. As arrows are in the hand of a mighty man; So are children of the youth. Happy is the man that hath his quiver full of them: They shall not be ashamed, But they shall speak with the enemies in the gate.
>
> —Psalm 127

Barry Denzil Haney, MD

Blessed is everyone that feareth the LORD; That walketh in his ways. For thou shalt eat the labour of thine hands: Happy shalt thou be, and it shall be well with thee. Thy wife shall be as a fruitful vine By the sides of thine house: Thy children like olive plants Round about thy table. Behold, that thus shall the man be blessed that feareth the LORD. The LORD shall bless thee out of Zion: And thou shalt see the good of Jerusalem All the days of thy life. Yea, thou shalt see thy children's children, And peace upon Israel.

—Psalm 128

In Malachi 2:14, the Holy Spirit tells us that children play an important part in fulfilling God's desire:

Yet ye say, Wherefore? Because the LORD hath been witness between thee and the wife of thy youth, Against whom thou hast dealt treacherously: Yet is she thy companion, and the wife of thy covenant.

In Titus 2:4-5, the Holy Spirit assigns duties to women in the church:

That they may teach the young women to be sober, to love their husbands, to love their children, To be discreet, chaste, keepers at home, good, obedient to their own husbands, that the word of God be not blasphemed.

The fundamental importance of motherhood is recognized throughout Scripture in the following ways:

- *Happiness for women in motherhood:* "He maketh the barren woman to keep house, And to be a joyful mother of children. Praise ye the LORD" (Psalm 113:9).

- *Mother's cleansing after childbirth:* "And when the days of her purification according to the law of Moses were accomplished, they brought him to Jerusalem, to present him to the Lord; (As it is written in the law of the Lord, Every male that openeth the womb shall be called holy to the Lord;) And to offer a sacrifice according to that which is said in the law of the Lord, A pair of turtledoves, or two young pigeons" (Luke 2:22-24).

- *Mother's role as teacher:* "My son, hear the instruction of thy father, And forsake not the law of thy mother" (Proverbs 1:8).

- *Responsibility to discipline children:* "The rod and reproof give wisdom: But a child left to himself bringeth his mother to shame" (Proverbs 29:15).

- *Sorrow of parents at their children's conduct:* "The proverbs of Solomon. A wise son maketh a glad father: But a foolish son is the heaviness of his mother" (Proverbs 10:1).

- *Negative influence of some mothers upon their children:* But when Herod's birthday was kept, the daughter of Herodias danced before them, and pleased Herod. Whereupon he promised with an oath to give her whatsoever she would ask. And she, being before instructed of her mother, said, Give me here John Baptist's head in a charger" (Matthew 14:6-8).

- *Children's responsibility to honor their parents:* "Hearken unto thy father that begat thee and despise not thy mother when she is old" (Proverbs 23:22).

- *Penalties for disobeying parents:* "And he that smiteth his father, or his mother, shall be surely put to death... And he that curseth his father, or his mother, shall surely be put to death" (Exodus 21:15,17).

Barry Denzil Haney, MD

Godly wisdom tells us when women devote themselves to their families, homes, and church; they are fulfilling God's will for their lives!

MY PERSONAL EXPERIENCE: MY MOTHER'S TESTIMONY!

On a spring morning in late May 2011, at the age of eighty-eight, my mother was outside working on her roses when she fell and struck her head on the fence. This began a three-week roller coaster ride of surgery, hospitalization, and hospice care ending in her death on June 17, 2011.

Within two hours of striking her head, she was transported to the hospital, evaluated in the emergency room, transported to the surgical department, where she underwent evacuation of a large subdural hematoma, which resulted in early transtentorial brain herniation and near-death during the surgical procedure. Over the next few days, her doctors concluded she had less than six months to live, which would require a gastrostomy tube be placed to feed her and confinement to a nursing home bed until she died.

During this hospitalization, the neurologist informed me of this shocking prognosis about a week before my mother died. Because he was a friend, he asked me if I would like to share this devastating news with her instead of him. I decided I would share this poor prognosis with her.

At that season of my life, I did not know Jesus. I did not know Jesus as my personal Savior. Although very difficult for me to do, I agreed I should be the one to inform my mother she had less than six months to live, only if she agreed to feedings through a tube and confinement to a nursing home bed. The other option was hospice care which would end her life in approximately seven days.

She was quiet for a moment, then asked me why hadn't the neurologist told her. I explained to her the neurologist asked me if I would like to share this with her instead of him. She turned her eyes from me, then said she was tired and closed her eyes.

After what seemed an eternity, but was probably three-four minutes, she opened her eyes wide and looked at me with an expression of joy and ecstasy. I asked my mother where she had been.

In a loud shout of exhilaration, she exclaimed, "I have been with Jesus, I am ready to go to heaven to spend an eternity with Him!" A few seconds later, she looked at me and said firmly, "I do not want anything done; I want hospice care!"

Needless to say, I was overwhelmed with sadness! But eventually, I was able to understand the miracle that occurred during this precious time with my mother!

The Holy Spirit used this precious moment I shared with my mother to convict me, beginning my search along the narrow path which led to my salvation, November 11, 2019!

PRAYER

Our heavenly Father

Thank You for providing us a mother who can under-stand our tears! Thank You for a mother who can inspire us through her daily prayers, sacrifices, and personal example!

Thank You for a mother who can soothe our disappoint-ments and mistakes! Thank You for a mother who, through her love, can share our heartbreaks!

Thank You for the angels who fashioned our mothers with a tender heart! Thank You for providing us with a mother's forgiveness and a fresh start!

In the precious name of Jesus Christ our Lord and Savior,

Amen!

Barry Denzil Haney, MD

CHAPTER 36

My Buddy, Little Bob!

"Make no friendship with an angry man; And with a furious man thou shalt not go: Lest thou learn his ways and get a snare to thy soul."

—Proverbs 22:24-25

WORLDLY WISDOM

In this passage, the Holy Spirit is teaching me not to have a relationship with angry people because their anger controls them, and this trait is not conducive to developing any meaningful relationship.

The Cambridge Dictionary defines friends in this way: "Persons you know well and like a lot, but who are usually not a member of your family."

The Dictionary of Bible Themes defines friends in this way:

> Those to whom one is close; Scripture stresses that friendship is often but not always a positive thing: where good friends can be invaluable in the life of faith, bad friends can be obstacles to the faith of believers, or even lead them astray totally.

Friendship was a regular ancient top of discussion. According to Craig Keener, in his book *Friendship. Dictionary of New Testament Background: a Compendium of Contemporary Biblical Scholarship 2000*, the kinds of friendship in antiquity included political friendship, pattern-client friendship, and nonhierarchical friendship, requiring the ideals such as loyalty, intimacy, shared confidences, sharing of all resources, and dying for others.

The Beatles, in 1967, released a hit song called "With A Little Help From My Friends." In this song, a memorable verse says, "*I get by with a little help from my friend.*"

This song still resonates today as an anthem for many of what true friendship means. Aristotle described a friend as a "single soul dwelling in two bodies."

In her article "11 Signs of A Genuine Friendship," Lindsay lists the following eleven signs of a genuine friendship:

- They push us to be more accepting of ourselves.
- They call us out when we're in the wrong.
- They're present.
- They really listen.
- They support us through adversity.
- They keep our stress in check.
- They keep us humble.
- They have our backs, even when life gets tricky.

Barry Denzil Haney, MD

- They make the friendship a priority.

- They practice forgiveness.

- They make us want to be better people.

As you read through the list of characteristics of a genuine relationship, does the list remind you of someone in your life?

Many of you will say yes to this question, but sadly, like me, many will say no, because you have not shared a genuine relationship with anyone during your life journey.

For those who say no to the question I posed, many will say they identify these characteristics in their pets, their closest friend. In a recent article "Pet Statistics," I found the following statistics about pets in the United States:

- Approximately six and one-half million companion animals enter US animal shelters nationwide every year.

- Each year, approximately one and one half million shelter animals are euthanized (six hundred seventy thousand dogs and eight hundred sixty thousand cats).

- Over three million shelter animals are adopted each year (dogs and cats equally divided).

- It's estimated that seventy-eight million dogs and over eighty-six million cats are owned in the United States.

In his article "Pet Industry Spending Trends Expected in 2019", Chris Rowland reports, pet industry spending has been steadily increasing and is expected to reach ninety-six billion dollars by 2020.

As I began writing this chapter, I realized my life journey was missing something, a genuine relationship with another human being. As a child, I was an introvert. I convinced myself, from an early age, I could not trust anyone because of the negativity I experienced when I tried to have a relationship with another person. Because of these disappointments I experienced, I found it much easier to live in my own imaginary world, with my own imaginary friends, and I actively built up impenetrable walls of separation from other people to prevent them from entering my imaginary world, preventing them from hurting me!

This wall-building has continued and become more sophisticated, more formidable, more elaborate during my life journey. This continued until two years ago when I finally established a genuine relationship with God. When I look back at my life journey until that moment, I cannot think of one single person I could count on as a genuine friend.

Sounds like a pretty lonely, pathetic, self-centered life journey, doesn't it?

Sure, I have had many superficial relationships with many people throughout my life journey because of my life experiences, which demanded, or I should say, required me to have. But, in all honesty, I never had a genuine relationship with anyone, not even with a family member, my children, or even my loving, supporting wife of fifty years.

Another reason for refusing to develop relationships with another person was my refusal to let them discover my deep, dark secret, my imagined, unpardonable sin, the one thing even God could not keep me from doing, despite many cries for His help over the years! I could never let anyone get close enough to me to learn of this terrible, unpardonable sin. I was enslaved by the one thing which controlled my life, the one thing which eternally separated me from my Father God, the one thing which condemned me to hell for an eternity!

From 2011 to 2017, I marked off of my bucket list, one of the major goals in my life, to own a sizable piece of land in the backwoods of Kentucky. From the time I was a Boy Scout hiking the trails at Camp McKee Scout Reservation, where Daniel Boone reportedly roamed, I dreamed of owning a piece of God's country in the forests of Kentucky. That dream became a reality when I purchased nearly two hundred fifty acres of essentially undeveloped land, called Muse Hollow, in south-central Kentucky, near the Tennessee border.

Barry Denzil Haney, MD

Because of health concerns, I sold the property after only five years of ownership, but during that five-year period, I experienced "heaven on earth," my own "Garden of Eden," a place I affectionately called "God's Country."

MY PERSONAL EXPERIENCE: LITTLE BOB!

During this time at Muse Hollow, I developed the first genuine relationship with another creature God created, my dog, Little Bob.

Little Bob was my buddy, my devoted friend!

Although small in stature, he more than made up for his lack of size, with his brash and fearless personality when confronted with danger. He once held off a pack of coyotes at Muse Hollow, who were determined to have him for lunch, but a pistol shot from my brother Clay sent the coyotes running for cover.

His exploratory and hunting instincts were legendary!

His whole purpose in life was to survey the ridge tops surrounding Muse Hollow, to protect his human companions from the dangers lurking in the deep, dark forests beyond the tree line in the hollers. Of course, he was always hunting for the trophy bone, from the dead carcasses of animals or wayward calves, who had ventured into the shadows of the forest.

One triumphal day, he couldn't wait to show my brother Clay, the carcass of a successful hunting expedition, standing over the fresh remains of a dead skunk he had killed earlier. But of course, the skunk got his revenge when he sprayed the victorious Little Bob, with a healthy dose of his vile-smelling scent, from his glands right before he died!

One evening while my brother, wife, and I were sitting on the porch of the cabin, enjoying the cool breeze of a summer evening, Little Bob arrived on the front porch, obviously injured.

After careful examination, I found two different fang mark bites on his back legs, evidence of two successful attacks from resident timber rattlesnakes, who reluctantly shared God's Country with us. Over the next few minutes, I recognized the death rattles of impending death; sure Little Bob was going to leave this paradise soon!

My wife, a nurse, went into the cabin and brought back a Benadryl tablet, quickly stuffed it down the back of Little Bob's throat, trying to prevent what I thought was his soon demise.

To my amazement, this small dog made a miraculous recovery from what I was sure, certain death. His bright, clever, determined, hard-as-nails personality soon returned, as he was ready for new adventures in God's country!

GODLY WISDOM

In his book *Face to Face: Meditations on Friendship and Hospitality*, Steve Wilkins makes this observation about the difficulties we have in this modern age to develop any sort of godly friendship:

> The nature of the world itself, the lack of community in our age, and the fact that we have been brought up in a world that is so barren of godly friendship, all mean that we are crippled to some degree in understanding what it means, what its demands are, and how to obtain it.

The Bible tells us God is the only friend whose love is always unconditional and unlimited, but as I discussed in Chapter 14, God's love requires two conditions to be met. The first condition was met by the death of Jesus on the cross at Calvary, when he paid the price for our sins. The second condition is met by the believer, by God's grace through faith.

In James 4:4-10, The Bible tells us instead of focusing on getting friendship in the world; we should focus on our relationship with God:

Ye adulterers and adulteresses, know ye not that the friend-ship of the world is enmity with God? whosoever there-fore will be a friend of the world is the enemy of God. Do ye think that the scripture saith in vain, The spirit that dwelleth in us lusteth to envy? But he giveth more grace. Wherefore he saith, God resisteth the proud, but giveth grace unto the humble. Submit yourselves therefore to God. Resist the devil, and he will flee from you. Draw nigh to God, and he will draw nigh to you. Cleanse your hands, ye sinners; and purify your hearts, ye double minded. Be afflicted, and mourn, and weep: let your laughter be turned to mourning, and your joy to heaviness. Humble yourselves in the sight of the Lord, and he shall lift you up.

In her book *Biblical Counselling Keys on Friendship*, June Hunt offers these guidelines on how to fan the flame of friendship based on the listed Scriptural passages in parentheses:

- Recognize that you need wise friends (Proverbs 13:20).
- Look for others in need of a friend (Philippians 2:4).
- Ask God to bring a faithful friend into your life (1 John 5:14).
- Be approachable by smiling at others (Proverbs 15:13).
- Speak to others by name (Jesus speaks to you by name John 10:3).
- Listen attentively to others (Ecclesiastes 3:7).
- Give genuine compliments and encouragement (Proverbs 16:21).
- Ask open-ended questions (Proverbs 20:5).
- Help others verbalize their feelings (Proverbs 27:9).

- Look for the kernel of truth in your friend's criticism (Proverbs 27:17).

Finally, in Philippians 2:1-11, the Holy Spirit gives this advice on how to have a genuine godly relationship:

> If there be therefore any consolation in Christ, if any comfort of love, if any fellowship of the Spirit, if any bowels and mercies, Fulfil ye my joy, that ye be likeminded, having the same love, being of one accord, of one mind. Let nothing be done through strife or vain glory; but in lowliness of mind let each esteem other better than themselves. Look not every man on his own things, but every man also on the things of others. Let this mind be in you, which was also in Christ Jesus: Who, being in the form of God, thought it not robbery to be equal with God: But made himself of no reputation, and took upon him the form of a servant, and was made in the likeness of men: And being found in fashion as a man, he humbled himself, and became obedient unto death, even the death of the cross. Wherefore God also hath highly exalted him and given him a name which is above every name: That at the name of Jesus every knee should bow, of things in heaven, and things in earth, and things under the earth; And that every tongue should confess that Jesus Christ is Lord, to the glory of God the Father.

———

ILLUSTRATION

The following illustration concerning friendship is taken from Michael P. Green's book *1500 Illustrations for Biblical Preaching*:

A new homeowner's riding lawn mower had broken down, and he had been working fruitlessly for two hours trying to get it back together. Suddenly, one of his neighbors appeared with a handful of tools. "Can I give some help?" he asked. In twenty minutes, he had the mower functioning beautifully.

"Thanks a million," the now-happy newcomer said. "And say, what do you make with such fine tools?"

"Mostly friends," the neighbor smiled. "I'm available any time."

PRAYER

Our heavenly Father,

Please help those struggling with relationships in their lives! Help them realize they must first establish a relationship with You. You are a God of relationships, and before we can have a relationship with You, we must first remove the obstacle of sin, separating us from Your eternal love. Help us to realize, a genuine relationship requires trust! We must first put our faith in Jesus, in order to have an eternal loving relationship with You!

We also must ask forgiveness of our sins and repent of our sins. Then by Your grace, Your mercy, we become born again! We become a child of God! Jesus resides in our hearts, and the Holy Spirit begins the miraculous cleansing of our spirit, preparing us for the glorious day in our future, You have promised us, when we will stand before You, on final judgement day, and Jesus will be at our side and will confirm to You, He knew us, and then we will begin an eternal loving relationship with You in heaven!

In the precious name of Jesus Christ our Lord and Savior,

Amen!

CHAPTER 37

Family Thanksgiving: "Poppy Talk"

"Speaking to yourselves in psalms and hymns and spiritual songs, singing and making melody in your heart to the Lord; Giving thanks always for all things unto God and the Father in the name of our Lord Jesus Christ."

—Ephesians 5:19-20

WORLDLY WISDOM

In this passage, through the hand of Paul, the Holy Spirit is telling me to sing and make music in our heart, always thanking God for His love, for imagining us in His dreams, and for creating us in His image.

In his article "A Special Exegesis of Ephesians 5:19 and Colossians 3:16," John McNaugher summarizes what Paul means when he says "the psalms and hymns and spiritual songs" of these passages:

> That the "psalms and hymns and spiritual songs" of these passages included nothing that was inspired, nor any compositions newly inspired in the apostolic age...that they are all embraced in the book of Psalms, this finding being based upon the impregnable testimony of the Greek Bible

and Psalter used by Paul and the Pauline churches, upon the usage of contemporary Hellenistic writers, upon the witness of the gospels according to Matthew and Mark, upon the conformity of the Psalter to this threefold characterization, and upon the fact that an exclusive reference to the Psalms satisfies every postulate of the context.

The Cambridge Dictionary defines thanksgiving in this way: "The acts of saying or showing that you are grateful, especially to God."

The Dictionary of Bible Themes defines thanksgiving in this way:

> The offering of thanks, especially for gifts received; Scripture emphasizes the importance of giving thanks to God for all his gifts and works, both as an expression of our dependence upon him and gratitude to him.

Thanksgiving Day is an annual, national holiday in the United States, Canada, some of the Caribbean islands, and Liberia, celebrating the harvest and other blessings of the past year. The American holiday is rich in legend and symbolism. It is modeled after the 1621 harvest feast shared by the Pilgrims and the Wampanoag people in the Plymouth colony. The traditional fare of the Thanksgiving meal typically includes turkey, bread stuffing, potatoes, cranberries, and pumpkin pie.

For Christians in the United States, Thanksgiving is celebrated as a day to give thanks to God for His gracious and sufficient provision. However, because of secularism, many in our culture think of Thanksgiving as a day of feasting, football, and family gathering.

Barry Denzil Haney, MD

MY PERSONAL EXPERIENCE: ONE SPECIAL THANKSGIVING DAY SHARED WITH THE FAMILY!

I would like to share with you the following conversation I had with my family at a Thanksgiving Dinner in 2019:

"As most of you know, I have been diagnosed with moderate dementia, for which I receive daily medication. Although this helps me think faster, my wife says, the medication has sped up my thinking process so much, it makes me talk too fast. Despite this, I still have memory problems from time to time. Because of these memory problems, I find myself relying on my 'smartphone' when giving a presentation.

I used to be so vain, I would spend hours memorizing my presentation prior to delivering it; I'm sure to impress the listener, a little prideful, I think you would agree, but now that I'm a Christian, I am striving to be more humble. So, '*Let's humor the old man!*' Maybe a future title for a book?

Since I am the oldest person at this gathering, I ask you to humor me. As most of you know, although officially retired from secular work, I now work for Jesus. Therefore, I ask for your indulgence as I tell you about Jesus.

As we get ready to eat the delicious thanksgiving dinner lovingly prepared for us, and before I give the traditional blessing before we eat, I would like to pose this question to each of you: 'What comes to mind when you think of 'Thanksgiving?' Like most, do you picture a time of eating, partying, watching parades, or watching football, or do you picture a time of thankfulness, thanking God for all your blessings?'

I would like to read you an excerpt from an article I recently read entitled 'What Should be the Focus of Christians on Thanksgiving?'

The event we commonly call the 'First Thanksgiving' was celebrated by the Pilgrims after their first harvest in the New World in October 1621. It was truly a time of thanksgiving, with the feast lasting three days, and according to Edward Winslow, it was attended by ninety Native Americans and fifty-three Pilgrims. These Pilgrims, seeking religious freedom and opportunity in America, gave thanks to God for His provision for them in helping them find twenty acres of cleared land, for the fact that there were no hostile Indians in that area, for their newfound religious freedom, and for God's provision of an interpreter to the Indians in Squanto. Along with the feasting and games involving the colonists and more than eighty friendly Indians (who added to the feast by bringing wild turkeys and venison), prayers, sermons, and songs of praise were important in the celebration. Three days were spent in feasting and prayer.

From that time forward, Thanksgiving has been celebrated as a day to give thanks to God for His gracious and sufficient provision. President Abraham Lincoln officially set aside the last Thursday of November, in 1863, 'as a day of thanksgiving and praise to our beneficent Father.' In 1941, Congress ruled that after 1941, the fourth Thursday of November be observed as Thanksgiving Day and be a legal holiday."

Unfortunately, I'm afraid, for many in the United States, thanksgiving today is more about eating, partying, and watching football, than for thanking God for all His blessings in the past year.

GODLY WISDOM

In the Bible, what does godly wisdom tell us about thanksgiving?

In Psalm 107:21-22, the Holy Spirit tells us how to praise the Lord: "Oh that men would praise the LORD for his goodness, And for his wonderful works to the children of men! And let them sacrifice the sacrifices of thanksgiving and declare his works with rejoicing."

In both the Old Testament and New Testament, thanksgiving is mentioned as an activity involving the community of faith.

In the Old Testament offerings were expressions of thanksgiving in Leviticus 7:12-15:

> If he offer it for a thanksgiving, then he shall offer with the sacrifice of thanksgiving unleavened cakes mingled with oil, and unleavened wafers anointed with oil, and cakes mingled with oil, of fine flour, fried. Besides the cakes, he shall offer for his offering leavened bread with the sacrifice of thanksgiving of his peace offerings. And of it he shall offer one out of the whole oblation for a heave offering unto the LORD, and it shall be the priest's that sprinkleth the blood of the peace offerings. And the flesh of the sacrifice of his peace offerings for thanksgiving shall be eaten the same day that it is offered; he shall not leave any of it until the morning.

In Jerusalem, temple musicians played the lyre and were leaders in praise. During David's reign, trained leaders conducted "songs of praise and thanksgiving" (Nehemiah 12:46). In many of the Psalms, thanksgiving is mentioned in the following ways; thanks for deliverance from enemies, hostile accusers, and death; songs of thanksgiving; exhortations to enter God's presence with thanksgiving; and calls to give thanks.

In John 6:10-11, Jesus gave thanks as he fed the five thousand:

And Jesus said, Make the men sit down. Now there was much grass in the place. So the men sat down, in number about five thousand. And Jesus took the loaves; and when he had given thanks, he distributed to the disciples, and the disciples to them that were set down; and likewise of the fishes as much as they would.

Thanksgiving is described as limitless by Paul's admonition to Ephesian believers in Ephesians 5:18-20:

And be not drunk with wine, wherein is excess; but be filled with the Spirit; Speaking to yourselves in psalms and hymns and spiritual songs, singing and making melody in your heart to the Lord; Giving thanks always for all things unto God and the Father in the name of our Lord Jesus Christ.

In his book *Worship: Adoration and Action,* D. A. Carson says this about praise and worship, "Biblical religion is God-centredness: in short, it is worship."

In closing, the sense of thanksgiving as recognizing God as the Creator is made clear in Revelation 4:9-11:

And when those beasts give glory and honour and thanks to him that sat on the throne, who liveth for ever and ever, The four and twenty elders fall down before him that sat on the throne, and worship him that liveth for ever and ever, and cast their crowns before the throne, saying, Thou art worthy, O Lord, to receive glory and honour and power: for thou hast created all things, and for thy pleasure they are and were created.

Barry Denzil Haney, MD

ILLUSTRATION

The following illustration concerning thankfulness is taken from Michael P. Green's book *1500 Illustrations for Biblical Preaching*:

A little boy was asked by his father to say grace at the table. While the rest of the family waited, the little guy eyed every dish of food his mother had prepared. After the examination, he bowed his head and honestly prayed, "Lord, I don't like the looks of it, but I thank you for it, and I'll eat it anyway. Amen."

PRAYER

Our heavenly Father,

You are the beginning and the end, the Alpha and the Omega, You are the divine Creator, You are the great, I am, You are my personal Savior, You are my Creator God, You are the one and only. Hallelujah, we bow down before You and praise and worship Your name. Thank You for being my Creator!

Thank You for imagining me in Your dreams! Thank You for Your unconditional love, mercy, kindness and grace. Thank You for caring for me so much, You died on the cross, so that my sins are forgiven so that I might spend an eternity with You in heaven, even though I don't deserve it. Thank You for forgiving my sins.

Thank You for the hope that You give me each day. Thank You for the opportunity to please You each day. Thank You for giving me the opportunity to play a small part in Your grand plan of salvation for the world. Thank You for all the blessings You have bestowed on me.

Thank You for everything You have given me and blessed me with. There are so many things I have to be thankful for! Help me to always have a thankful attitude and mindset. You are so good, You are so gracious, You are so faithful, thank You Lord Jesus! Thank You, Father, thank You, Son, thank You Holy Spirit!

Thank You for my church; thank You for my pastors. Thank You for my family, thank You for my friends, thank You for my home, thank You for my country.

Thank You for the simplicity of the Gospel. Help us to trust in You as we do Your will. Help us to have a sensitive heart when it comes to this country, not to criticize, but instead look for common ground and consensus!

By the power and the anointing of the Holy Spirit, help us to regain the tender heart we once had. Remove any calluses within us through repentance, by a commitment to live by the law of love. By a renewed devotion to the Word, through daily prayer and meditation, and by fellowship with You.

In the precious name of Jesus Christ our Lord and Savior,

Amen.

Barry Denzil Haney, MD

CHAPTER 38

Pass The Briny Salt & White Light, Please!

Ye are the salt of the earth: but if the salt have lost his savor, wherewith shall it be salted? it is thenceforth good for nothing, but to be cast out, and to be trodden under foot of men. Ye are the light of the world. A city that is set on a hill cannot be hid. Neither do men light a candle, and put it under a bushel, but on a candlestick; and it giveth light unto all that are in the house. Let your light so shine before men, that they may see your good works, and glorify your Father which is in heaven.

—Matthew 5:13-16

WORLDLY WISDOM

In this passage, the Holy Spirit is telling me, once we have faith in Jesus, we *are* the salt of the world and the light of the world.

By our witness, we are instrumental in helping Him convict others of their sin, preventing the moral decay in their life. We are a light to the world because He will use us as a vessel for the fruits of the Spirit to radiate out from us, serving as a beacon of light for the unsaved, so He, by His grace, can convict them of their sin, so they too can spend an eternity with Him in heaven.

The Cambridge Dictionary defines *salt* in this way:

> "As a common white substance, found in sea water and in the ground, used to add flavor to food or to preserve it."

The Dictionary of Bible Themes defines *salt* in this way:

> "As a basic commodity, used for seasoning and preserving foods in biblical times."

The Dictionary of Bible Themes describes *light* in this way: "As the brightness that enables sight in the darkness; Scripture often uses light as a symbol of the saving presence of God in a fallen world, with darkness being used as a symbol of sin or the absence of God."

SALT

Salt is a mineral substance of great importance to human and animal health, as well as to industry. Since ancient times, salt has been a valuable commodity. Salt is not fancy or expensive. It is a common household product.

Salt is sodium chloride, an ionic compound with the chemical formula $NaCl$, which represents a 1:1 ratio of sodium and chloride ions. It can be created in the laboratory by adding together two very reactive elements together, sodium metal and chlorine gas. Sodium is necessary for life. Sodium ions are one of the main ions in the human body and are necessary to regulate the fluid balance of the body. Chlorine ions are necessary for proper nerve function and respiration. Both of the ions are supplied by salt.

Most of the salt we used comes from natural brines, hence the term briny salt. Brine is water containing a high concentration of salt, with the most commercially important natural brines found in the Dead Sea, Austria, France, Germany, India, the United States, and the United Kingdom. These natural brines not only contain a high concentration of salt but also usually contain chlorides and sulfates of potassium, calcium, and magnesium, as well as carbonates and the element of bromine.

Salt has a variety of uses. It is used universally as a seasoning from ancient times until now. Livestock requires salt, often made available in solid blocks. The meat-packing, fish-curing, and food-processing industries use salt as a preservative or seasoning or both, a process used to preserve food since ancient times as well. Salt is used for preserving hides and as a brine for refrigeration.

Salt is very important in the chemical industry. It is required in the manufacture of baking soda, caustic soda, hydrochloric acid, chlorine, and many other chemicals. Salt is also employed in soap, grace, and porcelain enamel manufacture and enters into metallurgical processes as a flux, a substance promoting the fusing of metals.

Large amounts of salt are used in northern climates to help get rid of accumulated snow and ice each year because of salt's ability to lower the melting point when applied to snow or ice. Salt is used in water softening equipment to remove calcium and magnesium compounds from water.

In ancient times, salt was very important to their culture and religion. Salt was used in sacrificial offerings to their gods. Covenants were made over a sacrificial meal, in which salt was a necessary element. One of the oldest roads in Italy is the Via Salaria, the Salt Route, over which Roman salt from Ostia was carried into other parts of Italy. Cakes of salt were used as money in Ethiopia and other parts of Africa and Tibet. Officers and men in the Roman army were given an allowance of salt. In the Middle Ages, people used salt as currency, and it was called "white gold."

LIGHT

Light is electromagnetic energy that can be detected by the human eye. Electromagnetic radiation occurs over a wide range of wavelengths, from gamma rays, with wavelengths less than 1×10^{-11} meters, to radio waves, measured in meters. The wavelengths visible to the human eye are within a very narrow band, from seven hundred nanometers for red light down to about four hundred nanometers for violet light.

If you ask the question, *"What is light?"* no single answer can satisfy the way light is experienced, explored, and exploited. In a general sense, light is the primary tool we use to perceive our world and to communicate within it. Light warms the Earth, is responsible for the weather, is necessary for photosynthesis, and interacts with matter, shaping our universe. Without light, we could not exist.

Because of the importance of salt and light to mankind for daily existence, you can understand why Jesus used salt and light to teach the importance of salvation during the Sermon on the Mount!

ILLUSTRATION

The following illustration concerning witness is taken from Michael P. Green's book *1500 Illustrations for Biblical Preaching*:

> Two Texans were traveling together on vacation. They
> decided to stop at one of the natural wonders of the world,
> Niagara Falls. As they took the beautiful drive from Lake
> Erie to the falls, they were filled with admiration and awe
> at the size and power of the Niagara River. They were
> particularly impressed with the rapids just above the falls

and stopped there to look. From there, they could see the massive mist cloud that always hangs over the precipice.

One of the men, having already been there, said, "Come, and I'll show you the greatest unused power in the world." Taking him to the foot of Niagara Falls, he said, "There is the greatest unused power in the world."

"Ah, no, my friend, not so!" was the reply of the other. "The greatest unused power in the world is the Holy Spirit of the living God."

GODLY WISDOM

In Mark 9:50, the Holy Spirit is warning us to stay committed and dedicated to pleasing God, do not let your dedication and commitment to spreading the good news of the Gospel to others *"leech out:"*

> "Salt is good: but if the salt have lost his saltness, wherewith will ye season it? Have salt in yourselves and have peace one with another."

In Genesis 1:3-5, the Holy Spirit tells us God is the source of natural light:

> And God said, Let there be light: and there was light. And God saw the light, that it was good: and God divided the light from the darkness. And God called the light Day, and the darkness he called Night. And the evening and the morning were the first day.

In 1 John 1:5, the Holy Spirit tells us that Light is a symbol of God: "This then is the message which we have heard of him, and declare unto you, that God is light, and in him is no darkness at all."

In his book *The Living Church: Convictions of a Lifelong Pastor*, John Stott offers this insightful take on the truths of salt and light:

> Both images (salt and light) set the two communities in contrast to each other. On the one hand there is the world, which with all its evil and tragedy is like a dark night, whereas on the other hand there is 'you' who are to be the dark world's light. Again, on the one hand there is the world, which is like rotting meat and decaying fish, whereas on the other hand there is 'you' who are to be its salt, hindering social decay. We might have said in our idiom that they are as different as oil from water. But Jesus said we are to be as different as light from darkness and salt from decay.

Historically salt is used to preserve food, purify it, and prevent it from decay. This is the same thing the Holy Spirit does when he enters into a born-again Christian. The Holy Spirit enters into the person's heart to purify and cleanse, to prevent further decay of the person's spirit. This begins the process of sanctification that occurs in a new Christian's life from the time the Holy Spirit first enters, to the day he reaches heaven on final judgment day, to that time when he finally becomes pure, becomes Christlike, becomes holy as Christ is holy. This progressive sanctification that takes place in us is like the purification of salt used in the Israelites temples during the Old Testament.

In his book *The Bible Guide*, Andrew Knowles tells us this about light:

> Light is utterly different from darkness. It shines out to conquer gloom, reveal a situation or show the way. Jesus says his followers give spiritual light to this world—their

good deeds shining out for the glory of God. So—don't fail the Father by hiding away!

Light is God's Word. When God said, *"Let there be light!"* He was speaking not only about the visual sense of light and darkness but also about the spiritual nature of His love entering into the universe He was creating, replacing darkness, the separation from the Creator God.

We are to be His Light to the unsaved when we are born again, when we have faith in Jesus. We are to be a beacon of light, a ray of hope to those who are unsaved.

Once we become Christians and have faith in Jesus, the Holy Spirit then uses us as a conduit for the fruits of the Spirit to radiate out from us, so others can see the glory of God's kingdom in us. This gives the Holy Spirit the opportunity to convict the unsaved of their sin through God's grace. Again, the only reason the unsaved, those blinded by Satan, can see your light, the fruits of the Spirit radiating from you, is because of God's grace.

Satan has insinuated his self into the very core of each person's soul, like the moss growing in the darkness on the north side of the tree.

Satan covers the unsaved with a blanket of deception and lies, preventing them from seeing the light, from seeing God's absolute truths, from seeing Jesus. Instead, he exists in darkness, believing the many falsehoods that Satan perpetuates through the various secular world-views, all the "isms." The only voice the unsaved can hear is the voice of another nonbeliever who is being deceived by Satan.

In their book *A Critical and Exegetical Commentary on the Gospel According to Matthew,* the authors W. D. Davies and Dale C. Allison make these concluding observations about the disciples as salt and light:

> The followers of Jesus are salt and light for all, for Jew
> and Gentile the world over. So Matthew's universalism is
> once more apparent. No less apparent is the evangelist's
> exalted estimation of the ecclesia's role in the religious life

of humanity. If the church does in fact consist of those who are "the salt of the earth" and "the light of the cosmos," then the church must be the primary locus of God's activity in and for all people.

Isn't it funny, the human brain? We can study the brain using tools such as microscopy, gross anatomy, MRI, intra-operative electrode manipulation, EEG, and other man-made tools. Through histology, pathology, MRI studies, and other means, we think we understand the human brain or at least in the future will understand the human brain.

Those who are blind think the human brain is an organic representation of a supercomputer. These people think the human brain; the small human brain can comprehend the omniscience and omnipotence of the creator God. How vain we are! How proud and arrogant we are!

PRAYER

Our heavenly Father

This time on Earth is such a mere speck of time when compared to eternity! Help us to take up our cross while we are on earth, and help us to do everything we can to fulfill Your purpose for our life. Then we will truly become witnesses to those around us.

Help those we come into contact with experience the fruits of the Spirit flowing through us, because of the work of the Holy Spirit within our hearts. So, they too will see God's inexpressible joy, God's love, God's peace, God's patience, God's faithfulness, God's kindness, God's goodness, God's gentleness, and God's self-control.

Barry Denzil Haney, MD

Then, the day we die, when we stand in front of You, to give an accounting for our lives on final judgment day, and You say, "Does anyone know him?" Jesus will say, "I knew him, I knew him well!" Then You will tell us, "Welcome, my child, welcome to an eternity with me in heaven!"

In the precious name of Jesus Christ our Lord and Savior,

Amen

CHAPTER 39

Finally, Total Surrender, Submission!

I am crucified with Christ: nevertheless I live; yet not I, but Christ liveth in me: and the life which I now live in the flesh I live by the faith of the Son of God, who loved me, and gave himself for me. I do not frustrate the grace of God: for if righteousness come by the law, then Christ is dead in vain.

—Galatians 2:20-21

———

WORLDLY WISDOM

In this passage, the Holy Spirit is telling me, when we finally totally surrender, when we have faith in Jesus, our life becomes a display of Christ; we become more and more Christ-like each day of our lives while here on earth.

We undergo progressive sanctification, we become more holy, until the day we arrive in heaven when we will then be pure, we will then be perfect, we will then be holy, we will then be Christ-like! This miracle takes place because of the Holy Spirit's presence in our heart, working in us and through us, cleansing and preparing our decaying, rotting spirit for heaven!

The Merriam-Webster Dictionary defines surrender in this way: "To yield to the power, control, or possession of another upon compulsion or demand."

In the Dictionary of Bible Themes, submission is defined in this way: "A humble attitude where obedience is rendered within a relationship; whether it be to God, authorities or other people at work, in the church, in marriage or in the family."

From a worldly, psychological standpoint, what does surrender mean? In her article "When It's Time to Let Go of Control and Surrender," Nancy Colier gives us this definition:

> Surrender happens when we know that we don't know. It arrives when we know that we cannot think or see our way through where we are. We don't have the answers. In true surrender, we don't know if what's to come will be better or worse, more comfortable or more awful. All we know is that we can't do it this way, the way we've been doing it, a moment longer. Surrender happens when it can not happen.

When we finally decide to surrender our will over to someone else's control, in her article "The Art of Surrender," Jennifer Hamady offers us this advice:

> When we are able to move from resistance to surrender—of either positive or negative experiences and circumstances—we lose neither control nor ourselves. Rather, we are given the clarity and tools that enable us to manage those changes powerfully, regardless of how radical or even traumatic they may be.

Surrender, in a spiritual sense, means a believer completely gives up his own will and subjects his thoughts, ideas, and deeds to the will and teachings of a higher power. Submission is the acknowledgment of the legitimacy of the power of one's superior or superiors.

In the world today,
we see the acknowledgment
of submission all around us.

In the Arts, the title *Submission* is used in four films produced from 1976 to 2017. In the music world, the song title, "Submission," is used by Ash, Basement, Gorillaz, and the Sex Pistols, from 1977 to 2017. In the non-Christian religions, Ibadah has an Islamic principle of submission to divine will, the religion Islam means submission, and Submission/Submitter, a member of United Submitters International, an Islamic sect.

The computing and technology world uses terms such as electronic submission, submission servers, mail submission agents. In the sports world, terms such as submission related to combat sports, submission hold, and submission wrestling. Finally, the term sexual submission is used in a sexual context.

ILLUSTRATION

The following illustration concerning the day of salvation is taken from Michael P. Green's book *1500 Illustrations for Biblical Preaching*:

> The story is told of a time when Satan held a strategy session for subverting those who were close to salvation. "What shall we do?" asked Satan. A daring demon stood and shouted, "I have it! I know what we can do! We can tell men that there is no life after death, that they die like animals." Satan's face fell as he answered, "It will never work. Man is not ignorant; even atheists admit of times when they sense a tomorrow after death."
>
> Another demon spoke, "Here's the solution! Let's say there is no God or if there ever was; He is dead—because even if He started the universe, He has left it now." Satan replied in dismay, "That won't work either; most of them know there *is* a God, even though they don't seek Him."
>
> Other ideas were presented, but none brought hope to Satan and his underlings. Finally, as they were about to give up, one demon leaped in glee, "I have it! A sure solution!" The other demons crowded around to hear the plan. "Go tell them that God is real and the Bible is God's Word." A gasp came from the audience as the demon continued, "And tell them that Jesus is God's Son and frees men from sin." The other demons were horror-stricken, thinking that their associate had gone bananas, until, with a smile, he added, "*Then* tell them that this is not the best time to choose Christ. Help them make excuses for delaying their decision. Tell them there is no hurry!" The demons danced in delight, realizing a workable plan had been discovered.[11651]

Barry Denzil Haney, MD

GODLY WISDOM

Before discussing what Biblical surrender and submission mean, let me share with you what June Hunt, in her book *Biblical Counseling Keys on Submission: Yielding from a Spirit of Strength*, says godly submission is not:

- Submission is not...bowing and cowering.
- Submission is not...subservient or second class.
- Submission is not...inferior or self-effacing.
- Submission is not...degradation or humiliation.
- Submission is not...nonassertive or non-confrontational
- Submission is not...indecisive or indirect.
- Submission is not...flattery or manipulation.
- Submission is not...peace at any price.

Although lengthy, the following passage in 1 Peter 2:13-3:22, teaches us, as Christians, what surrender and submission means, advice, I feel we should all heed:

> Submit yourselves to every ordinance of man for the Lord's sake: whether it be to the king, as supreme; Or unto governors, as unto them that are sent by him for the punishment of evildoers, and for the praise of them that do well. For so is the will of God, that with well doing ye may put to silence the ignorance of foolish men: As free, and not using your liberty for a cloke of maliciousness, but as the servants of God. Honour all men. Love the brotherhood. Fear God. Honour the king. Servants, be subject to your masters with

all fear; not only to the good and gentle, but also to the froward. For this is thankworthy, if a man for conscience toward God endure grief, suffering wrongfully. For what glory is it, if, when ye be buffeted for your faults, ye shall take it patiently? but if, when ye do well, and suffer for it, ye take it patiently, this is acceptable with God. For even hereunto were ye called: because Christ also suffered for us, leaving us an example, that ye should follow his steps: Who did no sin, neither was guile found in his mouth: Who, when he was reviled, reviled not again; when he suffered, he threatened not; but committed himself to him that judgeth righteously: Who his own self bare our sins in his own body on the tree, that we, being dead to sins, should live unto righteousness: by whose stripes ye were healed. For ye were as sheep going astray; but are now returned unto the Shepherd and Bishop of your souls. Likewise, ye wives, be in subjection to your own husbands; that, if any obey not the word, they also may without the word be won by the conversation of the wives; While they behold your chaste conversation coupled with fear. Whose adorning let it not be that outward adorning of plaiting the hair, and of wearing of gold, or of putting on of apparel; But let it be the hidden man of the heart, in that which is not corruptible, even the ornament of a meek and quiet spirit, which is in the sight of God of great price. For after this manner in the old time the holy women also, who trusted in God, adorned themselves, being in subjection unto their own husbands: Even as Sara obeyed Abraham, calling him lord: whose daughters ye are, as long as ye do well, and are not afraid with any amazement. Likewise, ye husbands, dwell with them according to knowledge, giving honour unto the wife, as unto the weaker vessel, and as being heirs together of the grace of life; that your prayers be not hindered.

Finally, be ye all of one mind, having compassion one of another, love as brethren, be pitiful, be courteous: Not rendering evil for evil, or railing for railing: but contrariwise blessing; knowing that ye are thereunto called, that ye should inherit a blessing. For he that will love life, and see good days, let him refrain his tongue from evil, and his lips that they speak no guile: Let him eschew evil, and do good; let him seek peace, and ensue it. For the eyes of the Lord are over the righteous, and his ears are open unto their prayers: but the face of the Lord is against them that do evil. And who is he that will harm you, if ye be followers of that which is good? But and if ye suffer for righteousness' sake, happy are ye: and be not afraid of their terror, neither be troubled; But sanctify the Lord God in your hearts: and be ready always to give an answer to every man that asketh you a reason of the hope that is in you with meekness and fear: Having a good conscience; that, whereas they speak evil of you, as of evildoers, they may be ashamed that falsely accuse your good conversation in Christ. For it is better, if the will of God be so, that ye suffer for well doing, than for evil doing. For Christ also hath once suffered for sins, the just for the unjust, that he might bring us to God, being put to death in the flesh, but quickened by the Spirit: By which also he went and preached unto the spirits in prison; Which sometime were disobedient, when once the longsuffering of God waited in the days of Noah, while the ark was a preparing, wherein few, that is, eight souls were saved by water. The like figure whereunto even baptism doth also now save us (not the putting away of the filth of the flesh, but the answer of a good conscience toward God,) by the resurrection of Jesus Christ: Who is gone into heaven and is on the right hand of God; angels and authorities and powers being made subject unto him.

Help us to surrender, to realize this simple formula: all we need is faith in Jesus! All we need to do is believe Jesus Christ, is in fact, God incarnate, who came to this Earth in fleshly form, called the man named Jesus, the one and only begotten son of God and, as John tells us in John 3:16, "For whoever believeth in him shall not perish but have everlasting life."

Although the plan is so simple, because of our pride and arrogance, we find it difficult to believe! Satan deceives us and makes us think we do not need Jesus to save us; we can become our own god, whatever is right for us, whatever makes us feel good is the right thing to do. What we don't realize, our pride and arrogance are the very chinks in God's armor Satan uses to deceive us!

Pride and arrogance are the same sins that led to Satan being cast out of heaven, forever doomed to eternal separation from God, in a place called hell. Pride and arrogance prevent many from faith in Jesus! Pride and arrogance lead many to make the wrong choice, to make the choice not to accept God's payment for our sins through the death of Jesus on the cross at Calvary, to choose instead an eternity, separated from God!

MY PERSONAL EXPERIENCE: TOTAL SURRENDER AND SUBMISSION!

On October 19, 2019, during the "Dying Moments" ceremony, at my Emmaus walk, I finally totally surrendered and submitted my will to God's control. I laid at the foot of the cross, the one thing that I was still trying to control. The one thing that was preventing me from having a loving, personal relationship with Jesus. When I gave up control of my life completely to Jesus, at that moment, I finally trusted God completely. My chains were broken; I was set free. His unconditional love now flows through me! I am a conduit, through which His unending love, amazing grace, and mercy flow, allowing others to see the fruits of the Spirit! Praise

Barry Denzil Haney, MD

God, thank You, for Your unending love and mercy. I am now righteous, because of Christ's righteousness, holy, because of God's holiness![1]

PRAYER

Our heavenly Father

Oh, I pray for all the unsaved! I pray that they would understand, there's only one way to spend an eternity with You, our Creator God! Help them see the evidence all around them, for Your Divine design! Help them see all around them the marvels of the universe! Help them realize that just the fact they can imagine that a Creator God exists is testimony to Your existence!

Help each of us see everything around us was designed so mankind might be saved, might fulfill Your will for us, might spend an eternal loving relationship with You! Help each of us see You have provided us a way to spend an eternity with You! If we are really honest with ourselves, we know what we see in the secular world, the worldly pleasures, the depravity, the hate, the injustice, the sin nature of man, is not what we were created for!

We know deep down, absolute truth was instilled in us by You, our Creator. We know right from wrong! We have a code of conduct! We know we are missing something, and that something is Jesus! Oh God, help us to realize what we are seeking is You. Holy Spirit, help us to understand your instruction book, the Bible, Your inspired word help us to

---

[1] For those interested in finding out more about what the Emmaus Walk is all about, I invite you to go to this link: https://www.nwaonline.com/news/2014/sep/20/walk-to-emmaus-helps-renew-refresh-chri/

use the information You give us to navigate this rocky road we travel to our own salvation while we are here on Earth!

In the precious name of Jesus Christ our Lord and Savior,

Amen!

CHAPTER 40

Last Chapter: The Debate Is Over, But the Journey Continues!

For I am now ready to be offered, and the time of my departure is at hand. I have fought a good fight, I have finished my course, I have kept the faith: Henceforth there is laid up for me a crown of righteousness, which the Lord, the righteous judge, shall give me at that day: and not to me only, but unto all them also that love his appearing.

—2 Timothy 4:6-8

During our life journey, we all will come to a point where we need to address the *"elephant in the room."* We all have an elephant in the room, something that everyone knows about us but is afraid to address, afraid to confront us with, because of the fear of offending us or making us mad. When we finally recognize this elephant in the room, the thing that is preventing us from having a relationship with God, it is only then that the Holy Spirit is able to convict us so we too can spend an eternity with God in heaven.

As I shared in the chapter about my Emmaus walk, it took me over sixty-eight years to finally address my elephant in the room. Once I did, finally, I was able to accept God unconditionally, I was able to let God take complete control of my life, I was able to surrender completely to Him, I was able to trust Him with my life. At that moment, Jesus came to live in my heart; the Holy Spirit began to dwell in my heart, teaching me, guiding me, instructing me, protecting me.

Now, I spend my life trying to please Jesus. When I do this, the Holy Spirit uses me as a conduit to show those around me the fruits of the Spirit; love, joy, peace, patience, gentleness, kindness, goodness, faithfulness, and self-control.

My hope is that each person reading this book will address the elephant in their room, so they too will enjoy an eternal relationship with God in heaven!

In Ephesians 4:32, Paul instructs us, "Instead, be kind to each other, tenderhearted, forgiving one another, just as God through Christ has forgiven you."

In this spirit, I close with this:

> All of us, during our journey to salvation, come into contact
> with many people. We need to remember each person
> we meet was created by God in His image. He loves each
> person we meet; we should likewise love them as God loves
> them. Remember to strive to please God in everything you
> do. When you do this, you will be fulfilling God's plan for

your life. If you do this, when your fleshly body dies, when you open your eyes in heaven, you will stand in the presence of your creator God. He will ask, "Does anyone know him?" Then Jesus will say, "I know him, I know him very well!" Then God will say, "Welcome, my child, welcome to an eternity with me in heaven!"

To each one of you and your families, I wish you peace, joy, and all the best during your journey to salvation. May this incredible time of giving, serving God, and spending time with family and friends, bring you inexpressible joy that lasts throughout your lifetime. God bless each and every one of you!

CLOSING PRAYER

Paul tells us this in 2 Timothy 4:7: "I have fought a good fight, I have finished my course, I have kept the faith."

I offer this closing prayer to both Christians wanting to reaffirm their faith and to the unsaved wanting to know Jesus.

Our heavenly Father,

Like Paul in 2 Timothy 4:7, we come to a close. During the reading of this book, we have fought the good fight, finished the race, and kept the faith!

Holy Spirit help us apply what we have learned to do God's will, please Jesus, and be obedient to God's commandment to be fishers of men!

I am a sinner! I openly confess that Jesus is Lord! I believe in my heart. You raised Him from the dead! I do now receive and confess Jesus as my Lord and Savior.

In the precious name of Jesus Christ, my Lord and Savior,

Amen!

For those who, for the first time, have made a decision to receive Christ as their Lord and Savior, I encourage you to prayerfully seek a local church, congregation, or assembly that will assist you in growing as a new Christian by the clear teaching of the Bible.

In Romans 10:9, Paul gives the following assurance as a believer; "That if thou shalt confess with thy mouth the Lord Jesus, and shalt believe in thine heart that God hath raised him from the dead, thou shalt be saved."

Hallelujah, praise the Lord!

REFERENCES

Scripture references in this book are taken from the following source, which I own in my digital library purchased from Logos:

The Holy Bible: King James Version. *Electronic Edition of the 1900 Authorized Version.* Bellingham, WA: Logos Research Systems, Inc., 2009. Print.

————————

Dictionary references were obtained from the following sources:

Manser, Martin H. *Dictionary of Bible Themes: The Accessible and Comprehensive Tool for Topical Studies.* London: Martin Manser, 2009. Print.

Dictionary by Merriam-Webster: America's most-trusted online dictionary. https://www.merriam-webster.com

Cambridge Dictionary: *make your words meaningful.* https://dictionary.cambridge.org/us/

"74 Bible Verses about Absolute Truth." What Does the Bible Say About Absolute Truth? www.openbible.info/topics/absolute_truth.

"8 Things Toxic Mothers Do." Psychology Today, Sussex Publishers, www.psychologytoday.com/us/blog/tech-support/201905/8-things-toxic-mothers-do.

"A Special Exegesis of Ephesians 5:19 and Colossians 3:16." CPRC, cprc.co.uk/articles/specialexegesismcnaugher/.

"Absolute Truth in a Relativistic World." Focus on the Family, 21 Aug. 2019, www.focusonthefamily.com/church/absolute-truth/.

"Anticipating The Blessed Hope Titus 2:11-14." Word & Work, 28 Apr. 2016, www.wordandwork.org/2016/05/anticipating-the-blessed-hope-titus-211-14/.

"C.H.Spurgeon's Testimony." Precept Austin, www.preceptaustin.org/c_h_spurgeons_testimony.

"Conversion of St. Augustine." Midwest Augustinians, www.midwestaugustinians.org/conversion-of-st-augustine.

"Depression (Major Depressive Disorder)." Mayo Clinic, Mayo Foundation for Medical Education and Research, 3 Feb. 2018, www.mayoclinic.org/diseases-conditions/depression/symptoms-causes/syc-20356007.

"Depression." World Health Organization, World Health Organization, www.who.int/news-room/fact-sheets/detail/depression.

"Friday, December 8th: Psalm 150:1-6." 121 Community Church, www.121cc.com/121blog/2017/friday-december-8th-psalm-1501-6.

"Hell in Popular Culture." *Wikipedia*, Wikimedia Foundation, 28 Dec. 2019, en.wikipedia.org/wiki/Hell_in_popular_culture.

"Hell." *Wikipedia*, Wikimedia Foundation, 30 Dec. 2019, en.wikipedia.org/wiki/Hell.

"History." *Seven Deadly Sins*, www.deadlysins.com/history.World
Religious Religion Statistics Geography Church Statistics.
Retrieved 5 March 2015.

"How Do You Explain Human Cruelty?" Psychology Today,
Sussex Publishers, www.psychologytoday.com/us/blog/the-
couch/201010/how-do-you-explain-human-cruelty.

"How Much Control Do You Have in Your Life?" Psychology
Today, Sussex Publishers, www.psychologytoday.com/us/blog/
your-personal-renaissance/201404/how-much-control-do-
you-have-in-your-life.

"How Much Data Is There In the World?" Bernard Marr, www.
bernardmarr.com/default.asp?contentID=1846.

"Humanism." Humanists UK, humanism.org.uk/humanism/.

"In US, Decline of Christianity Continues at Rapid Pace." Pew
Research Center's Religion & Public Life Project, 31
Dec. 2019, www.pewforum.org/2019/10/17/in-u-s-decline-
of-christianity-continues-at-rapid-pace/.

"Is Thanksgiving Was a Civil Holiday or a Religious
Holiday?" Catholic Straight Answers, 22 May 2013,
catholicstraightanswers.com/is-thanksgiving-was-a-civil-
holiday-or-a-religious-holiday/.

"Is There a Gene for Loneliness?" Psychology Today, Sussex
Publishers, www.psychologytoday.com/us/blog/the-squeaky-
wheel/201612/is-there-gene-loneliness.

"IWA Publications." IWA Publications, www.iwapublishing.com/
news/brief-history-water-and-health-ancient-civilizations-
modern-times.

"Last Person to Know Everything." Hmolpedia, www.eoht.info/page/Last+person+to+know+everything.

"Many Americans Say Other Faiths Can Lead to Eternal Life." Pew Research Center's Religion & Public Life Project, 31 Dec. 2019, www.pewforum.org/2008/12/18/many-americans-say-other-faiths-can-lead-to-eternal-life/.

"Message: Beware! (Colossians 2:8-15)." RayStedman.org, www.raystedman.org/new-testament/colossians/beware.

"Message: Love Made Visible (1 John 4:7-12)." RayStedman.org, www.raystedman.org/new-testament/1-john/love-made-visible.

"*Message: Putting On, Putting Off* (Ephesians 4:22-24)." RayStedman.org, www.raystedman.org/new-testament/ephesians/putting-on-putting-off.

"*Message: Putting On, Putting Off* (Ephesians 4:22-24)." RayStedman.org, www.raystedman.org/new-testament/ephesians/putting-on-putting-off.

"Message: The Stranger of Galilee (John 1:14-18)." RayStedman.org, www.raystedman.org/new-testament/john/the-stranger-of-galilee.

"Message: The Way of the Cross (Mark 8:34-38)." RayStedman.org, www.raystedman.org/new-testament/mark/the-way-of-the-cross.

"Neanderthal flute - the oldest musical instrument in the world (60,000 years)." The National Museum of Slovenia. Retrieved 13 November 2019.

"Pet Statistics." ASPCA, www.aspca.org/about-us.

"Physiology of Anger." Mental Help Physiology of Anger Comments, www.mentalhelp.net/anger/physiology/.

"Procrastination Through the Ages: A Brief History of Wasting Time." Mental Floss, 11 May 2015, www.mentalfloss.com/article/63887/procrastination-through-ages-brief-history-wasting-time.

"Procrastination." Psychology Today, Sussex Publishers, www.psychologytoday.com/us/basics/procrastination.

"Psalm 91:5-6—Have No Fear—God and Anxiety." 828 Ministries, 6 Feb. 2013, www.828ministries.com/articles/Psalm-91-5-6—Have-No-Fe-by-Anthony-Wade-130206-217.html.

"Psychological Slavery." Psychology Today, Sussex Publishers, www.psychologytoday.com/us/blog/family-secrets/201405/psychological-slavery.

"Salvation: Can Non-Christians Be Saved?" Home Page of the ReligiousTolerance.org Web Site, www.religioustolerance.org/chr_savn.htm.

"Schwäbische Alb: Älteste Flöte vom Hohle Fels." epoc.de. Retrieved 28 March 2018.

"The 'Hornet' of the Conquest in Deuteronomy 7:20: An Alternate Meaning: AHRC." The "Hornet" of the Conquest in Deuteronomy 7:20: An Alternate Meaning | AHRC, www.ancient-hebrew.org/biblical-history/the-hornet-of-the-conquest.htm.

"The Absolute Existence of Truth." Billy Graham Evangelistic Association, billygraham.org/story/the-absolute-existence-of-truth/.

"The Art of Surrender." Psychology Today, Sussex Publishers, www.psychologytoday.com/us/blog/finding-your-voice/201307/the-art-surrender.

"The Cave Art Debate." Smithsonian Magazine. March 2012.

"The Mission of Jesus Christ According to Luke 4:18-19." Direction, directionjournal.org/41/2/mission-of-jesus-christ-according-to.html.

"The Neanderthal Flute." Divje-babe.si. 1 February 2018. Retrieved 13 November 2019.

"Trinity." compelling truth.org, n.d. https://www.compellingtruth.org/illustrations-of-Trinity.html.

"What Does God Incarnate Truly Mean?" A Matter of Truth, www.amatteroftruth.com/what-does-god-incarnate-mean.

"What Does It Mean To Have a Sound Mind?" Rick Renner Ministries, renner.org/what-does-it-mean-to-have-a-sound-mind/.

"What Is A Pagan? Is The Term Pagan Or Paganism Used In The Bible?" What Christians Want To Know RSS, www.whatchristianswanttoknow.com/what-is-a-pagan-is-the-term-pagan-or-paganism-used-in-the-bible/.

"What Is Fear?" Psychology Today, Sussex Publishers, www.psychologytoday.com/us/blog/recovery-road/201405/what-is-fear.

"What Were Jesus' Desert Temptation and What Can We Learn from Them?" CompellingTruth.org, www.compellingtruth.org/Jesus-temptations.html.

"What Were Jesus' Desert Temptation and What Can We Learn from Them?"

"When It's Time to Let Go of Control and Surrender." Psychology Today, Sussex Publishers, www.psychologytoday.com/us/blog/inviting-monkey-tea/201605/when-its-time-let-go-control-and-surrender.

"Where Are All the Pagans in Genesis?" The Hump of the Camel, potiphar.jongarvey.co.uk/2017/05/25/where-are-all-the-pagans-in-genesis/.

"Who Is This Divided Man? Part 1." Desiring God, 17 Jan. 2020, www.desiringgod.org/messages/who-is-this-divided-man-part-1.

"Wooden pipe find excites Irish archaeologists." abc.net.au. 10 May 2004. Retrieved 28 March 2018.

1701-1800. "John Wesley's Heart Strangely Warmed." Christianity.com, Salem Web Network, 3 May 2010, www.christianity.com/church/church-history/timeline/1701-1800/john-wesleys-heart-strangely-warmed-11630227.html.

Allen, R. Michael. *TH112 Doctrine of Christ and the Church: A Reformed Perspective.* Bellingham, WA: Lexham Press, 2017. Print. Logos Mobile Education.

Allen, R. Michael. TH112 Doctrine of Christ and the Church: A Reformed Perspective. Bellingham, WA: Lexham Press, 2017. Print. Logos Mobile Education.

Anderson, Neil T. Freedom in Christ: Small-Group Bible Study: A Life-Changing Discipleship Program (Student Guide). Ventura, CA: Gospel Light, 2004. Print.

Arichea, Daniel C., and Howard Hatton. *A Handbook on the Letter from Jude and the Second Letter from Peter.* New York: United Bible Societies, 1993. Print. UBS Handbook Series.

Baclagon, and Chuck Baclagon. "John 10:27-30: Have We Missed the Obvious?" Fide Quarens Intellectum, 27 July 2009, faithseekingknowledge.wordpress.com/2009/06/21/john-1027-30-have-we-missed-the-obvious/.

Bar, Shaul. A Letter That Has Not Been Read: Dreams in the Hebrew Bible. Monographs of the Hebrew Union College 25. Cincinnati: Hebrew Union College Press, 2001. Print.

Barbara Johnson (2010). *Moses and Multiculturalism.* University of California Press. pp. 50-52. ISBN 978-0-520-26254-6.

Barnhouse, Donald Grey. *God's Remedy: Romans 3:21-4:1-25.* Grand Rapids, MI: William B. Eerdmans Publishing Company, 1954. Print.

Barton, Bruce B., David Veerman, and Neil S. Wilson. *1 Timothy, 2 Timothy, Titus.* Wheaton, IL: Tyndale House Publishers, 1993. Print. Life Application Bible Commentary.

Benfield, Chris. "The Lord of Liberty (Luke 4:16-22)." Pulpit Pages: New Testament Sermons. Mount Airy, NC: Chris Benfield, 2015. 300-301. Print.

Bevere, John. The Fear of the Lord. Lake Mary, FL: Charisma House, 2006. Print.

Biles, Deron J. "2 Timothy 3:1-9." Preaching Source, preachingsource.com/sermon-structure/2-timothy-3-1-9/.

Broomall, Wick. *The Holy Spirit: A Scriptural Study of His Person and Work.* New York: American Tract Society, 1940. Print.

Brown, William P. Wisdom's Wonder: Character, Creation, and Crisis in the Bible's Wisdom Literature. Grand Rapids, MI; Cambridge, UK: William B. Eerdmans Publishing Company, 2014. Print.

Bunyan, John. The Fear of God. Vol. 1. Bellingham, WA: Logos Bible Software, 2006. Print.

Burgess, Adam. *"Dante's 9 Circles of Hell: A Guide to the Structure of 'Inferno."* *ThoughtCo*, ThoughtCo, 1 Nov. 2019, www.thoughtco.com/dantes-9-circles-of-hell-741539.

Butler, John G. *Jesus Christ: His Encounters.* Vol. 4. Clinton, IA: LBC Publications, 2003. Print. Studies of the Savior.

Butler, John G. *John the Baptist: The Herald of Christ.* Number Seven. Clinton, IA: LBC Publications, 1992. Print. Bible Biography Series.

Cable, Steve. "Procrastination: Conquering the Time Killer—A Christian Perspective." Probe For Answers, n.d. https://probe.org/procrastination-conquering-the-time-killer/.

Cajus, Diedrich G. (1 April 2015). "'Neanderthal bone flutes': simply products of Ice Age spotted hyena scavenging activities on cave bear cubs in European cave bear dens." Royal Society Open Science. 2 via Royal Society.

Cappa, S. A. "Loneliness." Ed. David G. Benner and Peter C. Hill. Baker encyclopedia of psychology & counseling 1999: 698. Print. Baker Reference Library.

Carpenter, Eugene E., and Philip W. Comfort. Holman treasury of key Bible words:200 Greek and 200 Hebrew words defined and explained 2000: 116. Print.

Carson, D. A. *Worship: Adoration and Action.* Wipf and Stock, 2002. Chapter 21

Cisler, Josh M, et al. "Emotion Regulation and the Anxiety Disorders: An Integrative Review." Journal of Psychopathology and Behavioral Assessment, US National Library of Medicine, Mar. 2010, www.ncbi.nlm.nih.gov/pmc/articles/PMC2901125/.

Collins, Adela Yarbro, and John J. Collins. *King and Messiah as Son of God: Divine, Human, and Angelic Messianic Figures in Biblical and Related Literature.* Grand Rapids, MI; Cambridge, UK: William B. Eerdmans Publishing Company, 2008. Print.

CompellingTruth.org, www.compellingtruth.org/Jesus-temptations.html.

Conard, NJ (2009). "A female figurine from the basal Aurignacian of Hohle Fels Cave in southwestern Germany." Nature. 459 (7244):248-52. doi:10.1038/nature07995. PMID 19444215.

Cosgrove, Charles H., and Mary C. Meyer. 2006. "Melody and Word Accent Relationships in Ancient Greek Musical Documents: The Pitch Height Rule." The Journal of Hellenic Studies 126:68-81.

Cosgrove, Charles. 2011. *An Ancient Christian Hymn with Musical Notation: Papyrus Oxyrhynchus 1786: Text and Commentary.* Heidelberg: Mohr Siebeck Verlag. ISBN 3161509234

Cross, F. L., and Elizabeth A. Livingstone, eds. The Oxford dictionary of the Christian Church 2005: 768. Print.

D'Angour, Armand. 2018. "The Song of Seikilos." In: Tom Phillips and Armand D'Angour (eds). Music, Text, and Culture in Ancient Greece. Oxford University Press ISBN 9780198794462, pp. 64-72.

David Sansone (2016). *Ancient Greek Civilization*. Wiley. pp. 275-276. ISBN 978-1-119-09814-0.

Davies, W. D., and Dale C. Allison Jr. *A Critical and Exegetical Commentary on the Gospel according to Saint Matthew*. Vol. 1. London; New York: T&T Clark International, 2004. Print. International Critical Commentary._

Deere, Jack. *The Beginner's Guide to the Gift of Prophecy*. Minneapolis, MN: Chosen: a division of Baker Publishing Group, 2014. Print.

Dish, The Daily. "What Do Atheists Think Of Death?" The Atlantic, Atlantic Media Company, 17 July 2013, www.theatlantic.com/daily-dish/archive/2010/05/what-do-atheists-think-of-death/187003/.

Draper, James T., Jr, and Kenneth Keathley. *Biblical Authority: The Critical Issue for the Body of Christ*. Nashville, TN: Broadman & Holman Publishers, 2001. Print.

Drury, Keith. *Spiritual Disciplines for Ordinary People*. Indianapolis, IN: Wesleyan Publishing House, 2004. Print.

Eastman, Dick. *The Hour That Changes the World: A Practical Plan for Personal Prayer*. Grand Rapids, MI: Chosen, 2002. Print.

Ecclesiastes 1:17 (KJV)—Forerunner Commentary, www.bibletools.org/index.cfm/fuseaction/Bible.show/sVerseID/17333/eVerseID/17333.

Eckhardt, John. *God's Covenant with You for Deliverance & Freedom*. First edition. Lake Mary, FL: Charisma House, 2014. Print.

Eckhardt, John. *Prophet Arise*. First edition. Lake Mary, FL: Charisma House, 2015. Print.

Elert, Glenn. "The Nature of Light." The Physics Hypertextbook, physics.info/light/.

England, Laura. "Dereliction of Duty: Be Angry." Ed. R. C. Sproul Jr. Tabletalk Magazine, June 1995: Anger 1995: 8. Print.

Fader, Sarah. "What Is A Toxic Mother And How Does She Affect Relationships?" Betterhelp, BetterHelp, 8 Jan. 2018, www.betterhelp.com/advice/parenting/what-is-a-toxic-mother-and-how-does-she-affect-relationships/.

Fairchild, Mary. "Learn the Key to Reconciling Faith and Works." Learn Religions, Learn Religions, 10 Sept. 2019, www.learnreligions.com/christian-justification-by-faith-or-works-700638.

Fitzmyer, Joseph A. *The One Who Is to Come*. Grand Rapids, MI; Cambridge, UK: William B. Eerdmans Publishing Company, 2007. Print.

Franklin, Jentezen. *Fear Fighters*. Lake Mary, FL: Charisma House, 2009. Print.

Geivett, R. Douglas, and Holly Pivec. *A New Apostolic Reformation?: A Biblical Response to a Worldwide Movement*. Bellingham, WA: Lexham Press, 2014. Print.

Gideons International, ed. *Conversations: A Simple Approach to Sharing the Gospel*. Gideons International, n.d.

Gideons International, ed. *Conversations: A Simple Approach to Sharing the Gospel.* Gideons International, n.d.

Goodman, Paul. "The 8 Main Reasons for War." Owlcation, 3 Dec. 2019, owlcation.com/social-sciences/The-Main-Reasons-For-War.

Greear, J. D. *"7 Truths About Hell." The Gospel Coalition*, The Gospel Coalition, 12 Nov. 2018, www.thegospelcoalition.org/article/7-truths-about-hell/.

Green, Michael P. *1500 Illustrations for Biblical Preaching.* Grand Rapids, MI: Baker Books, 2000. Print.

Green, Michael P. *1500 Illustrations for Biblical Preaching.* Grand Rapids, MI: Baker Books, 2000. Print.

Green, Michael P. *1500 Illustrations for Biblical Preaching.* Grand Rapids, MI: Baker Books, 2000. Print.

Green, Michael P. *1500 Illustrations for Biblical Preaching.* Grand Rapids, MI: Baker Books, 2000. Print.

Green, Michael P. *1500 Illustrations for Biblical Preaching.* Grand Rapids, MI: Baker Books, 2000. Print.

Green, Michael P. *1500 Illustrations for Biblical Preaching.* Grand Rapids, MI: Baker Books, 2000. Print.

Green, Michael P. *1500 Illustrations for Biblical Preaching.* Grand Rapids, MI: Baker Books, 2000. Print.

Green, Michael P. *1500 Illustrations for Biblical Preaching.* Grand Rapids, MI: Baker Books, 2000. Print.

Green, Michael P. *1500 Illustrations for Biblical Preaching.* Grand Rapids, MI: Baker Books, 2000. Print.

Green, Michael P. *1500 Illustrations for Biblical Preaching*. Grand Rapids, MI: Baker Books, 2000. Print.

Green, Michael P. *1500 Illustrations for Biblical Preaching*. Grand Rapids, MI: Baker Books, 2000. Print.

Green, Michael P. *1500 Illustrations for Biblical Preaching*. Grand Rapids, MI: Baker Books, 2000. Print.

Green, Michael P. *1500 Illustrations for Biblical Preaching*. Grand Rapids, MI: Baker Books, 2000. Print.

Green, Michael P. *1500 Illustrations for Biblical Preaching*. Grand Rapids, MI: Baker Books, 2000. Print.

Green, Michael P. *1500 Illustrations for Biblical Preaching*. Grand Rapids, MI: Baker Books, 2000. Print.

Green, Michael P. *1500 Illustrations for Biblical Preaching*. Grand Rapids, MI: Baker Books, 2000. Print.

Green, Michael P. *1500 Illustrations for Biblical Preaching*. Grand Rapids, MI: Baker Books, 2000. Print.

Green, Michael P. *1500 Illustrations for Biblical Preaching*. Grand Rapids, MI: Baker Books, 2000. Print.

Green, Michael P. *1500 Illustrations for Biblical Preaching*. Grand Rapids, MI: Baker Books, 2000. Print.

Green, Michael P. *1500 Illustrations for Biblical Preaching*. Grand Rapids, MI: Baker Books, 2000. Print.

Green, Michael P. *1500 Illustrations for Biblical Preaching*. Grand Rapids, MI: Baker Books, 2000. Print.

Green, Michael P. *1500 Illustrations for Biblical Preaching*. Grand Rapids, MI: Baker Books, 2000. Print.

Green, Michael P. *1500 Illustrations for Biblical Preaching*. Grand Rapids, MI: Baker Books, 2000. Print.

Green, Michael P. *1500 Illustrations for Biblical Preaching*. Grand Rapids, MI: Baker Books, 2000. Print.

Green, Michael P. *1500 Illustrations for Biblical Preaching*. Grand Rapids, MI: Baker Books, 2000. Print.

Green, Michael P. *1500 Illustrations for Biblical Preaching*. Grand Rapids, MI: Baker Books, 2000. Print.

Green, Michael P. *1500 Illustrations for Biblical Preaching*. Grand Rapids, MI: Baker Books, 2000. Print.

Green, Michael P. *1500 Illustrations for Biblical Preaching*. Grand Rapids, MI: Baker Books, 2000. Print.

Gritsch, Eric W. *Toxic Spirituality: Four Enduring Temptations of Christian Faith*. Minneapolis, MN: Fortress Press, 2009. Print.

Gritsch, Eric W. *Toxic Spirituality: Four Enduring Temptations of Christian Faith*. Minneapolis, MN: Fortress Press, 2009. Print.

Hannay, James O. The Wisdom of the Desert. Glass Darkly, 2012. Print.

Harvard Health Publishing. "How Addiction Hijacks the Brain." Harvard Health, www.health.harvard.edu/newsletter_article/how-addiction-hijacks-the-brain.

Harvard Health Publishing. "How Addiction Hijacks the Brain." Harvard Health, www.health.harvard.edu/newsletter_article/how-addiction-hijacks-the-brain.

Hawker, Robert. The Poor Man's Concordance and Dictionary to the Sacred Scriptures 1828 :356. Print.

Heiser, Michael S. *The Unseen Realm: Recovering the Supernatural Worldview of the Bible.* Lexham Press, 2015. Digital (Logos Edition).

Hengel, Martin. Crucifixion: In the Ancient World and the Folly of the Message of the Cross. Trans. John Bowden. Philadelphia: Fortress Press, 1977. Print.

Hobbs, Herschel H. *My Favorite Illustrations.* Nashville, TN: Broadman Press, 1990. Print.

Holmes, Lindsay. "11 Signs Of A Genuine Friendship." HuffPost, HuffPost, 7 Dec. 2017, www.huffpost.com/entry/qualities-of-real-friends_n_5709821.

https://bethanygu.edu/blog/guidance/7-missions-statistics-that-will-motivate-you-to-go/

https://blog.tms.edu/enslaved-a-theology-of-addiction

https://en.wikipedia.org/wiki/Holy_Spirit

https://www.goodtherapy.org/learn-about-therapy/issues/melancholia

https://www.harappa.com/indus/8.html

https://www.raystedman.org/old-testament/psalms/the-unthinkable-thought

https://www.uuamarillo.org/archives/sermons/2014-06-15-Grace-Humanist-Perspective.pdf

Hummel, Charles E. "The Church at Home: the House Church Movement." Christian History | Learn the History of Christianity & the Church, Christian History, 2 Mar. 2016, www.christianitytoday.com/history/issues/issue-9/church-at-home-house-church-movement.html.

Hunt, Josh. Surviving in an Angry World. Josh Hunt, 2013. Print. Good Questions Have Small Groups Talking.

Hunt, June. *Biblical Counseling Keys on Depression: Walking from Darkness into the Dawn.* Dallas, TX: Hope For The Heart, 2008. Print.

Hunt, June. Biblical Counseling Keys on Fear: No Longer Afraid. Dallas, TX: Hope For The Heart, 2008. Print.

Hunt, June. *Biblical Counseling Keys on Friendship: Iron Sharpening Iron.* Dallas, TX: Hope For The Heart, 2008. Print.

Hunt, June. *Biblical Counseling Keys on Loneliness: How to Be Alone but Not Lonely.* Dallas, TX: Hope For The Heart, 2008. Print.

Hunt, June. *Biblical Counseling Keys on Submission: Yielding from a Spirit of Strength.* Dallas, TX: Hope For The Heart, 2008. Print.

Idleman, Kyle. The Kyle Idleman Prodigal Collection: Aha, 40 Days to Lasting Change, Praying for Your Prodigal. Colorado Springs, CO: David C. Cook, 2016. Print.

In His Image, n.d. Accessed October 2020.

Inglis, Holly J. "How the Brain Works." Sticky Learning: How Neuroscience Supports Teaching That's Remembered. Minneapolis, MN: Augsburg Fortress, 2014. 32. Print.

Jaffe, Eric. "Why Wait? The Science Behind Procrastination." Association for Psychological Science—APS, www. psychologicalscience.org/observer/why-wait-the-science-behind-procrastination.

Jesus. "What Proof Do You Have That Jesus Is the Messiah? Jews for Jesus." Jews for Jesus, 10 Dec. 2019, jewsforjesus.org/ answers/what-proof-do-you-have-that-jesus-is-the-messiah/.

John Hick, Truth and Dialogue (London: Sheldon Press, 1974), p. 148.

Johnson, Elisabeth. "Commentary on Galatians 4:4-7 by Elisabeth Johnson." Galatians 4:4-7 Commentary by Elisabeth Johnson—Working Preacher—Preaching This Week (RCL), www.workingpreacher.org/preaching. aspx?commentary_id=1128.

Johnson, Elisabeth. "Commentary on Galatians 6:[1-6]7-16 by Elisabeth Johnson." Galatians 6:[1-6]7-16 Commentary by Elisabeth Johnson—Working Preacher—Preaching This Week (RCL), www.workingpreacher.org/preaching. aspx?commentary_id=613.

Jones, Beth Felker. Practicing Christian Doctrine: An Introduction to Thinking and Living Theologically. Grand Rapids, MI: Baker Academic, 2014. Print.

Jones, G. Curtis. 1000 Illustrations for Preaching and Teaching. Nashville, TN: Broadman & Holman Publishers, 1986. Print.

Jungkuntz, Theodore. "The Analysis of a Slogan: God's Unconditional Love." Currents in Theology and Mission 1995, Vol. 22 (3), pp: 210-212. ISSN: 0098-2113.

Keener, Craig S. "Friendship." Dictionary of New Testament background: a compendium of contemporary biblical scholarship 2000: 385. Print.

King, Barbara J. "Are You Hard-Wired For Compassion? How About Cruelty?" NPR, NPR, 23 Feb. 2012, www.npr.org/sec tions/13.7/2012/02/21/147199088/are-you-hardwired-for-compassion-how-about-cruelty.

King, G. R. D. (1985). "Islam, iconoclasm, and the declaration of doctrine." Bulletin of the School of Oriental and African Studies. 48 (2):267. doi:10.1017/s0041977x00033346

Knowles, Andrew. *The Bible Guide*. 1st Augsburg books ed. Minneapolis, MN: Augsburg, 2001. Print.

Lastoria, M. D. "Depression." Ed. David G. Benner and Peter C. Hill. Baker encyclopedia of psychology & counseling 1999: 335. Print. Baker Reference Library.

Latvus, Kari. God, Anger and Ideology: The Anger of God in Joshua and Judges in Relation to Deuteronomy and the Priestly Writings. Vol. 279. Sheffield: Sheffield Academic Press, 1998. Print. Journal for the Study of the Old Testament Supplement Series.

LeDoux, Joseph E. "Emotion, Memory and the Brain," Scientific American 220 (June 1994): 50-57.

Lesure, Richard G. (2011). Interpreting Ancient Figurines: Context, Comparison, and Prehistoric Art. Cambridge University Press. pp. 11-12. ISBN 978-1-139-49615-5.

Libretexts. "5.1: Sugar and Salt." Http://Chem.libretexts.
org/, Libretexts, 23 Feb. 2019, chem.libretexts.org/
Courses/College_of_Marin/Marin%3A_CHEM_114_-_
Introductory_Chemistry_(Daubenmire)/05%3A_Molecules_
and_Compounds/5.01%3A_Sugar_and_Salt.

Lowery, Doug. Christian Growth from A to Z: A Practical
Discipleship Manual for Both New & Growing Christians.
Greenville, SC; Belfast, Northern Ireland: Ambassador, 2007.
Print.

Lustig, Robert. *The Pursuit of Pleasure Is a Modern-Day
Addiction.* The Guardian, Guardian News and Media, 9 Sept.
2017, www.theguardian.com/commentisfree/2017/sep/09/
pursuit-of-pleasure-modern-day-addiction.

Lustig, Robert. "*The Pursuit of Pleasure Is a Modern-Day
Addiction.*" The Guardian, Guardian News and Media, 9 Sept.
2017, www.theguardian.com/commentisfree/2017/sep/09/
pursuit-of-pleasure-modern-day-addiction.

Lyon, Jim. Jesus B: The Calling of Every Christian. Anderson:
Warner Press, 2015. Print.

Lyon, Jim. Jesus B: *The Calling of Every Christian*. Warner Press,
2015.

Manser, Martin H. *Dictionary of Bible Themes: The Accessible
and Comprehensive Tool for Topical Studies*. London: Martin
Manser, 2009. Print.

Masci, David, and Michael Lipka. "Americans May Be Getting
Less Religious, but Feelings of Spirituality Are on the Rise."
Pew Research Center, Pew Research Center, 21 Jan. 2016,
www.pewresearch.org/fact-tank/2016/01/21/americans-
spirituality/.

Mazzalongo, Mike. "What Other Religions Teach About Salvation." BibleTalk.tv, 1 Jan. 1970, bibletalk.tv/what-other-religions-teach-about-salvation.

McDermott, Gerald. "The Bible's Many Gods: Gerald McDermott." First Things, Institute on Religion and Public Life, 20 Jan. 2014, www.firstthings.com/web-exclusives/2014/01/the-bibles-many-gods.

McDermott, Gerald. "The Bible's Many Gods: Gerald McDermott." First Things, Institute on Religion and Public Life, 20 Jan. 2014, www.firstthings.com/web-exclusives/2014/01/the-bibles-many-gods.

Michael P. Green. 1500 Illustrations for Biblical Preaching. Grand Rapids, MI: Baker Books, 2000. Print.

Moberly, R. C. Atonement and Personality. London: John Murray, 1907. Print.

Moltmann, Jürgen. *Sun of Righteousness, Arise!: God's Future for Humanity and the Earth.* Trans. Margaret Kohl. Minneapolis, MN: Fortress Press, 2010. Print.

Morris, Wayne. *Salvation as Praxis: A Practical Theology of Salvation for a Multi-Faith World.* London; New Delhi; New York; Sydney: Bloomsbury, 2014. Print.

Moshe Halbertal; Avishai Margalit; Naomi Goldblum (1992). Idolatry. Harvard University Press. pp. 1-8, 85-86, 146-148. ISBN 978-0-674-44313-6.

Mueller, J. Theodore. "Have We Outmoded Chalcedon." Christianity Today 1959 :180. Print.

Mullins, E. Y. Why Is Christianity True?: Christian Evidences. Chicago: Christian Culture Press, 1905. Print.

Murray, David, et al. *"A Letter to the Depressed Christian at Christmas."* ChurchLeaders, 10 Dec. 2019, churchleaders. com/outreach-missions/outreach-missions-articles/367332-a-letter-to-the-depressed-christian-at-christmas.html

Myers, Jeremy, and Owen Williams. *"When Jesus Gave Gifts to Men* (Ephesians 4:7-10)." Redeeming God, 9 June 2018, redeeminggod.com/sermons/ephesians/ephesians_4_7-10/.

National Museum, Seated Male in Namaskar pose, New Delhi, Government of India;

Nichols, Stephen. "The Story of Martin Luther's Conversion." Ligonier Ministries, www.ligonier.org/blog/story-martin-luthers-conversion/.

North American Division Corporation of Seventh-day Adventists. Adventist Men's Ministries Curriculum. Lincoln, NE: AdventSource, 2011. Print.

Offor, Geo. "Advertisement by the Editor." Light for Them That Sit in Darkness. Vol. 1. Bellingham, WA: Logos Bible Software, 2006. 391. Print.

Pao, David W. *Thanksgiving: An Investigation of a Pauline Theme.* Ed. D. A. Carson. Vol. 13. England; Downers Grove, IL: Apollos; InterVarsity Press, 2002. Print. New Studies in Biblical Theology.

Paul Kugler (2008). Polly Young-Eisendrath and Terence Dawson (ed.). *The Cambridge Companion to Jung.* Cambridge University Press. pp. 78-79. ISBN 978-1-139-82798-0.

Perdue, Leo G. The Sword and the Stylus: An Introduction to Wisdom in the Age of Empires. Grand Rapids, MI; Cambridge, UK: William B. Eerdmans Publishing Company, 2008. Print.

Peter Roger Stuart Moorey (2003). Idols of the People: Miniature Images of Clay in the Ancient Near East. Oxford University Press. pp. 1-15. ISBN 978-0-19-726280-1.

Phillips, Timothy R., and Dennis L. Okholm. Christian Apologetics in the Postmodern World. Downers Grove, IL: InterVarsity Press, 1995. Print.

Pierson, A. T. *A Spiritual Clinique: Four Bible Readings Given at Keswick in 1907.* New York: Gospel Publishing House, 1907. Print.

Pietz, Jennifer V. "Commentary on 2 Timothy 4:6-8, 16-18 by Jennifer V. Pietz." 2 Timothy 4:6-8, 16-18 Commentary by Jennifer V. Pietz—Working Preacher—Preaching This Week (RCL), www.workingpreacher.org/preaching. aspx?commentary_id=4268.

Pink, Arthur Walkington. The Nature of God. Bellingham, WA: Logos Bible Software, 2005. Print.

Pollice, Lucas R. *Open Wide the Doors to Christ: Discovering Catholicism.* Steubenville, OH: Emmaus Road Publishing, 2013. Print.

Pontifical Council for Culture. Where Is Your God? Responding to the Challenge of Unbelief and Religious Indifference Today. Vatican City: Libreria Editrice Vaticana, 2004. Print.

Pontifical Council for Culture. *Where Is Your God? Responding to the Challenge of Unbelief and Religious Indifference Today.* Vatican City: Libreria Editrice Vaticana, 2004. Print.

Powlison, David. "Anger Part 1: Understanding Anger." Journal of Biblical Counseling 1995, Vol. 14 (1), pp: 40-53. ISSN:1063-2166

Princeton University. "'Junk' DNA Has Important Role, Researchers Find." ScienceDaily. www.sciencedaily.com/releases/2009/05/090520140408.htm (accessed April 7, 2021).

Priolo, Lou. "Selfishness: Helping People with the Mother of All Sins." The Journal of Modern Ministry 6.1 (2009): 78. Print.

Publishing Association, 1877. Print.

Publishing Association, 1877. Print.

Ralston, Robert H., et al. "Salt." Encyclopædia Britannica, Encyclopædia Britannica, Inc., 31 Oct. 2019, www.britannica.com/science/salt.

Raymond. "Wit and Wickedness: Is It All in the Brain?" OUP Academic, Oxford University Press, 17 Oct. 2012, academic.oup.com/brain/article/136/3/980/316336.

Reber, Paul. "What Is the Memory Capacity of the Human Brain?" Scientific American, Scientific American, 1 May 2010, www.scientificamerican.com/article/what-is-the-memory-capacity/.

Redemption; or The Miracles of Christ, the Mighty One. Seventh-day Adventist Publishing Association, 1877. Print.

Redemption; or The Temptation of Christ in the Wilderness. Seventh-day Adventist

Redemption; or The Temptation of Christ in the Wilderness. Seventh-day Adventist

Redemption; or The Temptation of Christ in the Wilderness. Seventh-day Adventist Publishing Association, 1877. Print.

Roark, Warren C. The Holy Spirit. James L. Fleming, 2005. Print.

Rogers, Adrian. "The Sixth Commandment: Thou Shalt Not Kill." Adrian Rogers Sermon Archive. Signal Hill, CA: Rogers Family Trust, 2017. Ex 20:13. Print.

Rowland, Chris. "Pet Industry Spending Trends Expected In 2019." International Business Times, 28 Dec. 2018, www.ibtimes.com/pet-industry-spending-trends-expected-2019-2746276.

Ryrie, Charles C. Making the Most of Life. Chicago, IL: Moody Press, 1966. Print.

S Kalyanaraman (2007), Indus Script Cipher: Hieroglyphs of Indian Linguistic Area, Motilal Banarsidass, ISBN 978-0982897102, pp. 234-236

Sailer, William et al. Religious and Theological Abstracts. Myerstown, PA: Religious and Theological Abstracts, 2012. Print.

Sailer, William et al. Religious and Theological Abstracts. Myerstown, PA: Religious and Theological Abstracts, 2012. Print.

Sargent, Tony. Gems from Martyn Lloyd-Jones: An Anthology of Quotations from "the Doctor." Milton Keynes, England; Colorado Springs, CO; Hyderabad, AP: Paternoster., 2007. Print.

Scholl, Hans, et al. At the Heart of the White Rose: Letters and Diaries of Hans and Sophie Scholl. Plough Publishing House, 2017.

Scofield, C. I. *The Messianic Question*. New York: Publication Office "Our Hope," 1912. Print.

Scottsays, Tom, et al. "Is God's Love." Truthaccordingtoscripture. com, 17 Dec. 2019, www.truthaccordingtoscripture.com/ documents/articles/conditional-love.php#.XhRwQy2ZPOQ.

Shenton, Tim. Our Perfect God: A Summary of the Attributes of God. Leominster, UK: Day One Publications, 2005. Print.

Sidney H. Griffith (2012). *The Church in the Shadow of the Mosque: Christians and Muslims in the World of Islam*. Princeton University Press. pp. 143-145. ISBN 978-1-4008-3402-0.

Silverman, David J. "Thanksgiving Day." Encyclopædia Britannica, Encyclopædia Britannica, Inc., 16 Jan. 2020, www.britannica.com/topic/Thanksgiving-Day.

Smith, Ralph A. *Trinity and Reality: An Introduction to the Christian Faith*. Moscow, ID: Canon Press, 2004. Print.

Snyder, Howard A., and United Theological Seminary. "ARTICLE: Is God's Love Unconditional?" ChristianityToday. com, Christianity Today, 5 Nov. 2019, www.christianitytoday. com/ct/1995/july17/is-gods-love-unconditional.html

Sproul, R. C. *What Is the Trinity?* Vol. 10. Orlando, FL: Reformation Trust, 2011. Print. The Crucial Questions Series.

Stark, Glenn. "Emission and Absorption Processes." Encyclopædia Britannica, Encyclopædia Britannica, Inc., 7 Jan. 2020, www. britannica.com/science/light/Emission-and-absorption-processes.

Stecker, Chuck. Men of Honor Women of Virtue. Seismic Pub Group Inc, 2010.

Barry Denzil Haney, MD

Stott, John. *The Living Church: Convictions of a Lifelong Pastor.* Nottingham: Inter-Varsity Press, 2007. Print.

Strobel, Lee. *The Case for Faith: a Journalist Investigates the Toughest Objections to Christianity.* Zondervan.com, 2014.

Strong, Augustus Hopkins. *Systematic Theology.* Philadelphia: American Baptist Publication Society, 1907. Print.

Stufflebean, Steven. "Absolute Truth." Lamb and Lion Ministries, christinprophecy.org/articles/absolute-truth/.

Sylvia Estienne (2015). Rubina Raja and Jörg Rüpke (ed.). *A Companion to the Archaeology of Religion in the Ancient World.* John Wiley & Sons. pp. 379-384. ISBN 978-1-4443-5000-5.

Tabletalk Magazine, June 2008: Religious Pluralism 2008: 18-19. Print.

Tabletalk Magazine, September 2005: Redemption Accomplished 2005: 2. Print.

Teasley, D. O. *The Holy Spirit and Other Spirits.* James L. Fleming, 2005. Print.

The Editors of Encyclopaedia Britannica. "Hesychasm." Encyclopædia Britannica, Encyclopædia Britannica, Inc., 4 Oct. 2013, www.britannica.com/topic/Hesychasm.

The Editors of Encyclopaedia Britannica. "Messiah." Encyclopædia Britannica, Encyclopædia Britannica, Inc., 5 Oct. 2018, www.britannica.com/topic/messiah-religion.

The Editors of Encyclopaedia Britannica. "Phobia." Encyclopædia Britannica, Encyclopædia Britannica, Inc., 20 Aug. 2019, www.britannica.com/science/phobia.

The Hope of Survivors Staff. HopeSpeak. The Hope of Survivors, 2004-2014. Print.

The Workers' Bulletin. N. p., 1902. Print.

Tholuck, A., trans. "The Prayer of Jesus: 'Father, Forgive Them, for They Know Not What They Do.'" Light from the Cross: Sermons on the Passion of Our Lord. Philadelphia: William S. & Alfred Martien, 1858. 236. Print.

Tolbert, Mary Ann. "The Prodigal Son: An Essay in Literary Criticism from a Psychoanalytic Perspective." Ed. John Dominic Crossan. Semeia 9 (1977): 11-12. Print.

Toler, Stan. Rethink Your Life: A Unique Diet to Renew Your Mind. Indianapolis, IN: Wesleyan Publishing House, 2008. Print.

Torrey, R. A. *The Person and Work of the Holy Spirit as Revealed in the Scriptures and in Personal Experience*. New York; Chicago: Fleming H. Revell, 1910. Print.

Towns, Elmer L. *What Every Sunday School Teacher Should Know*. Ventura, CA: Regal; Gospel Light, 2001. Print.

Trites, Allison A. "Thanksgiving." Ed. David Noel Freedman, Allen C. Myers, and Astrid B. Beck. Eerdmans Dictionary of the Bible 2000: 1296. Print.

Van Til, Cornelius, and Eric H. Sigward. Unpublished Manuscripts of Cornelius Van Til. Electronic ed. Labels Army Company: New York, 1997. Print.

Villareal, Luis. "Counseling Hispanics." Healing for the City: Counseling in the Urban Setting. Eugene, OR: Wipf and Stock Publishers, 2002. 216. Print.

Vlach, Mike. "Does Daniel 7:13 Refer to the Ascension or Second Coming of Jesus?" Does Daniel 7:13 Refer to the Ascension or Second Coming of Jesus? 1 Jan. 1970, mikevlach.blogspot.com/2017/02/does-daniel-713-refer-to-ascension-or.html.

Vogel, Winfried. "Man and Knowledge: The Search for Truth in a Pluralistic Age." Journal of the Adventist Theological Society 7.2 (1996):184. Print.

Wallin, Nils Lennart; Steven Brown; Björn Merker (2001). *The Origins of Music*. Cambridge: MIT Press. ISBN 978-0-262-73143-0.

Warner, Daniel S. The Evening Light. James L. Fleming, 2005. Print.

Wax, Trevin. "I'm Afraid to Share My Faith." *The Gospel Coalition*, October 5, 2009. https://www.thegospelcoalition.org/blogs/trevin-wax/im-afraid-to-share-my-faith/.

Website, The Official. "C. S. Lewis as Atheist Turned Apostle—Official Site." Official Site | CSLewis.com, 2 May 2012, www.cslewis.com/c-s-lewis-as-atheist-turned-apostle/.

Weece, Jon. Sermon entitled "Pluged in—Tapping into the Power of God: His Power Over Sin." Southland Christian Church. 04/04/21.

White, Ellen Gould. *Confrontation; Redemption; or the Temptation of Christ in the Wilderness*. Review and Herald Publishing Association, 1971. Print.

White, Ellen Gould. *Confrontation; Redemption; or the Temptation of Christ in the Wilderness*. Review and Herald Publishing Association, 1971. Print.

Wilford, John N. (June 24, 2009). "Flutes Offer Clues to Stone-Age Music." The New York Times. Retrieved June 29, 2009.

Wilkin, Jen. "Why It's So Important to Know the Difference Between 'Godly' and 'Worldly' Wisdom." RELEVANT Magazine, 31 July 2018, relevantmagazine.com/god/why-its-so-important-to-know-the-difference-between-godly-and-worldly-wisdom/.

Wilkins, Steve. *Face to Face: Meditations on Friendship and Hospitality*. Moscow, ID: Canon Press, 2002. Print.

Wilson, Marvin R. Exploring Our Hebraic Heritage: A Christian Theology of Roots and Renewal. Grand Rapids, MI; Cambridge, UK: William B. Eerdmans Publishing Company, 2014. Print.

Wilson, Nancy. *Praise Her in the Gates: The Calling of Christian Motherhood*. Moscow, ID: Canon Press, 2000. Print._

Wright, N. T. *Evil and the Justice of God*. London: Society for Promoting Christian Knowledge, 2006. Print.

Zahl, Paul F. M. *Grace in Practice: A Theology of Everyday Life*. Grand Rapids, MI; Cambridge, UK: William B. Eerdmans Publishing Company, 2007. Print.

ABOUT THE AUTHOR

D r. Barry Denzil Haney was born in Lexington, Kentucky, in 1950. He grew up in Kentucky. He has been happily married to his wife, Judy, for fifty years, has three married daughters and six grandchildren. He has a surviving brother and sister.

He was a Boy Scout and achieved the rank of Eagle Scout and was an inductee into the Order of the Arrow.

While in undergraduate school, he received an undergraduate degree in Biology with high distinction.

He graduated from medical school in 1979. He honorably served in the United States Navy for thirty years, starting as an enlisted sailor in 1969, reaching the rank of Commander. While in the Navy, he received training as a Navy Flight Surgeon, Undersea Medical Officer, Submarine Medical Officer, became a certified Navy Diver, was in charge of a Hyperbaric Treatment Facility, and completed a residency in Diagnostic Radiology with special competency in Nuclear Radiology in 1990.

He retired from the Navy in 1999 and continued working as a radiologist in private practice until he retired in 2012.

During his lifetime, he has had many hobbies and interests including but not limited to: music, including playing the guitar, playing brass instruments in school (including the cornet, alto horn, saxophone, and baritone horn), attempting to play the cello; swimming; cycling, running (including participation in triathlon events in his thirties); hiking many of the National and State parks, including the Tetons, Hetch Hetchy Valley, Glacier Park, Yosemite, Zion National Forest, Daniel Boone National Park;

nature lover; camping; canoeing; traveling with his wife and family; and video gaming. In all of these hobbies and interests, what he values most is making "precious memories" with his family.

He now likes to say, "he works for Jesus," witnessing to others the Good News of the Gospel.

He, his wife, Judy, and dog, Marshmello now reside in Georgetown, Kentucky, and attend Central Church, affiliated with the Church of God Ministries, Anderson, Indiana.

For more information about this author, including forthcoming books, visit his website at www.barryhaney.com.

BACK COVER

In this book, Dr. Haney shares worldly and godly wisdom using personal reflections concerning his journey to salvation, along with supporting Bible verses, illustrations, and extensive research from Christian literature.

Masterfully done with the guidance of the Holy Spirit, in forty powerful chapters, the reader is given a sense of the changing, chaotic journey to salvation he experienced. He hopes the personal experiences he shares help each reader during their life journey.

His reason for writing this book is two-fold: to strengthen the faith of each Christian reading this book; by reading the book, allow the Holy Spirit to convict the unsaved, so they too might spend an eternity with God in heaven.

This is an excerpt from the book:

> "I sometimes can't believe God cares so much for me. I am nothing. But, I have to remind myself, I was created by Him in His image. He does love me. He does care for me. He wants me to crawl into his lap, and He wants to envelop me with His loving arms; He wants to have a relationship with me!
>
> Before He said the words, *"Let there be Light,"* He imagined me in His dreams, He imagined me writing this book. He worked out all the details of His grand plan of salvation.

Even as He spoke the words, *"Let there be Light,"* the creation event, the blinding flash, the explosion, the finely tuned Big Bang occurring in an instant, He knew I would be a passenger on a small blue planet, traveling through space and time, at this moment in time, in this moment of human history, in this moment of His plan of world salvation, during this moment of my walk with Jesus."